Inventing Politics

Inventing Politics

A New Political Anthropology of the Hawaiian Kingdom

Juri Mykkänen

University of Hawai'i Press
Honolulu

03 04 05 06 07 08   6 5 4 3 2 1

Library of Congress Cataloging-in-Publication Data

Mykkänen, Juri.
Inventing politics : a new political anthropology of the Hawaiian
kingdom / Juri Mykkänen.
p. cm.
Includes bibliographical references and index.
ISBN 0-8248-1486-X (alk. paper)
1. Ethnology—Hawaii. 2. Political anthropology—Hawaii. 3. Hawaii—Kings
and rulers. 4. Hawaii—Ethnic relations.
5. Hawaii—Politics and government. I. Title.
GN671.H3 M95 2003
305.8'009969—dc21
                                        2002014489

Designed by UH Press Production Department
Printed by the Maple-Vail Book Manufacturing Group

For the majority at home,
Annukka, Astra, and Siru

The whole fabric of heathen society, political, domestic, and religious, is based on the most absurd and rotten principles. There must be a tearing up of the very foundation and a building anew of the whole superstructure.

Rev. Sheldon Dibble, in the field 1831–1845

Contents

A Note on Conventions

I have followed the convention (e.g., Linnekin 1990b; Sahlins 1985, 1992; Valeri 1985b) of spelling the name of the whole archipelago without the glottal stop (') to distinguish it from the name of the Hawai'i island proper. Similarly, I have used the anglicized adjectival form Hawaiian instead of Hawai'ian.

Acknowledgments

First I would like to thank those people who had faith in my historical ethnography at the very earliest stages when I had very little to present to back up the project: Manfred Henningsen, Alan Howard, Deane Neubauer, Mike Shapiro, and Phyllis Turnbull. I hope this book makes you all think that you did something valuable. I also wish to thank my mentor at my home university, now retired, Ilkka Heiskanen, for his continuous support of my endeavors. I am grateful to Niilo Kauppi for the original suggestion of Hawaiian history as an ethnographic topic. Another good friend, Ilpo Koskinen, patiently listened to my worries while I worked to make sense of a very complex historical era. I truly benefited from my numerous discussions with him. Puakea Nogelmeier helped me in translating from Hawaiian, first in person and later through e-mail. He also shared his unique knowledge in locating Hawaiian language materials. Intellectually I am much indebted to Marshall Sahlins, whose summer course on Hawaiian history taught me the value of giving theory a documentary expression. Errors, stylistic choices, and interpretations are fully my own responsibility.

In fulfilling my endless requests for more material, the staff in the Bishop Museum Archives and Library, the Hawaiian and Pacific Collection at Hamilton Library, the Hawaiian State Archives, the Hawaiian Mission Children's Society, and the Hawaiian Historical Society always made me feel welcome. The Academy of Finland, Väinö Tanner Foundation, and the Finnish Foundation made this study financially possible. Phyllis and Murray Turnbull graciously shared their home with me during the final weeks of research. One can hardly imagine a more stimulating environment than the rooms on the hills of Mānoa Valley.

At the University of Hawai'i Press Pamela Kelley did a most wonderful job as an acquisitions editor. Without her guidance this book might not have been published. I was also lucky to have Masako Ikeda and Ann Ludeman looking after the project. David Akin copyedited the manuscript and did a hero's job in improving my English. Pauline Sugino at the Honolulu Academy of Arts helped me in locating the cover illustration.

Professionals doing research are often difficult spouses and inattentive parents. While I studied for this book and prepared it for publication, my wife and daughters have often seen my less-attractive side. But I hope that I have learned at least a little about the need to find a balance between various aspects of life. That, I think, would be the best way to thank them.

Introduction

This book is about cultural invention, contrasting and occasionally amalgamating interpretations of political being of two civilizations, Hawaiian and Euro-American. The focus of the study is Hawaii of the first half of the nineteenth century. This was an era of a steadily intensifying encounters between native and foreign cultures, and therefore one rich in cultural invention. Although civilizational encounter is never a prerequisite for cultural invention, it is nonetheless a catalyst, encouraging people on both sides to accommodate each other's ideas and actions. Invention is a controversial term, but I think it is an apt one to use here. Politics, especially native or "savage" politics, was a problem for nineteenth-century foreign observers, mostly Americans settled in Hawaii. It called up elementary parts of Western cosmology to be readjusted in the face of Hawaiian otherness. This alone would qualify as invention. But only if we consider the performance of the native Hawaiian culture upon foreigners simultaneously with foreigners' representations of Hawaiians can we arrive at a concept of invention that is appropriate to situations of culture contact (see Dening 1980, 44).

Today it is difficult to write about inventions of culture, at least in the sense that is often unfairly attributed to Hobsbawn and Ranger (1983) of production of inauthentic culture. Arguments that explicitly attribute cultural inauthenticity to current representations or appropriations of the past in the name of tradition have been rare (e.g., Keesing and Tonkinson 1982; Keesing 1989; Philibert 1986). But even the most benign and emphatic expositions of the relativity of cultural traditions, and hence their artifact nature, can be fatal for the present nativist struggles against domination by European culture, with the priority the latter so often give to the idea of cultural traditions as neutral, ahistorical (preferably

1

old), and stable. It is not only politically responsible, but also intellectually more fruitful to give up the project of exposing cultural fabrications, either as products of false consciousness or rational bids to power, and move toward what Sahlins has called "the inventiveness of tradition" (Sahlins 1999, 408). In doing so we underline not only the durability of cultures but also the necessary sense that accompanies any social act, whether driven by power motives or not. We must recognize fabrications, inventions, and social constructions as different and locally variable manifestations of living traditions. Because they are living, it is risky to assimilate the notions of inventiveness and cultural determinism, and to thereby deny historical agency all creativity and intentionality. Rather, to quote Sahlins again, "traditions are invented in the specific terms of the people who construct them," but culture itself does not by necessity cause people to act (Sahlins 1999, 409), nor is it always reproduced unproblematically (Brumann 1999)—there are always historical contingencies.

This position is almost identical with the original thesis of the invention of tradition *cum* culture as put forth by Roy Wagner.[1] What else was Wagner saying when he defined the efficacy of cultures as existing "through the fact of their being invented, and through the effectiveness of this invention" (1975, 10). Effectiveness here refers to Sahlins' specific terms. Any contingent event calls for meaning, and if it happens that a long-gone past is evoked to confer effectiveness, giving different appearances and shapes to tradition and legitimate meaning for the participants, it is neither a logical nor reasonable conclusion that an act of inauthenticity had taken place. In Pacific anthropology two notorious texts by Jocelyn Linnekin (1983) and Allan Hanson (1989) addressed the question of cultural invention along similar lines, although with the price of exposing mechanisms of invention that were too closely tied to the present-day politics of cultural identity. Hanson clearly stated that invention has always been part of cultural logic, as in the case of the New Zealand Maori who were his particular subject (p. 898), and Linnekin found no trace of inauthenticity when she analyzed the historical origins of today's "real Hawaiianness" (pp. 241–242, 249). Later Linnekin defended her position by saying that "if . . . tradition is always defined in the present, then all spurious traditions are genuine" (Linnekin 1991a, 173; see also 1991b; 1990a; Linnekin and Poyer 1990). Of course, we may ask if the concept of "spurious tradition" is necessary at all.

Even commercial usage of indigenous cultures, their selective objectification, deliberate pacification, and exploitation for profit, can be seen in this light as meaningful, and hence contextually authentic. If, say, the form of Hawaiian *hula* as it is performed for tourists in various locations in Waikīkī was culturally spurious, it would be difficult to comprehend the popularity of the shows and the dance itself. The shows carry meaning for the spectators, perhaps different from that of fairly similar performances in the early contact period. For those who are looking for authenticity, the attire of the dancers, for example, especially women's, is an easy object for a mundane deconstructive reading by pointing to imposed norms of Christian chastity and a radical transformation of culture. But should we reserve authentic *hula* only for those who claim Hawaiianness by studying early pictorial representations for the dress, and pass judgments of inauthenticity on others who take equal pride in the dance as it is today, designing elaborate costumes and attaching deep cultural meanings and spirituality to it? It is true that among the *hula* community different schools have themselves for years engaged in debates on the authenticity of different styles. But we will not get into these complexities except to note that the debate itself is a sign of culture in the making, and that a study of cultural innovation should not be separated from the study of culture in general. Cultures are always innovative, thanks partly to variations in specific competencies to resort to cultural meanings, and to inherent ambiguities in cosmologies and other fundamental beliefs. In this sense cultural tradition is by definition a "tool kit" which can be used selectively and creatively, but always meaningfully (Swidler 1986; Barth 1987).

Invention is an important concept in yet another sense. It emphasizes the important fact that cultures, all cultures, feed on external sources. Members of every culture draw upon their observations for various purposes and with various motives. They have their moments of reflection just as did the eighteenth-century European voyagers, for example, when their culturally defined idealism was shattered on the beaches of Tahiti. Relating to this, the editors of a recent book on Pacific encounters set out to qualify an important although not very tenable thesis, according to which "the privileging of the written record of the Pacific has involved such a radically binary idea of difference that it is difficult to articulate any cultural relation between voyagers and indigenes without its becoming starker" (Calder et al. 1999, 2). They referred to the European idea of savagery as either representing the greatest human antithesis to civilization or as a romanticized version of human natural existence not yet tarnished by the artificiality of civilization. Behind this binary image, they continue, lies the modern European theory of the origins of society, lifted out of the state of nature and formed into civil society by contract, the abstract expression for giving up part of the natural rights that belong to each member of society.

Later in the same book, J.G.A. Pocock explores the presence of these ideas in the writings of some Enlightenment thinkers. Pocock's analysis leaves these writers, Voltaire and Diderot in particular, with a fundamental ambiguity as to the cultural status of the "savage," who seems to have fallen into the category of murky in-betweenness, neither perfectly noble nor irrevocably ignoble. Pocock seems to maintain that for the European philosophers "the savage" was too important a notion in their own cultural critique of the European social order, and so they deliberately, in spite of evidence to the contrary, failed to provide this other with history. Given that Europeans had by the latter eighteenth century developed a profound sense of their own historicity and hence artificiality, it was remarkable that the Enlightenment was slow to make this a common character of all humanity. When this did happen and the noble savage was turned into his ignoble double, he became "the natural man historicized," yet he was too much part of his nature to be called civilized (Pocock 1999, 41). Here we witness a certain kind of cultural invention (if not inversion, see Thomas 1992) which uses established and institutionally important modes of representation to block non-Western people from disturbing Enlightenment politics.

These images still have some appeal and they continue to haunt anthropological knowledge despite decades of deconstructive criticism following Asad's (1973) attempt to question the value of anthropologists' representations of non-Western political systems. It is as if Asad saw an image of the romanticized state of nature in the works of British anthropologists studying African tribal societies, and an equally misleading image of a failed constitution of civil society in the writings of seminal orientalists. These ideological images (indeed, inventions) depicted African tribal organizations as benign and consensual, whereas Islamic societies were seen as despotic systems, ineffective and corrupt. Asad's accusations could not be sustained today, but there is a timeless core in his critique that still deserves our attention.

Asad reminds us of two related issues: first, that knowledge, as well as human existence since the Enlightenment, is historical and conditional on the position of the knowing subject; and second, that knowledge proceeds by objectifying and theorizing selectively. However, true as it is that in their representations of non-Western politics functionalist anthropology and European orientalism bore reflections of historical contingencies (phases of European colonialism), Asad was partly trapped by his own sources just as were the orientalist scholars whose work he was deconstructing. In quoting academic studies, Asad remained almost completely on the level of literary representation. Yet, he was attentive enough to find in the works under attack some indication of an alternative, for example, when he related a small vignette of Forte's description of local interactions between native chiefs and British colonial officers. This was in fact Asad's sociological explanation of the benign representations of African tribal politics: the power of the local chiefs depended on good working relations with the colonial administration, a fact known to, but unexamined by, the anthropologists of the time.

It is unfair to say that Asad was responsible for the subsequent rise of anthropological critique, which questioned the predominantly Western authority of scientific representation, opening it to literary criticism and making it look like a giant library of inauthentic inventions. But ever since, scholars trying to understand cultures other than their own have been drawn into debates in which their opponents try their best to demonstrate that this or that piece of "literature" is interesting only as a showcase of the elaborate use of some rhetorical technique. A meta-anthropology emerged that became a filing system of others' texts (Rabinow 1986), ignoring Asad's observant, although hardly original, sociology of anthropological knowledge. At the heart of this knowledge was, to quote his example again, the encounter between the local chief and the colonial officer. For the chief, a good and, most importantly, peaceful (the British might have said "civil") working relationship with the colonizer guaranteed some degree of autonomy and resources in maintaining his status among his people. A more focused literary criticism and more ethnographic description would have resulted in quite another sort of understanding of the knowledge of the other in colonial or nearly colonial situations. Further, our received notion of the African "savage" ruler would have included more variety than the "invented" image of benign and harmonious being, guided only by custom and traditional mutuality. Later anthropologists might have arrived sooner at the conclusion, which Pocock says Diderot was so reluctant to raise within the emerging European public sphere, that "the savage" was a cultured being, with intentions and motivations of his own. In fact this is exactly what Asad called forth, but his call was subdued and too often met only halfway. Scholarly work too often asserted the agency of indigenous people, colonized or otherwise marginal, and often became so inspired by that agency that the native sense of their action was replaced by what Sahlins has called "average Western common sense," and culture became as a mere smoke screen for motives of practical self-interest (Sahlins 1999, 407).

It was truly inventive, I would say, and paradoxical considering what the authors in the well-known volume edited by Hobsbawn and Ranger had to say about inventiveness at cultural boundaries. Hobsbawn himself gave the example of middle-class European patriotism, which was invented to serve the function of keeping new nation-states together (1983, 302). We might add that this function was possible because, as with all traditions, patriotism was meaningful, albeit invented, and in the new political context it was far more significant than, say, the older tradition of military honor and its rituals. Consider also what Terence Ranger said in the same volume about colonial Africa, where local people used their tribal identities, invented by European colonizers, "as clearly defined points of entry into the colonial world" (1983, 227). Similarly Bernard S. Cohn showed how in British India people appropriated the image created by colonial sociology in order to establish social ranks (1983). Again, a symbolic takeover by local people of traditions brought to them from the outside was possible because of the opportunities that these invented traditions offered them to realize their own cultural motives.

In this study I have worked amidst academic polemics regarding the status and usefulness of culture as an analytical concept (e.g., Bhabha 1994; Hartman 1997; Harrison and Huntington 2000; Nuckolls 1998; Sahlins 2000; Werbner and Modood 1997). I wish to go beyond accounts that highlight pure instrumentality and pretense in situations of culture contact, either to celebrate native intellects or to expose the calculating, ruthless mind of the colonizers, useful as these approaches may be in making sense of culture contact. I believe that events are interpreted through culture, new things are absorbed and accommodated, and used in new contexts to boost traditional arguments. In this analytical spirit, for example, we can observe how the abstract European notions of natural and civil society were reinterpreted by the "savages in-between," and how attempts to accommodate foreigners gave rise to more elaborate ideas of them and their society. I think Asad was correct all along in his analysis of colonial knowledge as a fusion of European theory, or ready-made cultural patterns, and the demands of the colonial encounter. However, in this book I have followed the more recent inclination in anthropology to consider both sides of the encounter simultaneously, without giving priority to either. I do consider what might be called colonial knowledge of Hawaiians and their politics, but I also give what I hope is equal weight to Hawaiian notions of foreigners' notions, and to the essential feature of any prolonged encounter: the interplay of each others' ideas across cultural borders.

Any cultural invention remains abstract if we do not consider the substance of the articulated culture, the discourse, together with the specific social relations that generated the invention (see Norton 1993). Failing this, we risk limiting our understanding of culture contacts to a listing of different types of cultural hybridity. This will eventually limit anthropological inquiry, as Sahlins says, quoting Friedman (1997), by substituting "an analytical construal of a people's history" for "an ethnographic description of their way of life" (Sahlins 1999, 412). If there is something hybrid in cultural encounters, it should be approached through specific historical events. Werbner (2001) has a point when she says that there is an embedded tension between different cultural elements, and these provide opportunity for reflection and improvised manipulation, and even resistance. But this idea has some redundancy in it, because, by extension, there is hybridity in every culture. We may think of a traditional tabu chief of Hawaii, whose fearsome powers were also the condition of land's fertility and the livelihood of the people living on the land. There was an inherent tension between the sacred chief's powers to give and take life, a sort of dialectic of legitimate and illegitimate use of tabus. Of course, culture contact was not necessary for this dialectic to be enacted in various contexts of everyday life or even on more ritual occasions. If the distinction of the chief's life-giving and lethal powers was enough to evoke a reflective state of mind among his subjects—who might have wanted to manipulate the circumstances in favor of the life-giving side—it is quite clear that what we would occur was in effect the same as the situation produced by conditions of cultural hybridity, a mixture of elements that are potentially and even by definition contradictory, heterogeneous, contextually varied, and subject to instrumental use.

Of course, culture contact is more fertile ground for hybridity and invention, because normal levels of cultural heterogeneity will be intensified, giving people a heightened feeling for agency, in Werbner's sense. Considering that cultural encounters involve two or more sides, this feeling of agency is not easy to describe; what is empowerment for one person may be quite the opposite for someone else. For example, the deep hierarchy that separated Hawaiian chiefs from commoners was a cultural puzzle for many foreigners. They mistook the strivings of common Hawaiians for culturally meaningful lives to be a lack of autonomy, simply because the Hawaiian cultural values prescribed a life in the service of a chief. The heterodoxy of contact culture is seen in the early attempts to produce sugar in Hawaii. The American owners paid their Hawaiian laborers in real money, which marked a moment of reflection because the native chiefs were in the habit of doing exactly the opposite. Native conceptions of a generous chief were subjected to brief but serious re-examination. This was at least partly premeditated by the white sugar growers, because they, too, wanted to contribute to the furthering of autonomy among common Hawaiians. In their terms the commoners were refusing the role of an independent, laboring, and free citizen, and were instead petitioning their chiefs to return to the generous way of life. The foreigners' money was a catalyst for native agency, but in a definitively native manner. If this is cultural hybridity, then contact cultures are typically and intensely hybrid.

In the history of Hawaiian politics this feature is often left unexamined, although for Pacific scholars the demise of the indigenous Hawaiian polity that began in the 1840s is a familiar story. Over the years, several works have been written about the disastrous effects of contact with the West. They tell us how the chiefs lost their lands, wealth, and will to live; how the chiefship was transformed into a "monarchy" led by missionary-politicians and wandering white men; how the traditional chiefly prerogatives were "contained," and a myriad of petty laws enacted in their stead; how the government grew into a "regular system" with increasing pecuniary needs that the common people experienced as intensified claims on their time, labor, and location. They tell about chiefs running into debt to foreign merchants, and warships blackmailing concessions to foreigners. They tell about the religious changes that made a once joyous and lively people into a nation burdened by gloom and anxiety. And they tell about the epidemics and venereal deceases that killed Hawaiians by the thousands, leaving ever-fewer chiefs to rule the land, and ever-fewer common people to provide for the chiefs.

This master narrative is often quite correct, but it tends to obscure events that took place on a more mundane level between people who could but rarely resort to outright violence in furthering their interests. As is the case in most encounters between people, the intent and meaning of their acts must be expressed through the medium of their language, and interpreted through patterns of their thought. Beneath the macroscopic history of political and cultural change lies a more modest history of cultural intercourse between people who held quite different ideas about the nature of rule, power, consent, divinity, and virtue. The overarching subject of this book is how these ideas were used to make sense of the less familiar, and how some of these very different ideas were fused together to form a common ground for understanding.

Because I am particularly interested in political ideas, this book is also about comparing cultures in political terms. It is not a comparative study in the objectivist sense of placing cultural contents along a continuum of abstract variables; rather it compares activities of Hawaiians and foreigners living in the Hawaiian islands during the early nineteenth century. In other words, my emphasis is on the historical people and the comparative descriptions they themselves created in order to make sense of the seemingly incomprehensible, and to enhance communication across cultures. Communication in culture contact situations is, of course, a complex matter. To find workable conceptual equivalents for staple foods or cooking utensils, for instance, requires relatively little effort since the referents of language can be shown and touched. More complicated is establishing ways to talk cross-culturally about abstractions such as governance and politics. In the chapters that follow my purpose is to show how this latter task was accomplished by both Hawaiians and foreigners, and to describe the historical contexts relevant to our understanding these efforts of mundane comparative politics.

I think that a venue for this can be found in a particular, localized history of how foreigners and Hawaiians used a set of Anglo-American political ideas, along with some Hawaiian notions, to create a language that depicted Hawaii as a political entity that had cross-cultural relevance for both sides. Admittedly, anyone who makes such a claim risks seeing too much in too little evidence. Vital to this approach has been my intention to avoid making preconceived judgments about the political nature of Hawaiian chiefly society, and to instead allow the participants of these historical events to do the judging. Although this strategy does not exempt me from the burden of interpreting history, I want to be clear that in approaching politics as a culturally relative notion this book is not a statement for or against the existence of indigenous Hawaiian politics. Rather it is an attempt to show how the people at one particular point of contact could meaningfully talk about each other's "politics." This is what I mean by the "invention of politics," in a fully cross-cultural sense.

Let me illustrate this very briefly. Early in my archival research I was drawn to a particular document that shows in an interesting way that politics had become a topic of cross-cultural discourse in early nineteenth-century Hawaii. The document is a missionary resolution with the title *Principles of Intercourse with the Chiefs, with Reference to Commercial and Civil Affairs*. It was drafted in Kailua, on the island of Hawai'i, in September 1826. Later it was submitted to the mission board in Boston and published in the *Missionary Herald* in April 1828 (MH 24:104), and two years after that a longer version was printed as an appendix in the *Minutes of a General Meeting of the Sandwich Island Mission* (SIM 1830). One paragraph of particular interest reads as follows: "That we consider ourselves required by our Instructions, as well as by the nature of our office as Christian missionaries, to abstain, like our Divine Master, from interference with the *political* and party concerns of the nation" (MH 24:104; my emphasis).

The reference to "instructions" reflects the origins of the mission about a decade earlier. It was then considered expedient to present foreign missions as neutral and universally benevolent enterprises, without the faintest hint of national interest. The American republic had the War of 1812 in recent memory, and maritime as well as commercial rivalry was gaining momentum. The missions also operated under Protestant theological principles, which justified a curious mixture of fundamental social reform and a deeply spiritual conception of divinity detached from earthly affairs. The document was meant primarily for the private use of the missionaries and their supervising officers in Boston. But since it was published in a missionary mouthpiece it also addressed a more general public, mainly those inclined to evangelical thinking and concerned with proper operation of the missions. The missions were financially dependent upon their charity. A few weeks after the document was first drafted, the missionaries wrote an explicitly public declaration with similar contents, challenging their critics to stand up in a formal hearing and bring their evidence to bear against the mission (SIM 1826b).

Why would American missionaries write in this way about interference in Hawaiian politics? Why this document, and why use this word? The immediate

context of these events tells us that this particular document can be characterized as the missionaries' attempt to put an end to a series of conflicts that marked
the ascent of the Hawaiian mission to a position of great local influence. As a collective, the mission tried to dispel the deeply rooted conviction, held up by several other conspicuous foreigners, that the mission had more than mere spiritual
interests in altering the traditional course of Hawaiian chiefship. Indeed, the missionaries had been accused of doing what they resolutely denied: interfering in
Hawaiian politics by inducing the chiefs to establish puritanical regulations, and
thereby turning themselves into effective rulers of the islands.

But there is another, less-immediate aspect to these events. In the pages that
follow I will argue that, as a matter of cross-cultural invention, politics had become an essential topic of public discourse in Hawaii by the mid-1820s. The exchange, to which the above documents are testimony, was also an occasion to
translate elements of a Western theory of society for Hawaiians. Moreover, had
the Hawaiian understanding of ruling been less a matter of mediation between
the worldly and the divine, the mission's involvement in native politics would
have been a trivial non-issue. But, the contrary being the case, the mission could
not help but become implicated in a complex and demanding network of cultural
translation.

The kind of translation I here refer to is not a simple matter of transposi-
tion, nor colonization of the mind. It is important to note that the translators
were in an awkward position, removed as they were from their own native sur-
roundings. It is elementary that the conditions in Hawaii were but rarely under
their control. This is generally true with translators, informants, and concept-
brokers during cultural encounters. Because they do their work within practical
areas of life, the stability of their environment cannot be guaranteed; nor can
the reception of their work because the natives already possess a load of cultural
significations, ready to be deployed to give novelties more familiar content.
Whatever they create, they do it by necessity as reaction to circumstances, and
often their work can be seen as being an answer to practical problems which
threaten the intelligibility of the situation, and their own place in it. Thus these
translators are also objects of their own translation. They have to allow native
conceptions to penetrate their own, and they witness alterations in their cultural base, or see its contradictions exposed (Thomas 1999, 133). A culture
shock, perhaps, but also an indication that the white man's (and his wife's)
story was more than a direct route back to his cultural source.

Anthony Pagden (1982) has said that for the early colonial Spaniards the
radical difference of Indians created a tremendous ontological problem, because their own society did not allow the notion of a natural difference of cul-

tures. The nineteenth-century Europeans and Americans were better equipped in the sense that they could appreciate differences and find places for them in their own world, now rendered profoundly historical. In Hawaii as elsewhere, they saw in the image of "the savage" their own uncultured past and an antipode of their present condition. In this they were backed by the Enlightenment tradition, represented, for instance, by the journalists of Cook's third voyage in their reflections upon the Hawaiians' politics (e.g., Cook and King 1784, vol. 3, 3, 95–96, 154–155). But they were also grounded in a century of European intellectuals who had engaged in comparative—and often didactic—political speculation, in the tradition of the early-modern cosmographers (Greenleaf 1964, 174). Thus, by the advent of the nineteenth century, the West had been changed dramatically by the discovery of the very historical nature of its people and institutions. The idealized image of the noble savage, invented as a criticism of Western artificiality, could not hold against the pressure to historicize the existence of the whole human race.

This does not mean that all Westerners could understand the differences or the reasons for them, or agree on their various explanations, not to mention approving of any of them. But in their ontological posture there was now a place for radical difference. In consequence, for some early nineteenth-century New England traders and missionaries, Hawaiians in general represented a blend of savagery and promise (cf. Pocock's notion of ambiguity, above), a radical difference that could be made to disappear by a civilizing influence. There was understanding that the "savage" people had developed distinctive forms of social life, one that represented not a lack but a perversion of humanity. In political analysis, which provided the paramount criteria of civilization, this thinking resulted in a proto-functionalist sweep that integrated Hawaii in a continuum of political orders. New Englanders—and practically all Westerners since the time of Cook—were capable of representing Hawaii, with its "despotic" government and the degraded condition of its people, in political terms, while still appreciating the substantial differences between the two worlds. A closer look would tell us that the cultural tolerance of difference was variously motivated. Others subscribed to an enlightened rationalism and made difference to be a natural condition of humankind. The Pacific peoples were soon depicted by them as having histories and customs of their own, which in some speculations were not even integrated with the common past of the West. Others looked to an older biblical paradigm and saw in difference a mask of the more fundamental depravity uniting humans in the face of almighty God.

As proponents of the continuum of differing stages of civilization, the Westerners were also capable of describing a lack of political organization in some societies. It is important to note that the recognition of a lack was not the same as facing something completely incomprehensible. It was rather a sign of the observer being ontologically comfortable with what was being observed, and an affirmative statement of difference, measured on a cultural scale that took the variation of the human condition into account. Whatever the case, the common criteria for judgment were presented by a distinctive form of political society, created as a contractual state underwritten by laws and a conception of restrained self that could subject itself to the rule of law. In the contexts of culture contact, the concept of politics was therefore used as an important instrument for cultural evaluation. For example, we could ask what circumstances resulted in the comments of the missionary George Turner on the social organization of Tana, New Hebrides, in the 1840s: " . . . no political constitution of any value whatsoever . . ." (quoted in Howe 1988, 295). This same instrument was also in use among the missionaries of Hawaii. When they attempted to organize a mission from Hawaii to the Marquesas in the early 1830s, they encountered a difficulty of special interest to us: for them, the mission was a failure because of "the entire want of civil government of any sort" in those islands (Armstrong, Alexander, and Parker to ABCFM, June 4, 1834, HP/HMCS). In their judgments about the political nature of "savage" societies, Western observers usually saw nothing but despotic politics or, in the worst cases of savagery, no politics of any conceivable nature.

Thus, fundamentally, for the West politics was a cultural construct that was and has ever since been used in organizing the great cultural variety that was opened up to the perception of the Western world, after the static view of the past was replaced by the uncertainties of historical existence. Mark Twain might have arrived a little too late to witness the historical process in Hawaii, but in 1866, forty-six years after the landing of the first missionaries and thirteen years after the closing of the mission, he had this to say about the cultural difference and civilizing influence: "The missionaries have clothed them, educated them, broken up the tyrannous authority of their chiefs, and given them freedom and the right to enjoy whatever their hands and brains produce with equal laws for all, and punishment for all alike who transgress them. The contrast is so strong—the benefit conferred upon this people by the missionaries is so prominent, so palpable and so unquestionable, that the frankest compliment I can pay them, and the best, is simply to point to the condition of the Sandwich Islanders of Captain Cook's time, and their condition today. Their work speaks for itself" (Twain 1990, 11–12).

Twain was an observant man, but he was surely a latecomer, and rather ignorant of the recent history of the place. His views are of course quite ethnocentric. Spirited by progressivist ideas, he joined those traveling writers who described the Hawaiian islands of the nineteenth century as rapidly ascending the ladder of civilization (in opposition to more romantic critics like Melville, who appreciated cultural difference to a degree of calling his own culture barbarous). Because progress in general was seen to coexist with Christianity, the Boston-based Congregationalist and Presbyterian missionaries usually received the credit for civilizing the Hawaiian heathens and enlightening their benighted minds. This praise was often accompanied by disapproving remarks that the missionaries promoted too austere an approach to life, and gained a little something for themselves along the way (Hobbs 1935). Such criticisms aside, the missionaries were credited not only with saving the immortal souls of the Hawaiians, but also with saving their more transient interests of a political nature—just as Twain wrote in 1866. They were even seen as helping Hawaiians to elevate themselves into the political world on equal footing with the civilized polities, and delivering an historical consciousness with all its accompanying anxieties and "artificial needs."

This idealized state, with the Protestant mission as its hero, is also the topic of our historical journey through the Hawaiian cultural landscape of the first half of the nineteenth century. More specifically, the journey is about comparisons between cultures and cultural stages, and constructions based on these observations. All this is done within the field of politics in order to specify what kind of a cultural invention politics was, or came to be, prior to Twain's remarks. Politics and missionaries is not a new topic in Pacific history (e.g., Sahlins 1992, 101–126; Kameʻeleihiwa 1992, 169–198; Gunson 1978, 280–300; Stewens 1968, 8–10, 24–31; Bradley 1968, 168–213; Dodge 1965, 138–146; Tate 1964; 1960; Strauss 1963, 43–82; Koskinen 1953; Wright and Fry 1936), but the field calls out for new ways to conceptualize the theme. For one thing, excepting the works of Sahlins, Linnekin, and Kameʻeleihiwa, the missionary influence in Hawaii has not often been questioned as a matter of indigenous cultural response. More importantly, functionalist and quasi-functionalist understandings of politics have resulted in an unquestioned orthodoxy, and the whole concept of politics has been taken too much for granted. Politics has constituted an objectivist framework, transcending cultural and linguistic boundaries and remaining one of the last unconquered bastions resisting "the native's point of view." In this study, my particular interest is in capturing the concept of politics in its particular historical contexts, and reshaping the conventional orientation toward that entity in cultural studies at large. While doing this, I shall emphasize the varying degrees of vagueness that, in many cases, characterize cultural categories such as politics, but which may become more focused if the historical context informs concrete perception by offering more precise referents for otherwise vague categories.

To say that I am approaching politics as a cultural invention is to argue, first, that all the power-thirsty cunning and self-interest in politics are more or less culturally motivated. This is the standard perspective of today's cultural studies, or nearly so. But the circumstances of seemingly rapid change in the Hawaiian Islands during the period in question require a more complex assessment of cultural motives. The complexity could be stated in a formula: where cultures communicate politics is not simply an arena for cultural practices, but also an object of the same practices. For example, when a Hawaiian chief had a church built, he did it because he wanted to promote his status and consolidate his power, as did his chiefly ancestors. The standard reading of church-building would involve a cultural interpretation of chiefly politics (e.g., Sahlins 1992, 71–72). But what if this church building caused a conflict between, say, traders and missionaries? And what if the conflict was represented—as it indeed was— in political terms by the participants themselves? I would say that the cultural interpretation of politics falls short of giving us a full account of church-building as a form of political activity. It would have ignored that the political nature of the conflict—whether it was overtly political or not—was also at stake when the conflict was interpreted culturally. Of course, no conflict is necessarily needed; church-building alone can be interpreted politically. It is tempting to question whether scholarly statements of this day are any different from those of participants 175 years ago. Consider the following: "On the whole, however, the conversion [to Christianity] of the Hawaiian population . . . can ultimately be explained in terms of the political control it offered the Hawaiian monarchy, especially Ka'ahumanu" (Howe 1988, 173). I take this as an example of approaches that use the concept of politics as an explanation in much the same way as the early missionaries and traders in Hawaii did concerning the status of church building. They, too, used politics as an explanation of motives.

However, there is a difference between interpretations made by participants in these events and observations made from a distance. Principally, the more distant observations are difficult to take as being part of the events they purport to describe. Let me illustrate this with an anecdote. For the late nineteenth-century French Ambassador to Hawaii, M.G.B. d'Anglade, Hawaiian politics was a matter of a happy surprise. A contemporary of Twain, who was practically an outsider, he commented: "One of the benefits of civilization has been the revelation to the natives of the existence of something known as politics" (d'Anglade 1987, 112). In an historiographical sense, this direct observation is a primary source for history writing. But this statement can also be treated as an expression of the cultural grid that frames interpretations. The cultural grid is part of the social and personal framing of the ambassador's perspective (the specific frame is his being an ambassador and an observer of political matters). Yet, he might also have been a participant in the Hawaiian social scene, hence contributing to the emergence of politics as a locally recognizable phenomenon. Therefore, his statement or recollection is not just a recorded fact that ostensibly describes an independent reality. I do not mean that we should discredit the ambassador for his bias, no more than Mark Twain for his, for their biases are constitutive of their identities, and those of others, and therefore of interest from the perspective of interpretive history. What may be biased in d'Anglade's or any other person's observation turns into a meaningful social act in an historical reconstruction.

But, from my point of view, outsiders' comments on Hawaiian politics essentially have value only as representations. It is important to recognize that these representations were founded on some prevailing ideas about history, human nature, and the constitution of society. But the more intriguing question is how and why these ideas became entangled with native Hawaiian culture. As in any analysis of representation, politics did not lie out there waiting—to use the Foucauldian expression—in some eternal identity, just to be discovered; rather, it was invented as an object of culturally relevant knowledge, thus becoming a category of thought that could claim in the voices of locally active people a place in an apparently incontestable reality. But it is one thing to reconstruct the political theory supporting these representations and quite another to study politics as a locally constructed idea. In the latter sense, politics cannot be understood merely by relying only on Western ideas about the place of Hawaiians in the scheme of civilization. This particular understanding of cultural invention calls for an equally particular understanding of the relativity of politics.

On Focus and Sources

I have already indicated the central position afforded in this study to the Protestant mission in Hawaii. In some sense, this book could be described as a cultural history of the mission, and yet I have tried to consider other relevant groups as well, mainly native Hawaiians, but to some extent also other foreigners. My particular focus on the position of the mission calls for justification. Following the growing appreciation among scholars of culture contact that the presence of white foreigners in the Pacific often "provided no more than contexts and opportunities for the working out of indigenous motivations" (Douglas 1993, 20), the received understanding of the role and importance of missionaries in transforming and, in some accounts, destroying the native Hawaiian culture has been modified in recent years. Most notably, Sahlins has argued that Hawaiian culture had elements in it that amplified the effects of the contact, with the unhappy result of eroding the legitimacy of the chiefly rule and collapsing the traditional land tenure system (1992). In their fierce mutual competition, the chiefs moved away from their prescribed virtue as being the benefactors of their people and assumed the haughtier image of insatiable extractors and uncaring tyrants, as they were so often described by contemporary observers. In these developments, a few American missionaries were less important than would ever have been allowed by the once-dominant glorifying history, or the subsequent standard of critical rejection.

It surely appears that the evangelical missionaries were caught in a Sahlinsian "structure of the conjuncture," and exerted their undoubtedly great influence only as useful dupes for the Hawaiian chiefs, and only so long as the chiefly establishment survived. However, being someone's dupe does not preclude the person's capacity to reason, to say nothing about their thinking culturally. Here it seems sensible enough not to confuse the power of indigenous cultures to signify with a corresponding *inability* of foreigners to do the same. The foreigners might have been surrounded by strange meanings and seriously incapacitated in their efforts to make their own meanings stick, and yet they were active in producing cultural objectifications that entered into contact with their cultural counterparts. The result being that they were far from inconsequential. In this sense, the missionaries were busier than the average foreigner.

We should also be careful not to accept wholesale the conception that the missionaries were simply pious errand boys for world capitalism. True as it is, the capitalist forces were already rampant when the first representatives of the American missionary movement arrived in 1820, as Lawrence Fuchs pointed out to us years ago (1961; also Bradley 1968). It might be tempting to marry commercial capitalism and the Protestant mission, because capitalism had propelled so frequent a traffic between New England ports, for example, and the Hawaiian Islands. Thus capitalism's contribution can be seen even in the creation, in 1810, of the American Board of Commissioners for Foreign Missions (ABCFM) itself, and the Foreign Mission School in Cornwall, Connecticut, a few years later. Although the mission, in some ways, grew out of commercial intercourse, it presented an ideological opposite to commercialism. Neither was it an agent of colonialism, but rather an offshoot of quite another battle, one fought in the West against the rising hegemony of the marketplace and the idea of founding social bonds on rational calculus. In this struggle, the evangelical mission was a living anachronism which succeeded by a whim of world historical irony to rise into a position of temporary influence.

The importance of the Sandwich Islands mission is, in my opinion, directly linked to its absorption into the strategies of the Hawaiian elite, on the one hand, and on the other to the ideology of spiritualism and professional calling, which were practically absent in the trader population in Hawaii. Among the foreigners, the evangelical missionaries were in fact best positioned to produce ideas and expressions that would translate cultural significations between Hawaiians and Westerners. First, the missionaries were, like some of the traders, domesticated and given an insider's status by the Hawaiian chiefs, and second, the mission, unlike any other group of foreigners, followed a calling to transform Hawaiian culture and hence to know it thoroughly and to compare it with their own ideals of civilization. It is true that the missionaries drew a clear line between themselves and Hawaiians, sending their children to the United States to be educated for the fear of their becoming more Hawaiian than American. In social terms, the missionaries kept to themselves even more than some traders who married Hawaiian women, but it was their special calling and their methodical interest in spiritual and social reform that turned them into mundane comparativists, and hence important subjects of this study.

To evaluate this role, we need to place the missionaries first in their own native context. This will be instrumental also in helping us understand the missionaries' incapacity for a positive disposition toward Hawaiian mores in general, which made them quite unreceptive to what they heard and saw. This is not to say that the missionaries were unable to comprehend what was going on, or helplessly inactive in their dealings with Hawaiians; only that they were seriously ethnocentric, perhaps more so than other foreign circles of the time. They were certainly set apart by their systematically dogmatic orientation and austere morality, both in their relations with Hawaiians and with other Westerners in the islands. Almost without exception, they were deeply committed supporters of religious orthodoxy, thoroughly steeped into revived Protestant evangelicalism. This was both the best predictor of their response to the new circumstances of "the field," and the most likely reason for their cultural myopia.

The missionaries were nevertheless able to perceive cultural differences, and they understood that sometimes they were having tremendous difficulties in communicating their views to Hawaiians. There was a touch of cultural relativism in their thinking, although they naturally did not let that compromise their primary objective: to eliminate heathenism. This attitude is displayed in remarks made by the prudential committee of the ABCFM after indulging in a mass of warnings sent by the missionaries not to take every description of Hawaiian progress so literally: "Language, when used in reference to geometry or mathematics, conveys precisely the same ideas to every mind. But not so when employed in describing the character and condition of mankind. Here the meaning is varied by a thousand causes. To give the people of Great Britain, for instance, a perfectly correct apprehension of the state of society in our own country, by means of mere descriptions, is perhaps impossible. The difficulty would be increased in France, and greater in Turkey, and greater still in China, and would, if possible, be farther magnified when we passed to the barbarous islands of the Pacific Ocean. The meaning of language is comparative" [i.e., relative] (MH 29, 55). This relativistic orientation, coupled with abominations of heathenism of all kinds, resulted in a feeling of ambivalence regarding the worth of Hawaiians. We shall see that this was an important twist in the missionary thinking. They learned native ways, realized the potential of the language, and defended Hawaiians against foreign intrusion, and yet they found the native culture guilty of every imaginable vice.

Although the missionaries were perceptive of difference, their thinking was imperialistic. It was based on a biblical version of reality that could be applied to almost anything, giving rise to gross occasional misapprehensions and frequent conflicts with those foreigners, mainly their fellow Americans, who did not share the demanding tenets of this universe. It made the missionaries quite impervious to criticism and provided them with a strong sense of being in the right. Of course, there is a sizeable dose of self-righteousness, and an even larger chunk of the rhetoric of Christian soldiery in their accounts, but I think these missionary accounts are no less important than the less dogmatic ones, because they contain the language and the ideas that most directly confronted Hawaiian culture, starting from a systematic study of the Hawaiian language.

Most of the time the confrontation is represented in an idiom that gives more evidence of the missionary way than what could be expected to qualify as good ethnography. As is so often the case, the descriptions could be said to be more about the observers than the observed (which we could say about Hawaiians as well). But we might challenge this position by pointing at one elementary feature of missionary writings: in general they were about the missionaries and their "labors," and intended to be so. The missionaries wrote about *their* presence in a heathen society, and most of what they saw was presented as colored by their evangelical efforts, and by the cosmology attached to them. In fact, the missionaries were writing a comparative history of their trials in the midst of a people (and not just Hawaiians) whose standards were quite alien to Protestant evangelicalism. So it is no wonder that we treasure those rare pieces of missionary writings that are forgetful of the evangelical objective, that is, when we are in need of more or less "objective" historical narratives of Hawaiian ways of life. When this is our need, the great bulk of missionary writings eventually become useless repetitions of pathetic lament and despair, or arrogant attacks on Hawaiian culture. But here we need to understand culturally not only Hawaiians but also the apparently self-righteous missionary dirge (I say "apparently" because their self-righteousness was, on its surface, of a "self-loathing" kind).

After the rise of Hawaiian historical ethnography (e.g., the work of Kameʻeleihiwa, Linnekin, and Sahlins), there is little need to argue that native Hawaiian sources are of equal importance to those produced by any other participants in the encounter. In this study, I have tried to use as many original Hawaiian language materials as possible. The various Hawaiian archives hold a great wealth of unexamined Hawaiian texts, too extensive for any one study to do it justice. Particularly important are the Hawaiian-language newspapers which were published from the 1830s into the mid-twentieth century. No student of late nineteenth-century Hawaiian history can ignore them, and those who, like myself, focus on the first half of the century can only lament that they were not published earlier (the first newspaper edited by natives began in 1861, earlier ones having been produced mostly by missionaries).[2] Also essential to understanding the genius of the encounter are books compiled, translated, and embellished by the missionaries. In translating the Hawaiian texts, whether letters by chiefs and other important persons, essays by Christian converts, or newspaper articles, I have followed the mode suggested by Walter Benjamin (1992, 70–82), who encouraged the translator to grasp the meaning of the text between the lines, and let the foreign language penetrate his own vernacular and transform it. I have attempted to do this by adapting my English to the expressive idioms of the original Hawaiian, and this has occasionally left me with awkward wordings. This, I think, is closer to the Benjaminian ideal than the use of rounded prose.

In historiographical terms, this study is a history in an anthropological key. As more experienced practitioners of this genre have noted (Comaroff and Comaroff 1991), it is impossible to subject every "significant" event to an interpretive act, and thereby recreate a chronological storyline that would trace events to their causal predecessors. By turning off from the main road of event-history, I risk reducing my text to a mere commentary on selected events, a kind of "best-of" collection of Hawaiian history. I have consciously (but as often instinctively) tried to avoid this, first, by arranging the historical material to form a narrative with a chronology—the text should appear more like a story with an inclination toward reflection than a series of commentaries. Second, I have tried to include events that appear less often in print, or have never before seen the light of day in the scholarly sense. This is not hard to do because the archival holdings in Hawaii alone will be feeding the profession of event-historians for a long time to come. Some of these "new" events have been integrated into the better-known "standard" history of the Hawaiian kingdom in order to indicate the richness of these archives, and the still unexplored possibilities that await researchers there. The more historians are willing to add abstract theory (read: anthropology) into their search for events, the richer the historiographic landscape will be.

CHAPTER

Natives and Foreigners
The Cultural Order of Hawaii's
Early Missionization

We must begin our study with an outline of broader ideas that Hawaiians traditionally had concerning the origins of their culture. These ideas long predated contact with Western society, and were part of Hawaiians' traditional lore, and directly linked with their understanding of chiefly rule and the nature of the chiefship. These traditions would become constitutive of the Sandwich Islands Mission's position as well. These Hawaiian ideas have been analyzed before by others, and will be familiar to many Pacific Islands scholars. But they are key to understanding my argument, and where possible I will illustrate them with examples and events that are less often seen in print.

The received understanding of Hawaiians' relationship to foreigners as a class is based on a reading of the traditional Hawaiian culture as entailing an accentuated and constitutive difference between foreigners, *haole*, and native or true people, *kānaka maoli* (Sahlins 1981, 64–65; Dening 1982, 427). In general, Hawaiians were eager to co-opt foreigners and institute *haole* customs. This was a natural thing to do, at least according to their oral traditions. These traditions claimed that the social hierarchy, the chiefly lineages and the gods and other deities had their origins in the strange lands beyond the horizon. But in Hawaiian society not all *haole* were equally admired, elevated, or treated with friendship. Not all *haole*, especially after Cook's proven mortality, were treated like minor chiefs; *haole* was an ambiguous category that could also evoke fearful sentiments. Among those *haole* who stayed (beginning in 1787; Ralston 1993, 176), a few got lands and wives, and thus became domesticated (Kamakau 1992a, 251). Others got along as best they could, employing themselves as carpenters, masons, or petty traders, but they were always at risk of losing their status, sometimes with good reason (Campbell 1967, 87; Gast and Conrad 1973, 248, 281; Journal of Levi Chamberlain, Sept. 23, 1823; Journal of Daniel Chamberlain, June 30, 1820). Some became common farmers on a little spot of land granted by a chief, while others, mainly deserters from merchant ships, merely wandered about without being much employed.[1] This white and sometimes industrious middle-class was, however, functionally if not symbolically inside Hawaiian society and, through intermarriages and loyalty ties, they were socially linked to the domestic order of island life (Turnbull 1805, II, 81; Bradley 1968, 41, fn. 160).

True foreigners, those who passed through without integrating into the local order, evoked quite different standards of conduct. Thus, for instance, a lieutenant of the Russian navy, Otto von Kotzebue, was denied access to the Honolulu fort during his visit in November 1816. Later he found out that no foreigner could enter the fort (Kotzebue in Barratt 1988, 144; see also Golovnin 1974, 22), making it less likely that he was refused entry because he represented Russia, with which the high chief Kamehameha's men had troubles just prior to Kotzebue's landing. "No foreigner" referred to those not in the service of Kamehameha or his chiefs; namely traders, whalers, and visiting captains and officers (and probably also to *haole* workmen hired by the chiefs). On the other hand, in the cultural order, these "wild" foreigners indeed had a place—they were categorically dangerous.

To appreciate why Hawaiians feared or admired foreigners, we must know why they feared or admired their *ali'i*, or chiefs. In oral traditions as well as in their cosmology, Hawaiians traced the ancestry of their chiefs from a great genealogical distance—both in time and place. They could easily count the generations separating the original ancestor and the living chief, but the cosmic dimensions of the sea and the sky were left unmeasured. When memory ceased, these dimensions were translated into cosmic language, and stereotyped within the paradigmatic theme of migrations from the distant homeland of Kahiki to the islands of the Hawaiian chain and back. In one common variation, a priest brings a chief from the radiant stock of Kahiki to rule in Hawaii; in another a brave Hawaiian chief visits Kahiki, bringing home a new plant, animal, tool, or ritual object (Malo 1991, 6–7; Kamakau 1991b, 3–5, 90–111; Kepelino 1932, 76–79, 98; Fornander 1916–1920, vol. 5, 590–595; Masse, Carter, and Somers 1991, 46–47).[2] The gods, too, were said to have arrived from Kahiki (Kamakau 1991b, 112–115), which, according to the Hawaiian cosmic geography, was located in heaven, again divided into different regions of Kahiki (Malo 1991, 10; Kamakau 1992a, 5–6). The earliest post-contact evidence of Kahiki is the recollection of James King, Cook's second lieutenant, who recounts how the Hawaiians at Kealakekua Bay on the island of Hawai'i indicated that the god of the Hawai'i high chief Kalaniʻōpuʻu, Kūnuiākea, lived with the Englishmen (King in Beaglehole 1967, 621). This "national" god was represented in the temples by a wooden image nearly one meter high (King in Beaglehole 1967, 505–506), but he was said to live in the highest heaven. He manifested himself in Hawaii through his several forms, like Kūkāʻilimoku, the war god later adapted by Kamehameha, the most famous conquering chief of the post-contact period (Kamakau 1991a, 7; 1992b, 211; Beckwith 1989, 363–364). By coincidence, when the Cook expedition first sighted the islands in January 1778, they were coming from Tahiti, which they communicated to Hawaiians at Kauaʻi (Samwell in Beaglehole 1967, 1222). The prevalence of *t* over *k* in the Kauaʻi dialect, and the vague general distinction in the Hawaiian language between *t* and *k*, suggest that the Hawaiians of Cook's time knew where the foreigners were coming from. The new era of voyaging began much as any Hawaiian relying on the received tradition could have expected; the intercourse with the land of Kahiki had always been extraordinary and pregnant with magnificent events.

The glory—as well as the danger—associated with Kahiki is particularly clear in the famous chant of Kūaliʻi, a legendary Oʻahu chief. The following quotation is from the early part of the chant, where Kūaliʻi's wars of conquest are symbolically equated with the appearance of humans on earth.[3]

Kolohia kau mai ana Kona i ka maka,	Invited, Kona meets the eye,
Hoʻoulu ilalo o Kumuhonua,	Caused to grow under Kumuhonua,
ʻO nakeke ka papa i Hawaiʻiākea.	Rattling the foundations of Hawaiʻiakea.
ʻO kuhia i ka muʻo o ka lā;	Pointed to the early rays of the sun;
Kau mai ana Kona i ka maka—	Kona meets the eye—
Ke kau lā Kona,	Kona appears,
Ke moe lā Kohala.	Kohala lies behind.

(Fornander 1916–1920, vol. 4, 374–375; Kamakau 1991b, 115–116)

A typically Hawaiian way to construct a chant requires the composer to integrate the story line with built-in hidden meanings *(kaona)*. In order to interpret a chant one is advised to find *kaona* by linking the poetic sentences with typical motives of Hawaiian cosmology, and what Sahlins calls "heroic chiefly life" (Sahlins 1985). In this sense, chants could be treated as historical and social indices, which contain valuable information about the Hawaiian understanding of the fundamentals of their society.

The chant relates to Kūaliʻi's fame as a conqueror, who is by ancestry connected to the divine land across the ocean. In the excerpt we have first a description of a voyage nearing its end, land appearing in the horizon. There is immediately a play on words as the arising land is called Kona. Besides a land section on the southern side of Hawai'i island (we know it is Hawai'i because Kohala is mentioned), it also means leeward in general, the coast that first meets anyone coming from the south, the direction of Kahiki. We also have the names Kumuhonua and Hawai'iākea, the first being the original ancestor of the old chiefly line of Olōlo (Kamakau 1992a, 446), and the second, following Fornander, a form of the god Lono, who ruled the land under the sea (Fornander 1916–1920, vol. 4, 370, fn. 14 and 374, fn. 10; cf. Kamakau 1991b, 129). Both names refer to original times when the land was born and humans began to dwell upon it. The rattling of this Lono's foundation (*papa*, see Beckwith 1989, 24) is probably an allusion to a violent separation of the archipelago from the sea bottom and at the same time an indication of a conquest of land and freeing of it from the tabu of the god. In Hawaiian cosmogonic logic, human life was thus made possible (cf. Beckwith 1990).

Alternatively, and perhaps even intentionally, this part of the chant may refer to an outright conquest of the land of an autochthonous line, which formed the ancestral foundation (another meaning of *papa*) of Kūali'i's opponents. Thus Kūali'i's line, and hence Kūali'i himself, is a traditional usurping foreigner-chief (Sahlins 1985, 73–103; cf. Howard 1985), who, by sacrificing the vanquished chief and marrying the sacred women of the conquered side, establishes himself as the new ruler with a crafted link to the autochthonous chiefly stock. Kūali'i's whole existence is at stake here, and through him the lives of his people. The early rays of the sun also bear witness to the original times of humankind, because in the shared Polynesian tradition daylight is associated with the appearance of humans in contrast to the darkness of night, which evokes the time of gods and dangerous tabus. The symbolic effect created by combining images of the arrival of a chief's canoe, the appearance of land and the rising sun, on the one hand, and the latent cosmogonic ideas of the arrival of humans in general, on the other, reminds us of the paradigmatic function of the highest ranking chief as the foundation of humankind and the divine condition of life.

Kūali'i is a conqueror *ali'i* who arrives to establish his rule, or *aupuni*, which in the Hawaiian cultural order was synonymous with order and organized social life in general. Kūali'i's *aupuni* was a symbolic conquest of the earth for the enjoyment of his people, making him not just a ruler in some legalistic or contractual sense, but a true paramount without whom no order was conceivable. The highest *ali'i*, as Valeri remarks (1985b, 158–159), was a condition of all social activity and, in fact, of the society itself. According to Kamakau, the highest-ranking chiefs "could release *(wehe)* the *kapus* [tabus] of the gods, hence they were called 'life here on earth,' *he ola ma ka honua nei*" (Kamakau 1991a, 10). It has often been pointed out (e.g., Ellis 1979, 120; Kamakau 1992a, 222; Handy and Pukui 1972, 46; Charlot 1985, 1) that after the death of a high chief all tabus upon which normal social order rested were abrogated for *anahulu*. This was a ritual period of ten days during which "various forms of ritual inversion took place" (Sahlins 1981, 65), as in a kind of Saturnalia, until the new high chief restored the tabus, and returned the society to the cosmic order which he represented through his divine ancestry.[4]

For Hawaiians, the concrete environment being of divine origin, their arduous duty was to negotiate their mode of being with the divine. People were profoundly appropriators of divine nature, hence their delicate status and thoroughgoing ritual existence. Although every Hawaiian participated in this negotiation in daily life (Malo 1991, 81), not just anyone could secure nature for humankind as a whole. A person with sufficient *mana* was required. The Hawaiian means of demonstrating this power was a genealogy extending back to the realm of the divine, called *pō*, which in the Hawaiian cosmic chronology predates human culture and the profane, *ao* (these are terms also used for night and day). Thus the person genealogically closest to gods, who was also called *akua*, a god (Malo 1991, 54; Kamakau 1991b, 25), could also defy them, that is, appropriate nature for humankind.

Schematically, humankind, as represented by the high chief, was really a usurper of divine powers. For example, in the best-known Hawaiian creation chant, Kumulipo, the emergence of divinity and humanity are framed within an archetypal competition (Beckwith 1990, 94–106, lines 595–707). The chant describes gods and the first man as being from the same source, but through the first child of the woman, the man, instead of god whose right it duly was, initiates the senior line that appropriates the land.[5] An analogy of this mythical concentration was witnessed in the marital strategies of the Hawaiian elite, but, as Sahlins remarks, it also served as a model for the typical process of usurpation: ". . . an iconic realization in the mode of social relations of the appropriation of the bearing earth (= the wife) from the god (= the chief of the senior line) by and for the humankind (= the usurper, the warrior). The problem was that this apparent harmony of act and myth led to struggles without end" (1991, 42).

The possibility of war reached its climax at the death of a high chief, when a new life on earth was to be installed, often according to the high chief's *kauoha*, dying wish. The new high chief showed his generosity and productivity by redistributing the lands to his followers. In this way, he truly was the life on earth and the source of all power. This dividing of lands often bypassed the closest male relatives of the high chief, particularly because they were his main genealogical rivals. It was safer to give land to lesser *ali'i* and thereby keep the potential "gods" without land resources, which simultaneously deprived them of manpower. Therefore, for any chief of the junior line, the new high chief represented an object of usurpation, for he, as a closest link to pō, became a "god." By becoming a land-giving "god," the high chief paradoxically jeopardized his divine status by being subject to serious responsibilities as "god," as the guarantor of general welfare. The smallest misfortune in his position could lead to rebellion by any one of his closest relatives, who had the same genealogical connection to the divine and who were his virtual doubles (Valeri 1985b, 165–166).

So it was not always clear who would receive the greatest possible honor of being the life on earth. In principle, at least, the closest relatives were all potential enemies to each other, for they all possessed the claim to godliness. In this model, warfare through the worship of Kū could, and often did, elevate an otherwise junior ranking chief to the paramount status of the first-born. It should, however, be remembered that not just anyone could choose this path; a connection to a chiefly line was needed. As Sahlins suggests, the victorious usurper, to capture the divine mana, sacrificed his prime opponent and married the highest ranking women of the defeated side so as to secure his status and that of his descendants. In a recurrent theme in Hawaiian lore, an adopted son discovers his royal origins and finally usurps the position of his elder brother. It is not merely that this sequence can be read as metaphoric expression of humankind appropriating fertile earth; the point is also that the son's high-ranking origin had been concealed from him. In cases of succession and usurpation, the actual relations of different ali'i and their supporters received their coherence from the principle of genealogy, or the transformation of "power into rank" (Valeri 1985b, 157).[6]

The Hawaiian mode of establishing chiefly rule was therefore essentially a matter of cosmic dimensions. A conquering foreigner-chief, epitomized in the chant of Kūali'i, would use his mana to transform chaos into order with useful tabus. The chief would establish his rule by creating a tabued and thoroughly ritualized system of hierarchical social relations, land divisions, and circulation of material goods, the aupuni. So far, I have given only an approximation of this notion. For a more thorough understanding we must turn to the actual performance of the creation of aupuni. This took place during the temple rite called hono. Documentation of the rite goes as far back as the early contact period, and it was practiced until the critical year of 1819.[7] Although the hono rite did not survive the changes of time, it has value in describing Hawaiian ideas of social order which were far more durable than the rite itself; the principle of social organization did not disappear together with its ritual representation (see Sahlins 1981, 64–66).

The hono rite was an important part of the consecration of a luakini temple, the site of human sacrifice and royal privilege. The royal privilege to consecrate *luakini* through human sacrifice was also a privilege to establish the proper social order and the necessary tabus—or better to render the tabus useful for the continuity of society. According to Valeri, the performance of the *hono* rite was itself a mirror image of the universe in creation, now scaled down to minimal symbolic elements. By recreating an orderly universe, it also reproduced the high chief as the living condition of the same order. This was actualized most concretely after a war of conquest. Following the decisive battle the victorious chief would tour his dominions, consecrating temples as he went along. This was done most regularly during the *makahiki* ceremonies at the turn of the year, when the fertility god Lono was ceremonially defeated by the forces of Kū and driven to exile, thus leaving the rejuvenated land for humans.[8]

The participants in this rite were seated in eight rows before images of gods, so that each row began from an image and ended at the sacrificial altar, *lele*, which was surrounded by priests. The high chief and the high priest stood behind the *lele* facing the gods. The people sitting in rows had turned their backs to the images. All sources seem to agree that this rite required great effort on the part of the participants because they had to hold up their arms and bend down their heads during the long prayers, which, according to 'Ī'ī and Kamakau, lasted a full hour. After the prayers, the participants ate sacrificial pigs particularly reserved for this occasion.

In this rite we are interested in the interpretation of both the spatial arrangement of the participants and the contents of the prayers. According to Valeri, "the *hono* rite depicts the final transfer of the divine form into the social relations" (Valeri 1985b, 326). Arranging the participants in rows by god images is a clear sign of the divine ordering of society. But the people in rows are more passive in their roles; though all pray in unison, they do not initiate prayers, nor do they face the gods represented by the images. Instead they face the priests and the high chief, who remain, through sacrifice, the privileged mediators between the visible society and the invisible gods. Besides being an enactment of the separation of gods and humans, this is also a recreation of the necessary social hierarchy. Hence the indispensability of the chief.

The prayers of the *hono* rite add an important element to the reconstruction of the Hawaiian theory of society, and, as we shall see, to the understanding of the cultural interface that produced peculiar Western political interpretations of the chiefship. After the first prayers, there followed the prayer of the ruling chief, who at the same time grasped the human victim by the mouth with an ivory hook:

Ē Kū ē, ē Kūnuiākea,	O Kū, O Kūnuiākea,
Ē Lononuiākea,	O Lononuiākea,

Ē Kānenuiākea me Kanaloa,   O Kānenuiākea, and Kanaloa,
Eia ka 'ālana, ka mōhai;   Here is a gift [and] a sacrifice;
He 'ahu ko'o kea,   A cape of white tail feathers,
He palaoa pae,   A whale ivory cast ashore,
He kipi 'āina, he lawe 'āina.   [And] a rebel, a grabber of land.
Ē mōlia aku i kipi owaho me loko,   Curse the rebels outside and inside,
I ke kūnou po'o me ke kuhi lima,   Who, with bowed head and pointing finger,
A i ka lawe 'āina ho'i.   Plot to take the land.
E ola ia'u, i ka pouhana o ke *aupuni*,   Grant life to me, the support of the government,
A me nā ali'i a pau,   And to all the chiefs,
I ka hū, i ka maka' āinana,   To the masses, to the common people,
I ke *aupuni* mai 'ō ā 'ō.   To the domain, from one end to the other.
'Āmama, ua noa,   'Āmama, [tabu] is freed,
Lele wale aku lā ho'i.   The prayer has gone on its way.

(Kamakau 1992b, 143, translation slightly modified, my italics in the Hawaiian)

In this brief prayer the whole establishment of the traditional Hawaiian society is at stake. The chief, now hooked to the sacrificial victim, channels the divine *mana* of the gods into society. He becomes the support *(pouhana)* of his government *(aupuni)*, which in this case is much more than an organization of the functions of ruling (cf. Kamakau 1992a, 135). Here, the chief is in fact creating the society, not merely securing some fundamentals of an already existing social community; the Hawaiian *aupuni* did not, as a Western observer might easily think, leave the members of society as they were before the establishment of *aupuni*. On the contrary, *aupuni* was the society and the high chief was its condition. The importance of the chief's monopolizing the dedication of *luakini* and the human sacrifice is also clear, for those were the most visible media to the divine, and hence the keys to his own position atop the social hierarchy. Any subordinate chief performing these rites would indeed be considered a rebel, not to mention a commoner (Kamakau 1992b, 129). Further, rebels who threatened to rise against the chief were truly *his* enemies, but because the chief was the founding principle of society, rebellion had a wider significance for social organization and cultured human existence as a whole. Such a rebellion was never a mere coup d'état.

So important was the chief's person that even in the Christian era the chiefs tended to give orders to God while praying, in close functional resemblance to their facing the god images in the *hono* rite. According to a son of a missionary, the chiefs used the word *kauoha* (to order, to command) in their prayers, while the common Hawaiians were much more modest and used the word *nonoi*, to ask, to petition (Emerson 1928, 159). This comes as no surprise if we remember that the chief was, besides the medium, also the natural adversary to gods, and vice versa (see Valeri 1985b, 225–226; Sahlins 1985, 93). The chief's task was to control gods through his sacrificial cult.

By appropriating the land through sacrifice, the chief became associated with that particular piece of land—or should we say that the land came to bear the identity of the chief (Kepelino 1932, 74; Valeri 1985b, 146). The principle of extension of the chief's person to incorporate physical landscape and people living on the land belongs to the same phenomenon. The recorder of native traditions David Malo might have had this in mind when he composed a small vignette of a typical *aupuni*. For Malo, *aupuni* was like a human body, the *ali'i nui* being the head (which was the most sacred part of the natural body), and the other *ali'i* forming the shoulders and chest. The head counselor, *kālaimoku*, and the high priest, *kahuna nui*, were the arms of *aupuni*, soldiers the right foot, farmers and fishermen the left. The fingers and toes represented the people employed in miscellaneous activities (Malo 1987, 121–122). "Here are the things that belong to the true body of *aupuni*, all the people from the commoners to the chiefs under the high chief. That is the true body of *aupuni*, because where there is land without people there is no *aupuni*" (Malo 1987, 121, my translation; cf. Kepelino 1932, 146).

In the same vein, but a generation later, Kamakau pictured a united body of chiefs and commoners, *ali'i* and *maka'āinana* (Kamakau 1865a). It seems that Kamakau was employing the same bodily metaphor primarily to criticize the chiefly establishment for its traditionally unacceptable methods of self-aggrandizement. However, in evoking the traditional past, Kamakau framed the three elements— the high chief, lesser chiefs, and commoners—in a state of *becoming* a united body under the high chief. The product of this unification (without entertaining any romantic ideas of tribal consensus) was called *aupuni*. Later, in chronicling the passing of the chieftainship to Kamehameha's son Liholiho, Kamakau again stressed the image of the extended body of a chief: "When Liholiho became king he gathered about him the young chiefs of every rank and the children also of warriors and many of the commoners and made them members of his household as friends (*aikane*), favorites (*punahele*), and foster children (*ho'okama*), just as the old chiefs had done before him. The kingly crown in those days was represented by the circle of chiefs and commoners who surrounded the king" (Kamakau 1992a, 249).

Thus, in a state of *aupuni* people are united through and under a chief, whose identity becomes the identity of the people living under him. This was then repeated throughout the social classes so that each person was known to have an identity of his or her superior. Such a group was designated by adding the word *mā*

to the head person's name. Although the term was rejected as being impracti-
cable, the people of *aupuni* were theoretically the high chief's *mā*. Malo in fact implies just that, while capturing the traditional passivity of a Polynesian chief: "The
high chief was like a house. The house merely stands but the wooden fence makes
it firm and secure. The high chief is like that, the chiefs under him and the people
everywhere are the things that secure him" (Malo 1987, 125, my translation).[9]

For such a chief, his or her genealogical rank and the link it provided to the
divine were the ultimate source of a legitimate rule. The best way to prevent a
chiefly genealogy from diminishing in respect and glory was to couple with his
closest relative, a biological sibling. An offspring from such union was genealogically closest to gods and was also called *akua*, a god (Malo 1991, 54; Kamakau
1991b, 25). An *akua* chief could also defy gods, that is, secure the appropriation
of nature for humankind. This ideal of the genealogically purest possible mating
between a sister and brother *(nī'aupi'o)* was represented in the *hono* rite by coconut fronds plaited with coconut fiber *(nī'aupi'o* actually means a bent coconut
frond, conveying the idea of self-generation) (Ii 1983, 38; Kamakau 1992b,
143).[10] The coconut fiber used in the plaiting was called, interestingly enough,
"kaula helehonua o ke aupuni" (Kamakau 1992b, 143); literally, "a binding cord
for the preparation of *aupuni*."

At least during the early contact period, from 1778 to 1819, the most powerful chiefs were worshipers of Kū, who became the avatar of the human progression on earth. However, a chief identifying with Kū had to claim legitimacy
by presenting a proper pedigree extending to the original times, and preferably
including several *nī'aupi'o* unions. To return to the name chant of Kūali'i (who
literally was a Kū chief), to his namesake god and alter ego was attributed what
a Hawaiian paramount needed, a connection to Kahiki, the origins of things:

'O Kahiki! Iā wai Kahiki?	Kahiki! For whom is Kahiki?
Iā Kū nō.	For Kū, indeed.
'O Kahiki moku kai ā loa,	Kahiki the island far across the sea,
'Āina o 'Olopana i noho ai.	The land where 'Olopana lived.
Iloko ka moku, iwaho ka lā;	Within is the island, without is the sun.
'O ke aloalo o ka lā ka moku	Approaching the island sun hangs low.
ke hiki mai.	
'Ane ua 'ike 'oe?	Perhaps you have seen it?
Ua 'ike.	I have seen it.
Ua 'ike ho'i wau iā Kahiki.	I have indeed seen Kahiki.
He moku leo pāha'oha'o wale	An island of strange speech is Kahiki.
Kahiki.	
Nō Kahiki kānaka i pi'i ā luna	To Kahiki belong the people who ascend

Ā ka iwikuamoʻo o ka lani;	To the backbone of heaven;
Ā luna, keʻehi iho,	And when above they tread,
Nānā iho ia lalo.	And look down below.
Aʻole o Kahiki kānaka;	There are no men in Kahiki;
Hoʻokahi o Kahiki kānaka,	Kahiki has but one kind of people, the
he haole.	*haole.*
Me ia la he akua,	Like them are gods,
Me aʻu la he kanaka;	Like me are men;
He kanaka nō.	Men indeed.
Paikau, a ke kanaka hoʻokahi	Wandering about, and the only one who
ia e hiki.	got there.

(Fornander 1916–1920, vol. 4, 374–375; Kamakau 1991b, 115–116)

Kūaliʻi was thereby depicted as a true representative of the *mana* of Kahiki. To him were given the violent yet potentially productive capacities, whose origin lay in the invisible land beyond the horizon. Then the famous character of ʻOlo-pana of Kahiki is cited to continue the association of Kūaliʻi with the land of gods,[11] which also brings us forward in the genealogical chain. The next line describes the space that divides earth and sky. This also has a double meaning, either a realist version, describing the sun's path as the traveler approaches the distant land (at this time Kahiki) or a poetic one, investing the chief with divinity and identifying him with the sun (cf. Sahlins 1985, 19, fn. 17) that travels along the firmament above the land, which is categorically common. The following line falls within the same metaphor: seen from Hawaii, Kahiki is the land of sunset, a land seen by the famous chief.

Then follows a description of Kahiki itself, which is said to be a land of strange speech. This may again tell us about a different culture and different people during the periods of migration, but it can also be an implication of the ritual and court language. As the forms of worship, these are supposed to have originated in Kahiki, and were not well understood by common Hawaiians (see Hinds 1968, 127; Botta 1984, 31). It was these proprietors of cryptic language that climbed up to the backbone of heaven. This was a common epithet for chiefly lineage, as was the identification of chiefs with high places.

Now this brilliant abode is said to accommodate no ordinary humans but only *haole*, who are like gods. This, of course, further affirms the link between divine forces and Kūaliʻi. The chant goes on to equate the characteristics of the god Kū with those of the *haole*.[12]

He ulele Kū mai ka lani,	Kū moving swiftly from the heavens,
He haole Kū mai Kahiki.	A *haole* from Kahiki is Kū.

(Fornander 1916–1920, vol. 4, 394–395; Kamakau 1991b, 116)

It becomes quite clear that, as indicated earlier, the god Kū and the person Kūaliʻi are at least symbolically interchangeable, since Kūaliʻi is an embodiment of the god's *mana* and since his own life is the image-turned-real of the legendary function of Kū as a conqueror. Hence the equation in the chant of *haole* and conqueror. However, as Sahlins says, a conquest is always a "sublunar creation" of society (1992, 180), hence a productive and, somewhat contradictorily, life-giving enterprise. So, for instance, Kamehameha's uncle and classificatory father, Kalaniʻōpuʻu, is celebrated in his name chant as,

Ka lālākea, ka manō keʻehiʻale,	. . . a white-finned shark riding the crest of the wave,
Ka niuhi moe lawa ʻo Kalaniʻōpuʻu,	O Kalaniʻōpuʻu: a tiger shark resting without fear
ʻO ka hōʻeloʻelo wela ʻole ia o ka maka,	a rain quenching the sun's eye-searing glare
ʻO ka umu ia nāna e hahao i ka ʻenaʻena.	a grim oven glowing underground.

(Pukui and Korn 1988, 5–6)

Here the images of destruction and death are combined with those of containment (resting shark, rain that cools off the heat, glow of the oven). The chief is a shark that cuts up the land (see Denning 1982), and allots the pieces for lower chiefs who repeat the process and give life down to the lowest commoner. The chief is a dual character; his is the life and the death, as Hawaiians used to say. In this sense, it is not surprising that the metaphors bring forth dimensions of chiefly powers, the sun may be warm and gentle, but it can also scorch and ravish. The chief is the man-burning fire breaking forth (*he momoku ahi kuni kanaka*), the dreadful one (*weliweli*) whose tabus would cause death by fire to defilers (M/BM 20; Kamakau 1991a, 10; Malo 1991, 57; NDOC/ 139). But the chief whose tabus placed him or her out of the reach of any ordinary mortal—commonly described as lonely (*mehameha*), distant (*mamao*), and heavenly (*lani*)—could also be, and was in fact prescribed to be, a patient (*ahonui*) and caring (*mālama*) head of the people, who did not forget the worship of gods (Malo 1987, 39). A useful chief had useful (i.e., contained) tabus. Schematically, the semiotics of a chief can be represented as a series of metaphors of life and death:

Life	*Death*
Stillness	Action
Distance	Closeness
Coolness	Heat

The right-hand column is characteristic of a conquering chief. Ideally the left-hand side resembles the symbolic universe of the post-conquest state (aupuni), the realm conquered from the fertilizing god Lono, or Kū's transformation from a destructive to a life-giving form (Valeri 1985b, esp. 262, 288, 331; Kameʻeleihiwa 1992, 44–49).

It is telling that the first opponents of the conquering chief Kūaliʻi in the battle of Waolani on Oʻahu were four high chiefs whose names were derived from the god Lono, the opposite of the god Kū (remember that the birth of the islands in the chant of Kūaliʻi was a symbolic conquest from Lononuiākea, the god of the submarine land base) (Fornander 1916–1920, vol. 4, 408–409).[13] By the same token, just before the victorious battle Kūaliʻi's companion remarked that they were surrounded by "the rain clouds," signs of Lono (412–413; Beckwith 1989, 31), and messengers of growth and comfortable coolness. The place where the battle took place, Waolani, is described in legends as being a site inhabited by spirits and gods who had built the first temple in Hawaii. Also, the first man, Wākea, was born there and later built the first human-made temple there—again an allusion to conquest (Kamakau 1991b, 20, 30, 129; Pukui 1983, nos. 1033, 2113, 2206; Pukui, Elbert, and Mookini 1976, 228). Evoking the appearance of humans on earth once occupied by gods only, what could be a more suitable location for the battle between the powers of Lono and the representative of humankind, or Kū? Kūaliʻi's first victory therefore marked at once his being singled out as the strongest chief of Oʻahu and an actualization of cosmic drama. Of course, the setting is almost too perfect with the four Lono chiefs, but historical accuracy is not at issue here. The point is rather how Hawaiians understood and made sense of the conquering chiefs by projecting the whole cosmology onto their actions, and passing the scheme down to their descendants in the form of the chant.

In this scheme, the origin of the haole lies in Kahiki, the ancestral homeland of all Hawaiians.[14] In the chant of Kūkanaloa, another god-like hero from Kahiki, he is described as haole and is even given the status of kupuna, ancestor, of Hawaiians (Kamakau 1991b, 114–115). Thus Kahiki, as a place of origin, had significant symbolic value for Hawaiians, who identified themselves as secularized (noa) descendants of divine (kapu) haole from Kahiki. Also Kūkanaloa, by marrying a Hawaiian chiefess, did what a foreigner should do: he became domesticated and retired into passivity, his tabus became useful and his offspring could trace its origin to Kahiki and ultimately to gods. The drawback was, however, that the closer to the present one came the more distant was this source and its divine perfection (Sahlins 1981, 13; cf. Valeri 1985a, 99). The appearance of Cook's ships and the dozens of others that followed gave Hawaiians a new possibility to inaugurate a direct intercourse with the lands and wonders of Kahiki. It is a whim of history that *haole* came to mean not only "foreigner" but also "white man."

In the Christianized Hawaiian tradition, the ancient *haole* are explicitly described as white men, especially in the accounts embellished by the Catholic faction (Yzendoorn 1927, 1–20). In the Catholic case, there seems to be a strong link between this story, the alleged discovery of Hawaii by the Spanish long before Cook, and the dissemination of Catholic faith in the islands, although the whole cluster is a product of genuine cultural reasoning rather than intentional forgery. The theory itself may have originated on the Protestant side (see Ellis 1979, 283–284, 318–320; Elisha Loomis, Journal, June 12, 1824). In 1823, when Ellis toured on Hawai'i, four years prior to the landing of the first Catholic missionaries, the word *haole* had already acquired its modern meaning of foreigner/white man. A deeper layer behind the hypothesis of Europeans visiting Hawaii prior to Cook may be sought in the vagueness of the term *haole* itself. The quotidian word for foreigner was *malihini*, which has more in common with a person's ignorance of local mores than his/her capacity to institute new ones. Because *haole* appeared as a special category in mythology, any arriving people could have added empirical content to the unknown, thus reformulating the story by providing a concrete referent which could be easily agreed upon. Therefore, it is hardly the case that Ellis merely mistook the meaning of *haole*. In principle, the category was open to all arriving creatures. For instance, in later years of contact an African American was termed *haole 'ele'ele*, dark foreigner (Kekāuluohi to Kekūanaō'a, Mar. 13, 1840, IDM/AH).

What was the place for *haole* then, especially when they began to remain in Hawaii? Their status must have been at least vague, if they were not categorically labeled as a dangerous species. They were extraordinary, and in that capacity also useful in enhancing the *mana* of those who came into contact with them, and especially those who could contain them in useful employment. But loaded with this unusual *mana*, the foreigners were also a constant object of Hawaiian envy and fear. In the early years of contact, it was easy for a wandering sailor with a little know-how of Western carpentry and ship building to settle down in the islands under some chief's protection. For common Hawaiians, such foreigners sometimes had chiefly qualities, and they were attractive to a people whose major objective in life had traditionally been to find a life-giving chief under whom they could live a meaningful life (*'imihaku*). On the same account foreigners could have been seen as competitors for the chiefs' attention. For the chiefs the *haole* arrivals meant perhaps an even greater threat. As Sahlins has attentively noted, the Hawaiian chiefs always appeared at the scene of contact a few days after the common people (Sahlins 1981, 36). If we take seriously the understandings carried by the traditional lore, foreigners were categorically rival figures for the chiefs. The danger they represented could be minimized by using the available indigenous social mechanism of attachment (ho'opili) to a chief, which the white men called employment.

In time, the problem of dangerous foreigners was more or less settled (until the arrival of warships in the mid-1820s). The foreigners became deliverers of desirable goods and skills, the Hawaiians provided necessities of food and drink, later sandalwood, and from the very beginning sexual gratification. In brief, Kahiki was secularized through its concrete manifestation. It became a giant storehouse, but remained a land of wonders where some sailed (the so-called holokahikis, as the Hawaiian sailors were called), and upon returning related more evidence of these wonders. For the chiefs it was more pressing to secure the goods than to worry about conquering foreigners. Not that this traditional wisdom was forgotten; the practice of trade had merely proven that the foreigners in general had no plans of war. Commerce was the order of the day. If, in practical terms, the opening up of Kahiki meant both a source of power and source of threat, a successful strategic response would transform external threat into local power, to which the post-contact arms deals and the more civilian commercial exchanges surely attest.[15]

The Foreign Priests of Jehovah

Commerce was still going strong when the threat grew markedly with the arrival of the first American missionaries off the coast of Kona, Hawai'i, in March 1820. Just the previous fall, following Kamehameha's death in May 1819, his son and follower Liholiho, and some other leading chiefs, had abandoned their gods and divine tabus and released the whole society into an ongoing state of freedom from tabus, or noa. What followed was a rather pleasurable period. Whatever the true reason for the abolition, it allowed people more flexibility in their dealings with the increasing numbers of foreigners. It found logical support in Hawaiian tradition as well. A native historian remarked that, "This custom was not so much of an innovation as might be supposed. In old days the period of mourning at the death of a ruling chief who had been greatly beloved was a time of license [noa]. The women were allowed to enter the heiau, to eat bananas, coconuts, and pork, and to climb over the sacred places . . . Free eating ['ainoa] followed the death of the ruling chief; after the period of mourning was over the new ruler placed the land under a new tabu following old lines. In this case Kamehameha II [Liholiho] merely continued the practice of free eating" (Kamakau 1992a, 222).

This so-called "cultural revolution," which can still provoke sorry comments from scholars (e.g., Obeyesekere 1992, 157), was in effect a premeditated act very closely tied to the Hawaiian understanding of their gods. To put it succinctly: gods were manipulable spiritual objects, whose tabus humans could control through ritual. An illuminating case is Liholiho's arrival at Kailua, Hawai'i, where the tabus were formally abolished. A messenger was sent to inform Liholiho that when he arrived at Kailua the tabu of his god would be neutralized by a *ti* leaf ritual. The leaf was a sign that the god had taken the tabu back to himself or herself and left humans *noa*, without the restrictions of tabu (Kamakau 1992a, 225). The newly arrived missionaries noted this in their peculiar way: "though they have abolished their Idols, they have not abandoned their vices" (Thaddesus Journal, June 28, 1820).[16] By this manipulative maneuver—which was unprecedented in its magnitude—the chiefs had established themselves as the sole sovereigns on earth. The gods had been defeated for the last time, thereby ending both Liholiho's constitutive privilege to human sacrifice and *hono*, and the possibility of human forces using gods against the ruling chiefs.[17]

Now the missionaries, burning with zeal, appeared on the scene, which they interpreted as being a religious vacuum ready to be filled with the spirit of the true God. The missionaries praised God for his wisdom, but they soon realized that a terrible landscape of atheism was laid open before them. Perhaps, after all, it was better to be a heathen and worship a deity than what as they perceived Hawaiians to now be: completely and consciously indifferent. That the Hawaiians were certainly not. It was simply that their conception of divinity included various shades. The gods were part of people's daily existence, and they were not kept outside of direct participation in human life, as God was in Protestant Christianity. This exclusionary tendency was particularly true in evangelical social theory, which placed God above everything as the ultimate source of rationality, while people were left to realize more or less successfully the divinely sanctioned moral duty to uphold the principles of civility. It will be seen that within this imagery alienation from the precepts of God was rooted in perversions in the social world. Atheism represented the worst kind of distortion of God-given reason. The distance between the true God and heathenism was shorter than that between the true God and a lack of all religious sentiments and beliefs in the otherworldly. The leader of the mission, Hiram Bingham, found cause for reflection: "irreligion, heathen amusements, licentiousness and revelry, abounded, and atheism took the throne"—it was "emboldened" (1849, 77; also Tyerman and Bennet 1831, 376, 379, 382). The order had been shaken, but perhaps more than was desirable.

It was perhaps difficult at first for the missionaries to understand that their mission was a potential threat to the existing Hawaiian regime, although they were soon informed of these fears (Thaddeus Journal, Apr. 10, July 17, 1820; Kahananui 1984, 123, 236). Perhaps they were blinded by the anxiousness of the Hawaiian *holokahikis* at the mission school in Cornwall, where these adventurous young men learned the great deeds of the living god Jehovah, who was worshiped in Kahiki (now divided into nations and well-known to these early converts). In the Hawaiian system, gods, *akua*, and "government," *aupuni*, belonged together, as could be expected in a conquest-oriented society in which the chiefs had personal gods. To hold fast to the reigns of *aupuni* and secure *mana*, one was obliged to take good care of one's gods and tabus (Malo 1991, 188–190; Kamakau 1992b, 226; Kahananui 1984, 95). This unity of worship and power was an essential part of the education of the chiefs, and also of the ruler in 1820 (Kamakau 1992a, 179, 209).

Now that the Hawaiian nobility had forsaken their gods and ruled without worshiping them, it was certainly a matter of great alarm if a group of *haole* from foreign lands would come ashore and begin to disseminate the word of a new god—ominously similar to the designs of traditional usurpers. If the priests were already there, the chiefs belonging to Jehovah would not be far behind (Holman to ABCFM, Nov. 21, 1820, HP/HMCS). The first intimation of new tabus— and thus a new regime—was the missionaries' refusal to make dresses for the female chiefs on their first Sabbath. The next Sabbath they declined to land their goods, and boldly informed Liholiho (Thaddeus Journal, Apr. 2 and 9, 1820). "We assured his majesty, that *Jehovah has a tabu*, once in seven days, and we were not permitted to remove our effects from the ship during his sacred time" (Bingham 1849, 89, my emphasis).

In Hawaiian tradition there is a famous story relating to this paradigmatic fear of foreigners imposing a new regime. When Hiram Bingham began to erect the first frame house in the islands in March 1821, rumors spread that the missionaries would smuggle in men in barrels and hide them in the cellar (a new thing in Hawaii but a matter of course in New England). Afterwards these men, led by the mission, would take the land. The same source relates other, similar fears that were apparently widely held at the time. The idea was clear and somewhat prophetic, effectively making the present rulers rather more domesticated than foreign, since there was in the islands a new class of foreigners: A prolonged *haole* presence would eventually lead to a demise of the chiefs, "and when no chief remains the land will belong to the *haole*" (Ka 'Ainoa 1842; HEN I: 223–227; Dibble 1839, 78; see also Journal of Sybil Bingham, Feb. 9, 1821; Tyerman and Bennet 1831, 471–472). Sometimes this fear resulted in explicit orders to expel all foreigners who did not hold land under any of the chiefs.

According to a long-time resident, such orders were issued or considered by the chiefs four times between October 30, 1814 and January 16, 1815, twice between August 8 and September 15, 1820, and on March 10, 1822 and October 9, 1823 (Gast and Conrad 1973, 214–215, 242–243, 262, 283).[18] The mass expulsions never materialized, although occasionally individual *haole* troublemakers were forced to leave. The fear of the *haole* did not completely diminish, even after the formal conversion of most of the population. When the Lahainaluna seminary was established in 1831 on Maui, some Hawaiians thought it best to be cautious: When the road to Lahainaluna had been finished, some people thought the missionaries planned to blow up the whole place, kill all the people, and then flee with their wives to the ships at the Lahaina harbor and sail away. Or, in another version, that they would kill all the people and then send for more Americans (HEN I: 223–227). The immediate comment of the chiefs after they had given the mission permission to stay followed the same logic: they warned against sending for more missionaries (Thaddeus Journal, Apr. 10, 1820). This, as we now know, they would have to take back.

In addition to their apparent fear of conquest (Stewart 1970, 161), the chiefs thought the missionaries might put at risk their relatively stable international relations and blooming commerce. This fear was closely tied to the Hawaiian conceptions of Kahiki and relations of power between the chiefly families. The rise of Kamehameha was mediated by his relation to Cook and Great Britain in general (Sahlins 1981). He was the chief noted for his ability to maintain warm intercourse with all foreigners and thus secure their support. But his prime asset was certainly the union with Great Britain, first inaugurated by the sacrifice of Cook and later confirmed by the so-called cession of Hawai'i island to the British crown in 1794 (Vancouver 1984, 1160–1164).

Although Kamehameha's only intention was to extend Hawaiian custom beyond the horizon and to secure an alliance with the most powerful nation to have sent ships to Hawaii, his actions were generally interpreted among foreigners in terms of international rivalry and Western treaty conventions. In time, other nations began to increase their presence in the islands, which naturally put Kamehameha's British connection on the spot. He was reminded of the sometimes strained relations between some of these nations and British representatives. Kamehameha was persuaded to continue the equal treatment of all nations, and even the difficulties with the Russians seemed to fade. As a sign of this policy of equality, Kamehameha accepted a flag in which both English and American insignia were recognized. Nevertheless, his British connection remained strong and was transferred to his son Liholiho, who in 1823 went to England to seek help from King George against rival chiefs, or, as his stepmother

Ka'ahumanu said, "to seek a *hakuaina*," a lord from whom Liholiho could hold the land (Bingham 1849, 204). It was said that Liholiho took some of his father's bones to England to enjoy their *mana*, and perhaps to hide them from the rivals who might have tried to defile the sacred remains (Ellis 1979, 258).

In a way, Liholiho's trip to England marked the end of the Hawaiian elite's British connection. Not that England would have been forgotten—as late as 1833 deified Cook was still prayed to by common Hawaiians in remote areas (Lorenzo Lyons to Anderson, Sept. 6, 1833, HP/HMCS). But a core group of active *ali'i* were turning toward the ascending America. For one thing, Liholiho died while in London, for another, a message arrived from King George in the summer of 1825 encouraging the work of the American missionaries. But no such confirmation had been received in 1820, when the first band of missionaries arrived. At that time the Hawaiian elite was very much attached to Great Britain and its *ali'i nui*, King George, or Kini Keoki (see Manby 1929, 23). In spite of this union, Kahiki began to be differentiated into nations—England, France, America, Spain, Russia, and so forth. As this detailed knowledge was gained from visitors and settlers it was fitted into a cultural scheme, adding more evidence to the conception of Kahiki. I cannot agree with Obeyesekere, for instance, that Cook could not come from Kahiki, the mythic land beyond the horizon, simply because it meant "Brittanee" already during the visit (1992, 61–62). On the contrary, we must make a distinction between the received mythological concept and its meanings as transformed through contact with foreigners. As detailed information was brought in concerning the concrete places and peoples of Kahiki, people's conception of it changed, and Hawaiian geographic awareness began to approach international (or at least European) standards. Nevertheless, at least two decades after the introduction of missionaries, Kahiki remained a synonym for Great Britain (Kahananui 1984, 88; Ka 'Ainoa 1842). Besides, in the precontact time, Hawaiians had used specific place names of Kahiki to add details to their legends (e.g., Kamakau 1991b, 92–95, 117). Consequently, far from asserting that Kahiki represented some physical reality, it is sufficient that we treat it as an organizational concept used by Hawaiians to make sense of the foreigners.

The differentiated Kahiki was also ordered hierarchically in such a way as to reserve the highest honors to Great Britain. The British were the safest alternative. After extensive visits to Hawaii, Vancouver, for instance, was lead to conclude that all foreigners employed by the chiefs were British (Vancouver 1984, 1191–1192). Spain and Russia, on the other hand, were perceived to be troublemakers and conquerors—not without good reason but also much due to some English and American opinions, which reflected strained relations between those countries (e.g., Colnett 1940, 220; Minson 1952, 40; Barratt 1988, 12–14). While Americans came for business (as did most of the early post-Cook Englishmen), the presence of the British Navy was an unparalleled reminder of the powers of that country. For the ritual-conscious Hawaiians, this naval presence gave a further impetus to regard the British as essentially different from other nationalities. Thus the presence of the American missionaries was perceived by the Hawaiian ruling *ali'i* as a possible offense to Great Britain, whose representative George Vancouver had even promised Kamehameha to send English priests to Hawaii (Thaddeus Journal, Apr. 10, 1820; Ka 'Ainoa 1842; Bingham 1849, 88; Kamakau 1992a, 246–247). The whole affair of the mission's landing, and the four and a half years that followed, were burdened with suspicion of its motives, for two interrelated reasons: preparation for possible conquest by Americans, and fear of endangering the British connection. Both were logical extensions of indigenous precepts for dealing with foreigners.

Hiram Bingham first met Liholiho on April 4, 1820, and immediately explained, with the help of interpreters, the purpose of his mission and asked for permission to settle in the islands. There was much discussion, and the highest chiefs gathered in Kailua, Hawai'i, to assess this unexpected turn in their relation to the *haole* world. A week later the permission was hesitantly granted, but only for a probational year. It seems that in the final argument, the technical know-how of the mission weighted more heavily in the decision to allow landing than any desire to embrace a new god. The chiefs were especially eager to monopolize the teaching of reading skills (Thomas Holman to ABCFM, Nov. 21, 1820, HP/HMCS; Thaddeus Journal, Apr. 10, July 15, 1820).

In a short time, the chiefly advocates of *noa*, the so-called Ka'ahumanu *mā*, as well as Kaumuali'i, the paramount of the semi-independent island of Kaua'i, adopted a favorable posture toward the mission. So much so that the leaders of the mission, the Reverends Hiram Bingham and Asa Thurston, could write in their public journal on July 17, 1820: "We want more missionaries and notwithstanding the scruples of the King [Liholiho] with regard to the *danger* of missionaries, most heartily would we welcome an equal number of additional laborers could they arrive tomorrow" (Thaddeus Journal, my emphasis). Judging by the mission journal, the three chiefs most eager to receive the missionaries were Ka'ahumanu's younger brother Kahekili Ke'eaumoku, alias Cox, her cousin Hū'eu Kalanimōkū, alias Billy Pitt, and her future husband Kaumuali'i, alias King George. The first two were reputed to have had a close rapport with foreigners already in the time of Vancouver (Vancouver 1984, 841).

Kaumuali'i's foreign contacts were also well-known, although he was more willing to engage foreigners against the Kamehameha regime, and thus also against Cox and Pitt. Between May 1820 and September 1821—that is, until his removal to O'ahu to be married with Ka'ahumanu—Kaumuali'i most graciously supported the missionaries on Kaua'i, Samuel Whitney and Samuel Ruggles, giving them "more than 200 acres of excellent land, two or three fish ponds, and 20 goats." Following the Hawaiian custom, the land was tilled by forty natives now under the missionaries, who themselves held the land directly from Kaumuali'i (Thaddeus Journal, Nov. 13, 1820). In the same manner, the chiefs provided lands and men for the missionaries on other islands, making the priestly foreigners petty chiefs in the Hawaiian style. For Liholiho this must have cost hours of lonely meditation.

The Native Chiefs of Jehovah

Although generally well-received by the chiefs—as they provided accommodation, food, and occasionally furniture (Lucia Holman 1986, 26, 28–29, 31–32, 35, 37)—the missionaries had a much more meager start in their evangelical objective. Successful execution of their work was hampered by two cultural and structural constraints. We are already familiar with one of these, namely, the ambivalence embedded in the Hawaiian conception of foreigners. The second was the hierarchical organization of Hawaiian society, which rendered the mission completely dependent on the goodwill of the chiefs. These two constraints combined to produce a situation in which the mission had its basic needs looked after, but missionaries were unable to extend their teaching outside the chiefly circles. The immediate response from the ruling chief Liholiho exemplified this old model of haole-Hawaiian relations. His desires were directed more toward material means of promoting his status as the ultimate appropriator of the earth. Excluding the physician Thomas Holman, he thought that the missionaries included too many useless people who could not build ships or otherwise increase his wealth. The system of reading and writing, or palapala, as Hawaiians had for years called literal communication—was good for nothing (Thomas Holman to ABCFM, Nov. 21, 1820, HP/HMCS). Nevertheless, Liholiho finally allowed the missionaries to teach the chiefs and their trusted men, but he only did so in order to see what these priests were up to. Liholiho also secured effective means to get information of the missionary proceedings. In a typically hierarchic manner he assigned servants and guards to the mission (Lucia Holman 1986, 27).

At the time, Liholiho was living in Kailua, Hawai'i, where he also wanted the Holmans to stay. The Holman couple was joined by the Reverend Asa Thurston and his wife Lucy, and the native helpers Hōpū and Kanui, from the Cornwall school. The rest of the band—the Reverend Hiram Bingham and his wife Sybil, Daniel and Jerusha Chamberlain and their five children, Elisha and

Maria Loomis, Samuel and Nancy Ruggles, Samuel and Mercy Whitney and two Hawaiians, Humehume and Honoli'i—headed for Honolulu, where they arrived on April 14, 1820 (Bingham 1849, 91–92). Meanwhile, the Thurstons and Holmans in Kailua were directly under Liholiho's eyes. The Holmans soon found that they were not suited for missionary life, quit the mission in July, and within a few months sailed back home. Asa and Lucy Thurston continued with the help of Hōpū and Kanui, although the latter took to the bottle and was excommunicated on July 22 (Thaddeus Journal, July 22, 1820). The first months of the mission in Kailua seem to have been a series of such hardships (especially the loss of the Holmans) that the Thurstons eventually joined the others in Honolulu (encouraged by news that Liholiho planned to move his court there). Hōpū, who had met his father and brother and had been given a piece of land by Liholiho, felt obliged to stay with his chief in Kailua. When Liholiho moved to Honolulu in February 1821, Hōpū loyally followed with the mission printer Elisha Loomis, who the previous July had gone to Hawai'i to instruct Kalanimōkū's household, after this chief's solicitation (Thaddeus Journal, July 17, 1820; Journal of Daniel Chamberlain, July 19, 1820; Bingham 1849, 99, 104, 125, 132; Gast and Conrad 1973, 246).

The island of Hawai'i was not left completely without Christian teachers, although the mission absented itself from that field for almost two years between 1821 and 1823. There were occasional visits to the former Hawai'i station, in October and November of 1822, and in the summer of 1823 (Barrère and Sahlins 1979, 21; Ellis 1979), but the dissemination of the faith was left to the Hawaiian helpers, Hōpū and Honoli'i, who sailed to Kailua in November 1822, to work under Kuakini, the chief Liholiho had left in charge of the island (Tyerman and Bennet 1831, 367). Hōpū's and Honoli'i's task was to continue the small select classes begun in 1820. We learn from a visiting English missionary, William Ellis, that in the spring of 1822 Kuakini had none of the missionary establishment with him (Ellis to Burden, July 9, 1822, HP/HMCS). Earlier, likely a year or two before the American missionaries arrived, Kuakini had engaged a Tahitian named Toketa, who had received missionary instruction in his native island. He could read and write—also in Hawaiian—and was, judging by his journal, on the verge of conversion to Christianity (Barrère and Sahlins 1979).[19] It was in Kuakini's court that the celebrated Hawaiian intellectual David Malo was first introduced to Christianity and the art of *palapala* (Piianaia 1987, vii–viii).[20] Besides supporting individuals somewhat versed in the worship of the new god, Kuakini took his own initiative in the propagation of *haole* culture. In 1823, this tea-drinking gentleman issued orders to observe the Sabbath and built a church of his own, much to the surprise of the missionaries, who found Kuakini's men at work when they returned from their inspection journey around the island in August (Ellis 1979, 293; Lucy Thurston 1934, 211; see also Kamakau 1992a, 390).

Kuakini's court is an early example of what a few years later developed into a mass scale organization of *palapala* and *pule*, or prayer, quite independently of the missionaries. For any Hawaiian chief, to be the center from which all activity emanated was equal to a purpose of life, whether it was building a temple (Kamakau 1992a, 155), weeding a taro field (Barrère and Sahlins 1979, 27–28), or organizing schools. Following this principle, which was a frequent subject of the missionaries' lamentations over the laziness of the chiefs, Liholiho placed his trusted servants ʻĪʻī and Kahuhu to Thurston's school in Kailua, and later to Bingham's in Honolulu. Afterwards ʻĪʻī and Kahuhu began to teach Liholiho's court. In the same fashion, Liholiho's younger sister Nāhiʻenaʻena was at the head of her own school, which was taught by a native Christian named Robert Haiā. To integrate her little organization, she saw to it that Haiā and one of her companions were married (Bingham 1849, 104, 322, 328–329).

Although we have only scanty information on what went on in Kuakini's court in 1821–1823, we can safely assume that these and similar stratagems were common there, as they were throughout chiefly households on every island. On Kauaʻi, the mission met practically no opposition. The two missionaries, Samuel Ruggles and Samuel Whitney, were strongly encouraged to stay by the island paramount Kaumualiʻi, whose son Humehume the mission had brought back home after some seventeen years of absence (Thaddeus Journal, May 28–29, Nov. 13, 1820; Journal of Samuel and Nancy Ruggles, May 3–June 26, 1820; Damon 1925, 205–207). However, Kaumualiʻi also had some misgivings about the motives of the missionaries. According to Nancy Ruggles, "Hoomhoome [Humehume] told us that his father had frequently enquired what he thought with respect to our coming to live with him and expressed his apprehensions that we should not come, but purposed to deceive him as other white people had done" (Journal of Samuel and Nancy Ruggles, July 25, 1820). This, of course, was soon effaced as the missionaries moved to Waimea on the leeward side of Kauaʻi and took up the teaching of Kaumualiʻi's household.

Kaumualiʻi was extremely anxious to have foreign teachers around him, but without Liholiho's permission he was unable to establish the tabu day for Jehovah (Damon 1925, 225), which would have been seen as a rebellious act. Although Kaumualiʻi was somewhat hesitant in carrying the orders of Jehovah very far, soon after Ruggles' and Whitney's arrival he ordered his men to build a church "on the ground lately occupied by a celebrated Morai [*heiau*, a temple]" (Thaddeus Journal, Aug. 23, 1820; Samuel Ruggles to Evarts, Aug. 2, 1820, HP/

HMCS). This church, the first in the islands, was located near Kaumualiʻi's own houses, as tradition prescribed, and it is believed that he seriously planned to take Jehovah as his new god. This speedy process on Kauaʻi was not taken lightly by Liholiho, who temporarily halted it by the removing Kaumualiʻi to Honolulu in late 1821 to be married to Liholiho's classificatory mother, Kaʻahumanu.[21]

After this incident Honolulu became the center of the mission until 1824, when developments on Kauaʻi launched native proselytizing with the full backing of a Polynesian hierarchy. As a prelude to what was to come, Kaʻahumanu, who had by now learned to read and write, sailed to Kauaʻi in late summer of 1822, and, after ordering eight hundred copies of the new spelling book, toured the area and gave orders to set up schools. This technique had always had a certain magic in it, and for a few days Ruggles and Whitney were more than fully employed in satisfying the educational needs of the sudden converts to *palapala*. And, as Bingham recalls, "their former pupils were now demanded as teachers for the beginners" (Bingham 1849, 172).

After Liholiho's arrival at Honolulu in 1821, the missionaries there were still employed mainly in teaching the chiefs. Apparently Liholiho was assured of the usefulness of *palapala*, because by 1822 he assumed a more positive stance toward teaching, and took up the slate and the sixteen-page spelling book released by the mission press in February. On August 5, Liholiho commenced his studies (Gast and Conrad 1973, 267; Tyerman and Bennet 1831, 475–476),[22] and on the 16th he wrote a letter to the high chief of Huahine, one of the Society Islands. In it Liholiho assured his Huahinean colleague that he was serving "the God of you and us *[kākou]*" (quoted in Bingham 1849, 172). This was by no means convincing for the missionaries, who held a quite different notion of divinity than the Hawaiian chiefs, for whom becoming a worshiper of a god was more a rational choice than a Christian-like epiphany. Not that the chiefs did not believe in their gods, as some of the missionaries thought of the Hawaiian priests, but their relation to their gods was instrumental rather than contemplative.

Just a few months earlier Liholiho had a talk with William Ellis, who reported that Liholiho liked the new teaching and the new god, but could not proceed in establishing Christian tabus because his chiefs were "of a different opinion, and seem, he says, satisfied with the present order of things" (Ellis to Burder, July 9, 1822, HP/HMCS; Tyerman and Bennet 1831, 439). The received wisdom in Hawaiian history appears to disagree with the idea that Liholiho was a hopeful convert to the ordinances of the foreigners' god. Rather, Liholiho is known to have been constantly drunk, a lover of feasts and good times, and disinclined to receive the "humiliating doctrines and self-denying duties" that the mission offered him. Without separating practice from theory, Liholiho's statement was in fact a paradigmatic expression of his social position. Chiefs who stand at the head of *aupuni* should have tabus to make their rule acceptable, and if not that, at least relatively enduring. Hawaii had been without tabus since November 1819, and after a brief rebellion by supporters of the old order, Liholiho's *aupuni* was the first to have stood without divine sanctions established in the *hono* rite. It is likely that Liholiho wished to have retained the old tabus; at the very least he was quite hesitant in abrogating them (Kamakau 1992a, 222–226). The chiefs who eagerly encouraged him to commit this extraordinary breach of tradition were mostly women of his father's household, who also belonged to the group of chiefs that Liholiho mentioned to Ellis as opposing Christianity. Obviously, they did not want to return to a tabu state in which their own elevated positions would have been threatened, first by Liholiho himself, and second by those ambitious chiefs who could resort to God's help in their bid for power, as had Liholiho's nephew Kekuaokalani following the abolition. It was better to let gods rest and continue their rather boozy but relatively secure existence. Liholiho, however, after assuring himself of the peaceful intentions of the missionaries, could add much to his own prestige by taking Jehovah on his side against the arrogant Ka'ahumanu chiefs.

Things were probably more complex than this, however. Toward 1823, after the arrival of Ellis and the Tahitians, the attitude of the chiefs toward Christian teaching gradually grew more approving, while Liholiho showed signs of withdrawal (Bingham 1849, 179). If his previous caution was marked by the traditional chiefly reserve where foreigners were concerned, this new opposition was primarily homespun, yet equally traditional. For whatever tabus there should be, everything must depend on his consent, not Ka'ahumanu's, although she had been made the co-ruler at the death of Kamehameha in May 1819, or at least so she claimed. However this may be, Liholiho was still the symbolic center of society, no matter how much a chief without tabus. As for so many other things, Hawaiians had a proverb to inculcate the people with the principles of proper order.

> O luna, o lalo; o uka, o kai; o ka palaoa pae, no ke ali'i ia.

> Above, below; the upland, the lowland; the whale that washes ashore—all belong to the chief (Pukui 1983, 273, no. 2505).

According to Pukui, this is a condensed expression of what has just been said: the chief has a say in everything, and all activity of life has a foundation in him. As against this, Ka'ahumanu *mā* was in effect usurping power for their Maui lineage, or, as Sahlins says, "Together, Ka'ahumanu and Kalaimoku usurped the active domain of Hawaiian sovereignty, leaving Liholiho in the position of ritual or sacerdotal king, in principle the superior and fixed condition of the social order. The dualism was in fact recursively applied, as Ka'ahumanu stood to Kalaimoku in the same relation of ritual to active ruler: thus war and business fell to Kalaimoku, whereas Ka'ahumanu was destined to become the great patron of Christianity" (Sahlins 1992, 61).

Before the latter could take effect, Liholiho had to be eliminated. In the old terms this would have meant war, an undesired alternative for the Maui chiefs of 1823, who wanted to "eat" from all the islands. An early attempt to accomplish something like a usurpation of Liholiho's symbolic space was Ka'ahumanu's order, given on August 13, 1822, to prohibit drunkenness. This coincided with her Kaua'i tour, Liholiho's short educational career, and the presence of the Tahitian converts (Gast and Conrad 1973, 268; Tyerman and Bennet 1831, 477–478). For a short time it seemed that Liholiho and Ka'ahumanu *mā* went hand-in-hand along the road of "improvement" as paved by the mission.

Not that Liholiho would have been sober for any length of time. On the contrary, amidst his studies Liholiho went on with the bottle and merrymaking, much to the disappointment of Ka'ahumanu *mā* (Bingham 1849, 108; Kaumuali'i to Hiram and Sybil Bingham, June 1823, JPL). This attitude is revealing in respect to the ambivalence that characterized the relationships between the highest chiefs. While the chiefs were extremely jealous of each other, they manifested a deep attachment to their superior Liholiho. This ambivalence was played out at the very top between Ka'ahumanu and Liholiho. It is thus improbable that Ka'ahumanu would have taken violent actions against her "son"; he was needed where he was. However, Liholiho was soon to discover that the more his "mother" and "uncles" took over the rituals of *palapala* (they already controlled much of the sandalwood business) the more his own authority diminished. In an attempt to check their usurping tendencies, he enrolled himself in the mission school. In September 1822, Liholiho, now instructed in the secrets of reading and writing, was quite conscious of the importance that *palapala* had recently acquired. Indeed, he insisted that none of his subjects should exceed him in learning (Journal of Maria Loomis, Sept. 1, 1822; Bingham 1849, 107). In a totalizing society this was the least Liholiho could do: exert effective control over the new things. This gave a special boost to the social importance of *palapala*.[23]

In the early weeks of 1823 Liholiho was still taking classes from his teachers, but apparently his mind was not really focused on the foreign lessons. It is likely that his mind was instead on his chiefs' mounting activities to appropriate the foreign culture all by themselves, without his traditionally vital instrumentality. In May the whole archipelago undertook festivities to commemorate the death of Kamehameha four years earlier. In an eyewitness account we can see clearly how the gulf between Liholiho and his chiefs had grown. In the ceremonial procession the chiefs wore, besides their native valuables, the best silks money could buy, producing a scene so full of luxury that our bystander could not help but proclaim it altogether "splendid." There was also some ritual destruction of fineries. In all this spectacle Liholiho came second. He was becoming poor. "The king and his suite made but a sorry exhibition. They were nearly naked, mounted on horses without saddles, and so much intoxicated as scarce to be able to retain their seats as they scampered from place to place in all the disorder of a troop of bacchanalians" (Stewart 1970, 119; see also Jarves 1843, 232). Not only was he becoming poor, but he also showed signs of turning against foreign customs.[24]

When the first missionary reinforcement arrived at Honolulu on April 27, 1823, the Maui chiefs saw an opportunity to harness these messengers from Kahiki to the service of their own ritual economies. At the time the paramount of Maui was Ka'ahumanu's younger brother, Kahekili Ke'eaumoku, or Governor Cox, who held the land under Liholiho's mother Keōpūolani, the most sacred chief alive. Ke'eaumoku was among the first high-ranking chiefs to have supported the mission. Even before the arrival of Ellis and his Tahitians, Ke'eaumoku had appeared favorable to *palapala* and he soon engaged Ellis to share prayers with him (Ellis in Stewart 1970, 275–276; Journal of Sybil Bingham, Aug. 9, 1822; Tyerman and Bennet 1831, 473). Keōpūolani was even more serious than her active chief, Ke'eaumoku. When Keōpūolani moved to Maui in May with about half of the nobility, she also included the newly arrived missionaries, William Richards and Charles Stewart, in the retinue of fifteen hundred common Hawaiians (Richards and Stewart to Evarts, Mar. 6, 1824, HP/HMCS). She gave Richards and Stewart good lands and ordered her people to build houses for them, and a little later she had a church built. Toward the end of the summer the now pious Keōpūolani fell ill. Before her death on September 16, 1823, she called Kalanimōkū and the future head of Maui, Ulumaheihei Hoapili,[25] to hear her *kauoha*, and told them to follow Jehovah and take care of her children by Kamehameha, Nāhi'ena'ena, and Kauikeaouli. At her deathbed Keōpūolani was baptized and elevated to legendary heights in Hawaiian tradition. Kamakau found just the right words to summarize her lifespan: "Thus the highest tabu chiefess became the first Hawaiian convert" (Kamakau 1992a, 262). We might recall her active role in the abolition of tabus; now she had again put her high rank to appropriate use.

Keōpūolani wanted a Christian burial, which was accordingly granted to her. At the time of her death Kalanimōkū and Hoapili personally saw that the most violent expressions of grief were suppressed, following the will of Keōpūolani

(Kamakau 1992a, 263). Soon after the funeral Hoapili took Kaheiheimālie (Ka'ahumanu's sister) as his new wife in a Christian ceremony, which at this point failed to set a trend (Richards to Evarts, Apr. 14, 1828, HP/HMCS). Yet it was a challenge: Liholiho collected his chiefs in Lahaina, Maui, and made known his determination to visit England. After appointing Kauikeaouli his regent and successor in case he did not return, Liholiho set out to prepare for the voyage, and left Honolulu harbor with a handful of favorites on November 27, 1823.

I have already referred to the likely reasons for his sudden departure as stemming mainly from his unfavorable situation vis-à-vis his hungry chiefs, who had recently flirted with the foreigners' god, his domain par excellence (Kamakau 1992a, 255–256; Kahananui 1984, 244; Bingham 1849, 204; Ellis to Burder, Nov. 20, 1823, HP/HMCS; Bingham to ABCFM, Nov. 21, 1823, HP/HMCS). It is said that sometime prior to his voyage Liholiho had attempted to establish the Sabbath and other forms of Christian tabus, but without much success (Dibble 1909, 180; Bingham, 1849, 177).[26] Liholiho's departure ended the attempts to turn him into a passive ruler of the traditional type. It also solved the problem of the mediation of divinity, for the chiefs no longer had to worry about trespassing on Liholiho's privileged area. Kauikeaouli being only ten years of age, Ka'ahumanu, assisted by Kalanimōkū, would take on the reins for the time being.

Ka'ahumanu's assumption of the mediative role to divinity was declared on December 21, less than a month after Liholiho's departure for England. On that day she had it publicly announced that from that moment on the Sabbath would be observed in the islands by abstaining from all the work from Saturday evening to Monday morning. Not even a fire could be kindled on the day of rest and prayer (Gast and Conrad 1973, 285; Reynolds 1989, 10; Journal of Levi Chamberlain, Dec. 21, 1823). Unlike Liholiho's attempts, this chiefly edict seemed to have bearing among the people, perhaps due to a better organization of its implementation and a wider support among the chiefs, particularly Ka'ahumanu *mā*, who had twenty days earlier made a collective decision to improve the treatment of foreigners (Gast and Conrad 1973, 285).

The next two years were decisive for the consolidation of the missionary presence in the Hawaiian social structures. At the time of Liholiho's departure in 1824, the missionaries, together with their native and Tahitian assistants, were already settled as teachers *(kumu)* under their Hawaiian patrons in four locations on the four major islands (fig. 1). But the knowledge they were prepared to propagate was still restricted to small circles of the chiefly households. As in other areas of life, the new and the prestigious were monopolized by the chiefs, and *palapala* had already gained much prestige. Prestige would soon characterize a form of social organization of schools and meeting houses, still controlled by the chiefs but properly distributed throughout the people. On April 13, 1824, the chiefs held a council in Honolulu, together with the native teachers and the missionaries, to make known their decision to extend the teaching of *palapala* and the word of God to the common people (Journal of Levi Chamberlain, Apr. 13, 1824; Bingham 1849, 211–212; Dibble 1909, 174).

Then an event of immense significance took place, one that compounded the Ka'ahumanu chiefs' ascension, questions of traditional land rights, and the worship of the Christian God. The paramount of Kaua'i and husband of Ka'ahumanu, Kaumuali'i, died on May 26, 1824, leaving his lands as they were under Liholiho. That is, the chiefs of Kaua'i would remain on their lands formerly held from Kaumuali'i. In his *kauoha*, Kaumuali'i deliberately ignored his son Humehume and ordered his nephew and Humehume's cousin, Luanu'u Kahalai'a, to assume the chieftainship of the island. This produced friction among the inheritors by evoking a familiar precondition of war. Because Liholiho had gone to England, these orders were carried out by Ka'ahumanu and Kalanimōkū, to whom the land control was temporarily assigned. When Kalanimōkū explained the state of affairs to the Kaua'i chiefs, he was met by much disaffection, and some demanded that Kaumuali'i's lands should be all put together and redistributed, as was usually the case when a new chief recreated the social order after a period of ritual tumult and upheaval. As a sign of the death of the one who controlled the land *(ka mea nōna ka 'āina)*, there certainly were extensive breaches of normal order; "fishponds were robbed, taro pulled, pigs killed, and other lawless acts performed" (Kamakau 1992a, 266). It seemed, "to take off all restraint. The laws respecting observing the Sabbath as a day of rest from all worldly employment & many others of a similar nature, were now wholly disregarded . . . No attention was paid to learning, but on the contrary, rioting & drunkenness were kept up . . . (Journal of Mercy Whitney, Mar. 1, 1825).

The people on Kaua'i expected to have a new holder of the land, for Kaua'i was still thought to be only allied to the ripening Kamehameha dynasty and Kaumuali'i was the chief who people considered to hold the land. And besides, ritual rioting and plunder after the death of a subordinate chief, who merely enjoys the benefits of the land *(ali'i 'ai moku)*, would surely be considered a declaration of war (Kahananui 1984, 145). But Kalanimōkū did not abide by the demands of the Kaua'i chiefs. He placed Kahalai'a above the lands, not as a land-holding chief but as *ali'i 'ai moku*, who would hold the land from his superiors in Honolulu, indicating that Kaumuali'i held the same subordinate position.

As several people had expected, the disaffected chiefs allied under Humehume, collected their followers, and on August 8, under the leadership of Kia'imakani and others, attacked the symbolic center of the windward (i.e., Maui

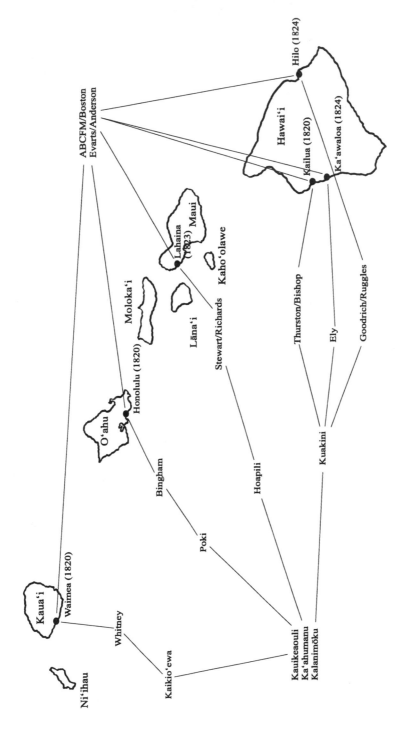

FIGURE 1. The dual organization of the Hawaiian mission in 1825.

and Hawai'i) rule, the coral block fort at Waimea. A brief battle ensued after which the rebel forces were repelled and chased far up into the mountains. In a few weeks' time all the leading rebels were caught or killed by the Ka'ahumanu people led by Kalanimōkū. The aftermath of the Kaua'i rebellion was equally bitter, and out of necessity Ka'ahumanu overruled Kaumuali'i's *kauoha*, stripped the chiefs of Kaua'i of their lands, and replaced them with her own people.

The raids of the rebels were directed also against the institutions of *palapala*, as the Hawai'i chiefs were easily perceived by Kauaians as usurpers allied with a foreign god. Bingham thought the foreigners were specially targeted, although there is only patchy evidence in favor of his opinion. Among the few killed at the fort were two foreigners, and Samuel Ruggles' mission station was ransacked. There were also reports that the opponents of *palapala* had attempted to burn the mission church. Whitney's place survived because it was located away from the rebels' route. In any case, Kalanimōkū told the missionaries that for their safety they should leave the island, and they did (Journal of Elisha Loomis, Aug. 9, 1824; Damon 1925, 232; Ellis to LMS, Oct. 26, 1824, HP/HMCS; Bingham 1849, 235; Stewart 1970, 312–313).

Before the missionaries left, however, Kalanimōkū, who had survived the rebel attack, sent for Whitney and Bingham—the latter was at the time visiting Kaua'i—to offer prayers to Jehovah for having preserved his life (Ellis to LMS, Oct. 26, 1824, HP/HMCS; Journal of Elisha Loomis, Aug. 9, 1824; Damon 1925, 231; Bingham 1849, 234). Later, before the decisive battle on August 20, Hoapili had his Tahitian teacher, Tau'ā, do the same (Kamakau 1992a, 268). After the prayers, as a sign of his acceptance of Christian ethics, Kalanimōkū gave strict orders to his men to save the lives of those who gave themselves up peacefully (Journal of Elisha Loomis, Aug. 22, 1824). Before departing Maui a week after the initial attack, the leaders of the reinforcement troops, Hoapili and another high-ranking Hawai'i chief, Kaikio'ewa, had a discussion with William Richards about Christian conduct of war, and were advised not to kill captives (Bingham 1849, 237–238; cf. Kamakau 1991a, 17). It is not certain to what extent these orders were followed, but some of the chiefs certainly boasted of abstaining from even taking captives. And those who were captured were "set to learn the *palapala*" (Ellis to LMS, Oct. 26, 1824, HP/HMCS).

We should further emphasize another interesting detail that once more exemplifies the strength of the native Hawaiian organization and its ability to mobilize the elements of *palapala* for the cause of the ruling families, as if everything would have happened without interference from the outside world. Reflecting the early ordering of *palapala* in the chiefly households, almost all the native teachers went to Kaua'i to help Kalanimōkū (SIM Journal to ABCFM, Aug.

14, 1824, MMCS; Damon 1925, 232; Stewart 1970, 315). To complete the picture and to signal the total encompassment of the mission by its Hawaiian patrons, Samuel Whitney boarded a ship to Kaua'i on August 18, "not to fight with carnal weapons, but to hold forth the word of life to those who are going to the field of danger and death" (Damon 1925, 231). To quote Ellis at some length:

> Among those who went down from Oahu were most of our teachers and scholars. I gave them every advice in my power before they went and as they were getting under weigh went on board the vessels and exhorted them to avoid all savage cruelty and act as became Christians. Their subsequent behavior demanded my gratitude to God and conveyed the most pleasing satisfaction to my mind. They forgot not to assemble together for prayer morning and evening and in the morning on which they marched to the battle. The teachers scholars &c formed the advanced guard on the right. They came in sight of the enemy at daylight [apparently August 20], and when the three companies into which they were themselves formed had halted, a teacher or chief gave a few words of exhortations to his companions, directing them to put their trust in God and not in their numbers, skill or muskets. Each company then kneeled down and united in prayer to that Being with whom are the issues of life and death. When this was ended they marched steadily on to the charge . . . It was nearly noon before the battles ceased but the prayers of the Christians were heard . . . They did not leave the field of battle till they had offered up their grateful thanks to Him who had covered their head in the day of battle (Ellis to LMS, Oct. 26, 1824, HP/HMCS; see also Bingham 1849, 239).

In the same vein, all around the islands, wherever a chief of some rank was present, the Sabbath was observed, fasts proclaimed, prayers uttered, meeting houses well attended, churches built, and schools established. In a word, the rituals of Jehovah multiplied as did the signs of his power.[27] The new head of Kaua'i island, Kaikio'ewa, began his rule by ordering his people to build a temple for Jehovah. To make the signs materially visible and known at every village—to transform the transcendent God into an immanent experience and part of the social order—Ka'ahumanu set out in February 1825 to tour all the islands, telling people to turn to *palapala*.[28]

The rebellion over, the new order began to take shape, but not as an entire, or even a partial, replacement of one culture by another. Much as Greg Dening has described regarding the Christianization of the Marquesas, the mission in Hawaii, in pursuit of a wider Christian environment, had to resort to representing and conveying Christian culture as "a series of moral rules" (Dening 1980, 200). These were then integrated and forged into Hawaiian structures of signification and social order by the Hawaiians themselves. The moral rules were grouped under *palapala*, which, as a social system, fared better in reproducing native culture than did the contact culture in the Marquesas, where local patterns of life were practically wiped out by the mid-1800s.

To *palapala*, which began as the small-scale instruction of elites in reading and writing, was now added the laws of Jehovah, *ke kānāwai o Iehova*, which were in fact an improvised selection of prohibitions and positive directives based on the commands of the Decalogue. Thus Kaʻahumanu gave orders to the district chiefs of Maui forbidding murder, drunkenness, boxing, fighting, and theft. She also enforced the observance of the Sabbath and ordered everybody to attend school once the schools should be established (Stewart 1970, 321). Hoapili, seeing to the fulfillment of the orders, would banish all those who disregarded *palapala* to the desolate island of Kahoʻolawe, in close vicinity to Maui (Chamberlain to Anderson, Nov. 14, 1824, HP/HMCS). After these events, the missionaries on Kauaʻi could, with some astonishment, write to Honolulu exclaiming that they had "never before seen the people give so good attention to the word of life" (quoted in Bingham 1849, 242).

The missionaries were not blind to the effects of the quelling of the Kauaʻi rebellion, but they had so much good faith in the instrumentality of the event that they saw in it a means to sow the seeds of true conversion among the rank and file Hawaiians, as well as the chiefs. The immediate reaction was colored with optimism and relief:

> I firmly believe the late contest will accelerate the progress of Christianity among the Sandwich Islands (Ellis to LMS, Oct. 26, 1824, HP/HMCS).

> It [the Kauaʻi rebellion] was the means of directing the minds of the Chiefs to the Lord of hosts, upon whose care they were led to cast themselves, and through whose Spirit, we trust operating on their minds, they were led to ascribe the victory to the interference of his hand (Chamberlain to Ellis, Nov. 3, 1825, MSL).

> He [Poki] managed his business well and ascribes his protection and success to the power and blessing of Jehovah, to whom he offered a public prayer before he demanded the arms of the opposing parts (Bingham to Burder, Sept. 13, 1825, HP/HMCS).

This optimism was partly spurred by the intensification of schooling as the chiefs sent their people to all parts of the islands to organize more schools, or what Sahlins calls "quasi-ritual centers." Their primary purpose was to serve as instruments of rule (see Sahlins 1992, 91–93). These schools, Kamakau says, were "conducted like the schools of the hula in old days" with a yearly exhibition of the talents of the scholars (Kamakau 1992a, 270). The usual method of starting a school involved first the permission or order from the chief of the place where the school was to be erected, and second the teacher's application to the missionaries for books, ink, pens, and paper or slates (Journal of Elisha Loomis, Apr. 14, 1825). According to missionary estimates, in 1825 there were from two to three thousand "scholars" in these schools, and a year later their number approached thirty thousand. At the time of Kaʻahumanu's death in 1832, the schools comprised nearly 53,000 students, or 40 percent of the total native population (Schmitt 1977, 211; Schmitt 1968, 42). Given these statistics, it is no wonder that the mission press churned out volumes in astronomical numbers.

It is certain that the battles on Kauaʻi in August of 1824 were a true field test for the power of Jehovah, and to some extent sealed the fate of the mission as an ally of the Kaʻahumanu regime. There were difficulties along the way, especially after Kaʻahumanu's death, but the alliance lasted well into mid-century. However, in the first half of 1825 there was nothing in sight that would shake the bonds of the union. Indeed, the editions of spelling books ran in tens of thousands (Judd, Bell, and Murdoch 1978, 6). According to Bingham, sixteen hundred books were distributed through the network of native schools in April alone (Bingham to Evarts, Oct. 18, 1825, HP/HMCS). And more were to come.

What finally secured the new position of *palapala* and the word of God were the deaths of Liholiho and Kamāmalu in London in July, 1824, the news of which arrived at Honolulu on March 8, 1825 (Reynolds 1989, 70). The British government had offered to ship their bodies and the surviving company of Hawaiian chiefs and attendants back to Hawaii. When the frigate *Blonde,* commanded by Lord Byron, arrived at Honolulu on May 6 with the Hawaiian delegation confirming the sad news, Kalanimōkū was quick to see that nothing of the old mourning customs were included in the reception of the ship. Excepting the news from the Hilo station that some of the Hawaiʻi chiefs had stopped the schools and turned their backs to *palapala* (Journal of Levi Chamberlain, May 10, 1825), which had now become the order of society, there were but few signs of the old ways. Kalanimōkū had his men publish orders forbidding drunkenness and crying, and at times the common Hawaiians were confined to their houses and prevented from seeing the coffins (Reynolds 1989, 79–80). Among the common people these prohibitions were perceived as utterly improper and that many a commoner thought Liholiho "might as well have been buried in England" (MR 1825, 600, copy in MSL).

The same ritual revolution prevailed during the funeral of Liholiho and Kamāmalu, who had the honor, although not by their own initiative, to inaugurate the new burial custom of the Hawaiian royalty (Keōpūolani was the first, to be sure, but at the time of her death she was not a formal head of the nation). If the mass of commoners was disaffected by all the disregard of tradition, the avant garde chiefs were all the more in favor of casting off the old ways, which they already called, reflecting the missionaries' conception of a gradual rise from the state of heathenism, the times of dark mindedness, or *na'aupō*.[29]

The funeral ceremony certainly manifested the ritualist order of *palapala*, although the climax of Lord Byron's visit was not the funeral but the council of chiefs, in which the new order was formally established and Kauikeaouli made the successor of Liholiho. The council was held on June 6 in the presence of the chiefs, two missionaries, Lord Byron, his chaplain, the recently arrived English Consul Richard Charlton, and some of the foreign residents.

Two important things were joined in the council: The chiefs under Kauikeaouli and Ka'ahumanu were given rights of inheritance, and Jehovah was made the god of Kauikeaouli's *aupuni*. Prior to the council, tradition had recommended that at the death of a subordinate chief the lands revert back to the paramount chief, who would then redistribute them, usually according to the wish of the deceased, but occasionally following some other scheme or direction. But beginning in 1825 the chiefs could pass their lands directly to their descendants. The break was not without some precedence. After Kamehameha's conquest there had been an increasing demand from the subordinate chiefs to make the positions of their families permanent, since the whole group was now under one ruler (Jarves 1843, 259; Kame'eleihiwa 1992, 86–87). However, total conquest and rights of direct inheritance formed a paradox, because as soon as land was given permanently to any one family, the unified chiefdom began to erode from inside, unless there was some motive to counteract that tendency. For the Ka'ahumanu chiefs, a unified *aupuni* under one paramount chief and dedicated to one god was just such a motive.

One of the missionaries may have understood the particulars of the occasion. According to him, all admitted "that the mere youth Kauikeaouli would never have been king had it not been for the influence of the gospel of peace. The king himself, I understand, has often admitted that he owes his kingdom to the controlling power of the true religion" (Dibble 1909, 183). The same was recorded in the Hawaiian tradition by Kamakau, according to whom "Ka'ahumanu went out to build a new government, a government founded upon God (*aupuni Akua*), and a government of knowledge (*aupuni imi naauao*). And it was knowledge (*naauao*) and God that secured the government of Hawaii" (Kamakau 1988, 38). Due to the structural arrangements of Hawaiian society, *palapala* became the proclaimed object of *na'auao* and the missionaries close companions for the chiefs.

At the council, after Kauikeaouli had been proclaimed king (the title had been in Hawaiian use since the days of Liholiho), and the Ka'ahumanu families established upon the land permanently, Kalanimōkū's younger brother Poki, the highest-ranking chief to survive the London visit, addressed the chiefs, relating the details of his interview with George IV. According to Poki, the King of England had encouraged the Hawaiian chiefs to attend "to the instruction of the missionaries, for they were sent to enlighten them & do them good—that they came to them not for secular purposes, but by a divine command to teach them the word of God" (Mission joint letter to ABCFM, June 6, 1825, HP/HMCS). It is obvious that Poki's message from "Kahiki" had a forceful impact on the chiefs, not simply because the messages from foreign lands would have been received uncritically, but because tradition provided the chiefs with a means to put things into an intelligible perspective. On this particular occasion, Poki's appearance mitigated the more serious skepticism among the chiefs and allowed them to pursue the course of refitting the land with the tabus of Jehovah. Lord Byron, on behalf of his king, secured a promise from the missionaries that they would completely disclaim "all right to interfere with the political and commercial concerns of the nation" (Mission joint letter to ABCFM, June 6, 1825, HP/HMCS). In this capacity, separating otherworldly affairs from the affairs of state, Byron could not have failed more profoundly. Just by bringing the news that legitimated the presence of the mission he made his own mission impossible.

This freed Ka'ahumanu and her closest relatives to redouble their efforts to turn the islands into a vast network of schools and churches, and to find a common cause in securing the unification. James Macrae, the botanist of the Byron expedition, was among the first outsiders to witness the effects of Liholiho's trip to England. As he recalls, immediately after the council, which of course had been closed by a public prayer, Ka'ahumanu and her sister Kekuaipi'ia boarded Byron's vessel and sailed to Hilo, where they proclaimed the new order to be established on their personal lands there (Macrae 1972, 54–56; Bingham 1849, 271). Several of the other chiefs did the same, and soon a new Christian nation had sprung up. The universal school edict was proclaimed on June 28, 1825 (Gast and Conrad 1973, 296), and when Ka'ahumanu and Kekuaipi'ia returned from Hilo, they immediately applied their organizational zeal to examining schools in Honolulu on July 13. And in the "afternoon Scholars went to the Meeting house" (Reynolds 1989, 99). In August, the chiefs' criers were heard in Honolulu calling people to stop sports and lewdness and to turn to *palapala* and go to prayer meetings (Journal of Levi Chamberlain, Aug. 20, 1825).

At this stage Christianity was truly an imposed doctrine of tabus and rituals of *palapala*. As it was, "many of them [common Hawaiians] say that if they do not go [to church], the chiefs will take their lands away, and cast them off from their presence" (Reynolds 1989, 105; also Kotzebue in Barratt 1988, 246; Ruggles to Evarts, Sept. 28, 1828, HP/HMCS). In the imposition itself there was, however, something that suggested a serious attitude toward the new tabus, perhaps not a mass conversion but a principle of social life through a chief (or *'imihaku*), a feature that the disillusioned missionaries later placed at the root of their failure to effect a more profound change in the "native mind." The schooling was taken very seriously by the common Hawaiians, who were in a habit of memorizing lessons and religious texts and passing them onto their friends and relatives, so that already in the fall of 1825 the missionaries were often surprised to "hear those who came from a distance and had never heard preaching, or obtained a knowledge of the alphabet, repeat whole hymns by heart" (Bishop to Evarts, Oct. 24, 1825, HP/HMCS). This, it can be said, the common Hawaiians did in order to make their best in a society dominated by the earthly counterparts of divine powers. To find a classic parallel, if the Nuer defined their social relations "in terms of cattle" (Evans-Pritchard 1940, 19), the Hawaiians did the same in terms of the chief. We shall see that this theory of society was also reflected in the rudiments of political theory that soon developed out of the inflamed encounter between the mercantile community and the missionaries, who were now de facto personal teachers and chaplains of the chiefs.[30]

It was difficult for the missionary mind to accept this fact of being supported and even patronized by "earthly princes" whom the missionaries would normally, in their own native environment, treat with cautiousness and reserve. The missionaries would naturally pay the princes their due respect, but all the while expressing a hope that they would eventually repent and be pacified by the miracle of grace. The foreign residents in Hawaii were also concerned about what they regarded as too close a relationship between the chiefs and the mission. For the foreign residents it was not so much the primacy of the almighty God threatened by the almighty chiefs that was at the bottom of their concern. Rather, it was the privileged place afforded to man and the freedom of his will that stirred up their feelings. The Western republican ideal of seeing politics and civil power as separated from religion and other matters of conscience was expressed in two different New England languages, one being the evangelical trust in God's sovereignty and everyone's duty to face Him alone and be reborn, the other being the language of new liberal individualism that saw in freedom of conscience a way to bar all authoritarian machinations, be they of the state or a priesthood. From this perspective, it was quite to be expected that the mission would interpret chiefly politics as a sign of hope, although not without ambivalence, whereas for the foreign residents the chiefs' decision to become Christian rulers put Hawaiian polity on the brink of tyranny.

The systematic encroachment upon what the foreigners called "conscience" was marked by two important texts that were published by the mission press in

Honolulu: the Hawaiian translation of the Decalogue by Bingham, and a collection of letters by the highest *ali'i*. Both were printed in December in editions of three thousand copies each (Judd, Bell, and Murdoch 1978, 8–9). The idea behind the first was to induce the chiefs to declare the Ten Commandments the new law of the land, or, as the missionaries themselves explained, to give the chiefs a definitive idea of God's commands, which they then could either accept or reject. (This was a strange suggestion, because the basic commands were already well-known to the chiefs and a standing fact in more populous areas.) The two texts were closely interrelated in that the chiefs' letters were written to encourage the people to turn to the new god Jehovah and his son Jesus, and to enforce the new tabus, the origin of which was in the Decalogue. The chiefs made it all appear very simple, and for an outsider it was easy to conclude that the new laws were declared arbitrarily from high above. Using their traditional prerogatives, the chiefs were determined to transform Hawaiians into a new nation that would forsake the old customs and turn to the morally sound Christianity. Good side (*'ao'ao maika'i*) and bad side (*'ao'ao hewa*) were distinctly marked out, the first being the realm of the new order and the latter that of the old ways. As Kalanimōkū put it, "Ua haalele i ka naau kahiko; eia wau ma ka naau hou." The old mind [lit. intestines, the seat of the mind for Hawaiians] is forsaken; I am of the new mind (*Ka manao o na alii* 1825, 3, my translation).

By this cognizant act, the self-proclaimed proselytes put their own past at a distance.[31] Kalanimōkū, as well as the other chiefs, were perfectly conscious of their choice in favor of Jehovah; all was well-organized and premeditated, to the extent that the cultural distancing, which was required by "the new life," *ke ola hou*, left the basic structure of their society intact. Kalanimōkū even recalled the decisive events that had led to his acceptance of Christianity:

> Keōpūolani said to me that I should serve God so that my soul is correct, so that we two shall live together in the good place of us all after death, the kingdom of God [*ke aupuni a ke Akua*].
>
> Then Keōpūolani died—I pitied her very much. I also liked her dying wish. Then the high chief [Liholiho] went to foreign lands—I lamented for his departure. Then died Kaumuali'i with his mind in the goodness [of God]. He ordered me to take care of Kaua'i, its lands, and all the people for the high chief. Then I went to Kaua'i and some made battle. And God took care of us. At that place my mind really dwelt on God (*Ka manao o na alii* 1825, 3–4, my translation).

Besides this historical consciousness, there also developed a more symbolic discourse in which the temporal kingdom, Kauikeaouli's *aupuni*, was made an extension of Jehovah's *aupuni*, the kingdom of heaven (not unlike Kamehameha's *aupuni*, which was dedicated to Kūnuiākea). Accordingly, the Devil's *aupuni* received the opposite characteristics, which, had any been detected, were conceived of as illustrations of a devolution of the established regime. Kauikeaouli's sister, the ten-year-old Nāhiʻenaʻena, expressed this idea in the briefest possible form. She wrote that she had prayed for God that he would make Hawaii a good *aupuni* and let the Devil have no *aupuni* at all in Hawaii (i nele loa o debelo i ke aupuni ole) (*Ka manao o na alii* 1825, 7). Although the evidence from early on is only suggestive, it seems that from the Hawaiian point of view the old forms of worship were, with the willing help of the missionaries, associated with the Devil, the enemy of God. In this light it is easy to understand the strict measures to suppress the old ways (cf. Kepelino 1977, 44). At this time Kalanimōkū, recalling the traditional wisdom of the chiefs who worshiped their gods (Malo 1839, 125; 1991, 190; Kepelino 1932, 140), told the visiting Kotzebue that it was high time they had a god to prevent the people from rebelling against the present rulers (Kotzebue in Barratt 1988, 251). So total was the reception of the new god that Kaʻahumanu's sister Kekuaipiʻia had already, in December 1824, reworked history to better correspond with the idea of sudden change. In her interview with Kotzebue, Kekuaipiʻia did not mention the abolition of the tabus in 1819, but let Kotzebue understand that Christianity had simply replaced the old worship: "In conclusion, the queen [Kekuaipiʻia] triumphantly made mention of yet another superior side of the new faith: previously, women had been compelled to be satisfied with dog meat, but now they could regale themselves on pork" (Kotzebue in Barratt 1988, 252), as if the removal of the eating tabu had began with the acceptance of Christianity.[32]

History having been adjusted, Kauikeaouli himself, watched over by Bingham and the native teachers, engaged in disseminating the new foundation of his *aupuni*. Samuel Ruggles witnessed one of these regal occasions, this time at Kaʻawaloa, Hawaiʻi: "The king's late visit did much good. His conduct was such as was desirable. On the Sabbath he addressed the congregation with propriety; recommended their strict attention to the instructions of their foreign teachers who he said were their real friends. He also told them not to follow their chiefs [local chiefs who were not church members] for they were 'blind, leaders of the blind' but all who persevered and were strong in the good way should be his friends, his brethren, but those who cleave to their old ways were Strangers,[33] they were not his people" (Ruggles to Evarts, Sept. 28, 1828, HP/HMCS).

We already know the function of such tours and chiefly visits. After the collective decision in favor of Christianity the missionaries, who from time to time toured their respective islands without the chiefs, gradually began to notice the effects of the introduction of the new god. Artemas Bishop, who held the station at Kailua, Hawaiʻi, from 1824 to 1836 (see fig. 1), made a general inspection tour to the more remote areas of Kohala and Hāmākua late in the summer of 1828. While staying in the villages he realized an altered situation: "When 5 years ago [1823, see Ellis 1979, 253–254] we visited this place [Kapulena] for the first time, I passed the sabbath at this place with one of my brethren [Joseph Goodrich], we had only a single fowl and a bunch of potatoes presented to us. But now [Aug. 29, 1828] as I sit in my hammock, I count 2 hogs, 12 fowls, ten bundles of pota- toes, ten calabashes of poi [water-pounded and fermented taro] and 20 fish, all which were sent in unto me within an hour after my arrival, and all except the fish is cooked" (Bishop to Evarts, Mar. 9, 1829, HP/HMCS).

It is possible that in 1823 there was a local shortage of food, and for that reason the visitors received a moderate welcome. But since Bishop experienced the same contrast wherever he went in 1828, it seems more likely that he was now received as Kuakini's priest, who was customarily entitled to a food tribute (for the priestly tribute in 1815, see Whitman 1979, 78–79). The people who organized the tribute were always minor chiefs or headmen of the particular places visited. In addition, they usually formed the core of the local church when that was formed (Baldwin to Anderson, Aug. 10, 1832, HP/HMCS).[34]

If the chiefs at this point made all look simple and clear-cut, the situation was more ambiguous among the common Hawaiians, whose plight was often the subject of foreigners' debate on the rights of individuals living in Hawaii. Although the chiefs had already in 1825 taken the traditional corvée labor sys- tem outside the acceptable limits by forcing a production of sandalwood on a massive scale—and almost equally massive church-building projects[35]—the so- ciety was still largely intact as far as the trajectories of commoner life. The com- mon people were still under their chiefs and, at least to some extent, ready to contribute to the honor and glory of these pillars of society. Despite the real and accumulating misery experienced by the common Hawaiians, the chiefs re- mained objects of commoner aspirations, for any honor associated with a chief and his or her project was extended to those who were below and performed the physical work. This commoner regard for their chiefs, and their attempts to place themselves in a favorable position vis-à-vis the chiefs, intensified any- thing that the chiefs chose to promote.

> So great was the desire to join the church that men and women flocked in from the country districts neglecting their duties to those at home. A wife would leave her husband or a husband his wife in order to devote himself to the service of God. Such a seeker after membership in the church would come first to Ka'ahumanu, braving the fear the people had of her because of her blood-red eyes, and would be sent on to another; perhaps at midnight they would be sent on elsewhere and their faith questioned. Finally they were told

that they must see one of the teachers who explained the word of God, for only so could their faith be known. It was these difficulties put in the way of their own simple manner of expressing their faith that made the chiefs and people so devoted to the word of God in the old days (Kamakau 1992a, 272–273, see also Bishop to Anderson, Mar. 9, 1829, HP/HMCS).

This does not mean that the commoners were not critical of the chiefs. They grumbled behind their backs and resorted to foot-dragging, moonlighting, and petty sabotage. But we can assume that they wished the chiefs would return to accepted custom and readjust the balance of burdens and benefits, that they would resume their caring for the people. The common people, hoping for the better, continued their reluctant toil for the honor of their chiefs.[36] On the foreigners' side, this fed into their political imagination, the foundations of which will occupy a large part of the next chapter.

CHAPTER

The Politics of Virtue

The Westerners who stayed in Hawaii during the intensifying contact era had a culturally defined place for the heathen chiefs, who in the native tradition were thought to be conditions of "life here on earth." In the Western scheme of things they were tyrants and despots, earthly princes who ruled the land as they pleased, absolute monarchs who cared but little for the restraint of law. The apparently unbounded charter of the ruling chiefs became the center of a lively debate regarding the direction in which the Hawaiian polity was heading in the 1820s. The mission was of course implicated, and accused of trespassing the privacy of all those who were subject to Christian tabus. Law, as these people understood it, could not by any means be applied to the faculty of conscience. The missionaries did not disagree, but their thinking sprang from a theory of society that placed social conformity and cohesion before the value of individual license. The mission reacted to foreign residents' sympathies for individualist social theory with suspicion, but also with some ambivalence, because the missionaries, too, thought that religion should be carefully insulated from the rulers' secular designs. For the missionaries, the freedom of conscience was at the heart of their enterprise, because they sought to transform the conscience of Hawaiians so that they would freely and sincerely choose God.

But the co-opted mission found itself navigating uncharted territory, because the worship of god in the Hawaiian thinking was not simply a matter of conscience; one could start a revolt by clinging too fast to the principles of one's mind if those principles were in competition with those of the chiefs. It was traditionally chiefly privilege to mediate between this world and the invisible world of gods, and thus to establish *aupuni*. In this cultural context, it was quite appropriate for the foreign residents to locate Hawaii in the political theory of the West as a deviation from received models of freedom of conscience. Of course, Hawaii was not alone among the nations governed by "despots"; a similar debate had surrounded the cherished tradition of the American Revolution, and would continue through the years of America's religious modernization in the nineteenth century. This debate, itself a cultural pattern, is important to our understanding not only the missionaries' and other foreigners' views on Hawaiian politics, but also the difficult position in which the mission found itself in the 1820s.

More generally, the debate over the freedom of conscience carried within it a major shift in the world view of Americans, and the emerging schism between worldly (mostly commercial) liberalism and religious orthodoxy. The social composition of the foreign community in the Hawaiian Islands during the first half of the nineteenth century provided fertile cultural ground for transplanting the controversy from the American continent. It is an historical paradox that without the motivation of the great engine of profit New England evangelicals might not have crossed paths with sea-faring Hawaiians, who in steady numbers ended up in the Cornwall school via personal tutelage of New England pastors. This clergy labored in an environment in which worldly capitalism had joined forces with a relaxed and more humanistic version of Protestantism. Liberals favored ethics and rational thought more than religious devotion. This was painfully felt by those who were more orthodox, who organized themselves into a counter-offensive through a dense network of voluntary benevolent and missionary societies.

This situation resulted from a slow development started in the eighteenth century. As Heyrman (1984) observes, the rising tide of commerce and secular forms of life generated varying local responses, and in many cases outside threats did not lead directly to a more liberal and individualistic society, but rather strengthened traditional communal life (Heyrman 1984, 407–414; see also Shain 1994). Seen in this light, the religious revivals, "the second great awakening" (McLoughlin 1978) that swept through New England and other eastern states in the beginning of the nineteenth century, can be interpreted as by-products of local resistances to the splintering effects of the worldly spirit of commerce. This is not to say that commercial capitalism would have, in itself, advanced the interests of Satan. But its effects were certainly tarnished by sin, since so many businesses were not controlled by proper Christian piety, which in this case meant orthodox Calvinism. The same was true in politics and higher education. The election of the liberal-minded Anti-Federalist Jefferson to the American presidency in 1800, and the defeat of doctrinal orthodoxy at Harvard in 1805, strengthened the conservative reaction, of which the missionary movement was "one symbol of the unity" against worldly dissent (Bradley 1968, 122). The more traditional element expressed its hopes for reform through revivals, which it hoped would recreate the moral unity. The missionary enterprise must be seen against this background of cultural reanimation and challenge.

Already in the 1790s the orthodox churches had formed missionary societies (Rohrer 1995) to promote the revivalist spirit and fight the rising tide of worldliness in the new frontiers. The formation of the American Board of Commissioners for Foreign Missions (ABCFM) was an important step in creating an atmosphere that united different denominations and attracted wide-spread support from around New England (Andrew 1976). From early on, the foreign missions program recruited young, relatively well-educated revivalists from surrounding communities into its ranks (fig. 2). It very soon became a center for a true Christian commonwealth, much in line with its English sister organization, the London Missionary Society, which already operated in the Pacific. The difference between the two organizations stemmed mainly from the particular historical situation in New England, which rendered the American enterprise generally more "hard-line" in character.

The missionaries that the ABCFM sent to Hawaii were typical orthodox evangelicals in that they came from small farming communities all across New England, and even beyond, and that they valued formal education as a way to the priesthood (Rohrer 1995). They differed from religious rationalists who, although well-educated, were largely from urban areas, especially Boston, and also from the north- and west-bound multicultural settlers who had not yet formed into permanent communities and were subject to itinerant preaching by often uneducated camp revivalists. Schematically speaking, the orthodox evangelicals were set apart from two modernizing forces: first, commercial capitalism and the growing rationalism of the elite that was its corollary, and second, the influx of migrants and the resulting diversification of the nation's religious outlook.

The agrarian background of the organization is important because the small, well-integrated, and homogeneous country communities were prime examples of Christian republicanism, centers of piety and orderly life. Cedric Cowing (1995) has argued that the cultural heritage of the small farming communities surrounding Boston placed these people on the more communitarian side of the scales relative to the "tidewater people," who were more properly avatars of new individualism, freed from the old reciprocal moral obligations. The revivals of the early nineteenth century witnessed this new type of urban, individualistic freedom in its infancy. As Barry Shain (1994) has amply demonstrated, the concept of individual freedom that informed Americans' orientations toward other members of their communities was traditionally corporate in character, involving an idea of moral

FIGURE 2. The northeastern United States and the birth places of the ordained ministers and licensed preachers of the Hawaiian mission. Compiled from the *Missionary Album* (1969).

liberty as opposed to natural liberty, which was thought to be shared by humans and animals alike. Moral liberty was made synonymous with political liberty, hence the strong bond between the ideas of individual freedom and communal responsibility, a bond that was now being challenged by commercial capitalism and frontier migrations. Evangelicalism was quite effectively used to check this challenge, and retard its progress.

Evangelicalism is thus the key to missionary thought, and contrasts markedly with other, more liberal, egocentric views of the world. According to Paul Conkin's definition, evangelicalism from the mid-eighteenth century onward "involved four defining commitments": a crisis-like conversion experience, finding a spiritual dimension in one's relationship with God, winning converts to this form of dedicated religiousness, and maintaining a high moral standard in life generally (Conkin 1995, 65). As Conkin is careful to point out, evangelicalism was not monolithic, but allowed various sectional interpretations to coexist. Perhaps the most important source of disagreement among the evangelical churches was the role of human effort in salvation. The orthodox churches clung to Calvinism, which regarded God as an all-powerful sovereign and could not accept the idea of human agency in God's grace, whereas those called Arminians reserved for humans an effective role in aiding their salvation by actively seeking the right way toward it. Arminianism, or versions of it, appealed to many, especially the poor and uneducated. Its principal evangelical manifestations were Methodism and Baptism, which in the early 1800s were gaining supporters faster than orthodox churches of the more prosperous classes.

In its purest form, orthodox Calvinism was declining when the second great awakening began at the turn of the century (Smith 1976, 32), but, as Rohrer (1995) argues, orthodox churches were not passive in facing these liberal challenges. In fact, orthodox ministers who were sent to frontier missions often adapted to new circumstances by emulating the emotional style of Methodist and Baptist preachers. Many also developed relationships with their congregations that lowered the cultural barrier that existed between the New England orthodoxy and the much-less-doctrinal ideas found in frontier villages. By combining affectionate evangelicalism and doctrinal purity, the missionary movement was inconspicuously reforming Calvinism from within.

It is worth noting that the once-dominant Calvinism was itself splitting into sections, with the evangelical missionaries accepting more popular forms of religion, supported by some authoritative theologians, while many parishes in New England remained committed to tradition. It would be wrong to say that the missions and the orthodox churches at home were in schism, because both objected to religious liberalism and worldliness. Both also shared the ideal of church purity, and maintained strict criteria of church membership, but the practicalities of the frontier forced missionaries to invent a ministerial style that would have been at odds with established practices. It seems that the frontier missionaries grew more democratic with their experiences than were the congregations of heartland New England, where the main concern was to defend the established order against the spreading tendency to substitute pure moralism for moral sentiment grounded in religious experience. But the established order itself, orthodox Congregationalism, was developing in different directions, the more moderate ones following the president of Yale, Timothy Dwight, who put more value on human efforts in the search for grace and regeneration. Dwight had himself served as a missionary, and during his presidency he continued to preach a form of active

Christianity, according to which it was the minister's duty to encourage people to use all proper means to advance their salvation. Dwight's most famous follower, Nathaniel Taylor, went even further, and was accused by the more traditional party of elapsing into Arminianism.

Among the traditionalists there were fears that Dwight's and Taylor's activism would lead to separation, and to their supporters joining the ranks of the newly created Unitarian church (Youngs 1998, 127). The New Haven Theology, as it was called, remained within the main body of the church, however, and the more dramatic challenge still came from Unitarianism. Behind the rise of Unitarianism was a bitter conflict that had erupted in the first years of the nineteenth century, as the principally Arminian and rationalistic movement of Boston liberals increasingly turned away from what they saw as the authoritarian "bigotry" and irrational "fanaticism" of Congregational orthodoxy. By the mid-1810s, the conflict had become more than a mere theological dispute, and in 1825 the increasingly popular Unitarians finally separated from the mother church by forming their own association. It is somewhat misleading to use the word "liberal" here because the members of this faction were mostly wealthy industrialists and large-scale merchants whose social views inclined toward the rather conservative. Their liberalism tended to be restricted to the faculty of consciousness, a position well-suited to their material interests. It is not altogether clear, but according to Mary Cayton the Unitarian churches in Boston generally catered to more influential people, both in wealth and position (and, we may add, political leadership), than did orthodox churches (1997). Even in urban Boston the members of orthodox churches were, although usually in good economic standing, more middle class, being often recently arrived from the countryside and engaged in small business or manufacture.

These petit bourgeois churches formed the breeding ground for evangelicalism. In cultural terms, orthodoxy and hence evangelicalism were attuned to believing, besides in the religious doctrines, in the values of equality, priority of the collective, and moral responsibility of the individual. With these core values, the orthodox held up a version of a covenanted society which was a real antithesis of liberal ideas based on free will and social contract. The idea of covenant as a model for society implied internalized and unlimited loyalty to the ordering principles, whereas contract implied a limited commitment for furthering the advantages of the contracting parties. The emphasis on inner experience through conversion merely served as a method of arriving at the ultimate truth about oneself, while the person, reborn in Christ, was wholly at the service of the community and ready to engage with any business sanctified by the covenant and within the bounds of law. Because covenant was unlimited, members

FIGURE 3. The four-year colleges attended by the members of the Hawaiian mission, 1811–1853 (the number of graduates in parentheses). Compiled from the *Missionary Album* (1969).

of society had a duty to participate in the common affairs of their community, thus becoming responsible citizens "by exercising the kind of freedom that appears in their taking upon themselves the obligations of unlimited loyalty, under God, to principles of truth-telling, of justice, of loyalty to one another, of indissoluble union" (Niebuhr 1954, 135; cf. Miller 1967, 90–91).

Although the evangelical movement was critical of certain social conditions, in its native environment it was not hailed as particularly progressive, and for good reason. As the criticism arose from the observation that the covenant society was disappearing, being replaced by a contracted society of morally less responsible individuals, a considerable number of concerned evangelists were drawn toward reactionary politics (Ashworth 1987, 198–200). Among other things, this was reflected in the educational choices of the future missionaries,

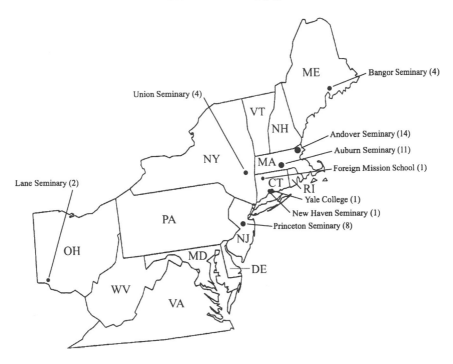

FIGURE 4. The theological seminaries attended by the members of the Hawaiian mission, 1819–1858 (the number of graduates in parentheses). Compiled from the *Missionary Album* (1969).

who predominantly entered the more conservative colleges and theological schools of Congregational and Presbyterian denominations (figs. 3 and 4).[1]

But whether the evangelicals really embraced a political ideology is unclear. It is true that the conservative but declining Federalist party was predominantly under Congregationalist control. But because Federalists also tended to promote the monied interests of the New England seaside, the evangelicals, opposed to wealthy Unitarians, were less likely to be drawn into the party, and many were listed under the Republican banner (Rohrer 1995; Heimert 1966). The evangelical republicans thought that the party was nonetheless closer to the egalitarian ethos of their rural ancestry. To them, Federalism implied aristocracy, a strange form of government to the liking of men committed to covenant society, in which the public good pervaded every aspect of private life. Although the evangelicals "accommodated many aspects of the democratizing republican society" (Rohrer 1995, 147), the majority were very reluctant to interpret their actions in political terms, despite their affinity to and defense of declining social values. Their evangelicalism involved a spiritual quest which was seen very much as an antithesis of worldly politics, and this view was largely shared by evangelical Federalists and Republicans (Rohrer 1995, 144; Bloch 1985, 219). It is not always easy to keep spiritualism separated from political activism, especially since evangelicals hoped to see the true religion become the guiding principle of "the earthly princes" as well. However, orthodox evangelicals often maintained a pointedly apolitical identity, particularly after it became clear that the French Revolution, the great inspiration for republicans, was assuming an anti-religious course.

Although evangelical missionaries subjected worldly affairs to their theocentric framework of thought, they did not generally engage actively in political debates of the day. Nevertheless, most of them shared a keen vision of a republic based on Christian piety. They built their notions of political society on the deeper foundation of a democratic culture that highlighted one's virtuous relationship to community, rather than assertion of one's rights as an individual. The great majority of evangelicals were not political theorists in any conventional sense, and many resorted to the common republican rhetoric when defending their own national heritage. This generic republicanism held that governments should be created by the consent of the people to promote and guarantee the natural and equal rights of citizens, but it failed to distinguish between those who made this a legalistic matter of compact, and those who said that rights would be best defended when people sought God for advice. Generic republicanism is quite frequently found in the missionary texts, as exemplified in the following quote by the leader of the first company of missionaries to Hawaii, Hiram Bingham: ". . . our own beloved country whose motto is 'that all men are free and equal' whose faith was pledged by solemn treaties, and whose early history and revolutionary struggle proved her high abhorrence of oppression and of every unreasonable encroachment of the powerful upon the rights of others" (Bingham to Evarts, Sept. 8, 1831, HP/HMCS).

But just as often the missionaries revealed their deep commitment to the virtuous utopia of human communities ruled by the word of God. In their minds, a covenanted community of regenerated people was the perfect condition in which freedom could mature. In these often pathetic meditations, the missionaries, to quote Bingham again, prayed to God that he would "cause the gospel to have free course in every land as the best means of checking the power of the oppressor, and delivering men from the bondage of Satan & slavery of Sin" (Bingham to Anderson, Oct. 2, 1832, HP/HMCS).

For evangelicals, the church was to become a community of the regenerate who would renounce earthly ambitions. The ideal of a pure church was easier to combine with low-key politics, as was the more conspicuous style of politics with liberal views on religion. These ideas led the evangelicals to accept and even welcome disestablishment. The orthodox organizer of moderate revivals, Lyman Beecher, wrote in his diary at the time of the disestablishment in Connecticut in 1818 that it was the best thing that ever happened to religion, because the churches would thereon have to rely on God only (Cremin 1980, 380). For evangelicals, the greatest fear was not that the state might be contaminated by the church, as the argument of Jefferson and his followers went. The church, if formed from a true center of believers, could not possibly contaminate the state, but the church members, in their civic duties organizationally disconnected from the church, were the best means to good government.

In contrast to this political theory held up by the American missionaries and other evangelicals who believed in the rectifying force of spiritual reform, the Anglo-American mercantile community in Hawaii, as well as in New England, was culturally united in their emphasis of the liberal spirit, without any biblical motivations to ground their actions. For the latter, there was in general no need for a moral reform. If such need ever arose, it was for a reform to end all reforms, which, in their view, were great and antiquated obstacles to human progress (and their profits). It seems that the republicanism of these merchants reflected a legalistic justification of freedom. Their ideal was a social contract based not on divine law, but on the reasonableness of adhering to it. A typical opinion might have followed the theme emphasized by Stephen Reynolds, a Massachusetts-born trader who settled in Honolulu in 1823 and was a keen observer of the various conflicts that raged between the mission and the mercantile community: "Mr Bingham told [Captain] Percival he (B) had sent to the Govt. of U.S.A. for protection. I wonder if he has sent for lands & Naval forces to force people to Heaven by powder & ball!! Mr Chamberlain [mission accountant] has gone to visit every part of the Island [Oʻahu] in company, or at the head, of two or three Native teachers—to tèll them (the people) they must make & subscribe to such laws as the Missionaries shall recommend—and the consequence will be they will all, by Law, go to Heaven" (Reynolds 1989, 140: June 23, 1826). The evangelical utopia was seen as one of the worst kinds of tyranny, because it demanded—or assumed—a mutual commitment to a standardized morality by all members of the community when they had been reborn in Christ. For the traders, and many others, that was a violation against contracted liberty and freedom of conscience. They denounced moral unity as a form of irrationality.

Take the concept of liberty, for example. When the mission began to exert its influence in 1825, the Hawaiian chiefs first raided against grog shops, gambling, and prostitution, continuing on this path for several years. The majority of foreigners interpreted this as a serious infringement of their "Liberties," and appealed to the chiefs for their defense. In the foreigners' jargon, liberty was referred to in its individualist, contract sense. It seems true that the businesses of some foreigners, so far as they pertained to selling spirits, and organizing horse races and pool tournaments, did suffer from the Bible-inspired laws, but for the most part their complaints rested on the assumption that the laws encroached upon their private sphere, upon what they did when they were not engaged in business. These activities they called "amusements," or all those things that one could find in the saloons of Honolulu and Lahaina. In view of their contract idea of liberty, to prevent them from enjoying these amusements was equal to tyranny. The mission found this idea of liberty repulsive. It made little sense to the evangelical mind, which interpreted every act, private or public, through its consequence for the covenanted community. Thus trying to place private amusements under the protection of liberty was a gross misrepresentation of liberty. In 1831, Bingham wrote to the mission board, with much disdain, that the foreign residents and captains "ask protection, not so much in their commercial pursuits, nor their avocations, nor their prayers or modes of worship, but in their 'harmless amusements'" (Bingham to Evarts, Nov. 25, 1831, HP/HMCS). The license to "amuse" oneself was not the foundation on which a nation with political virtue could be built.

Evangelicalism and Political Virtue

From the very beginning of their enterprise, the missionaries hoped to see in Hawaiians the signs of "that spiritual change, which alone could fit them to be useful to their countrymen in the highest sense" (MH 16, 568). They were careful to maintain the distinction between the form and the substance of Christian conduct, bringing to Hawaii a nineteenth-century version of visible sainthood, with its emphasis on deep conversion experience. The missionaries, as good evangelicals, were on a continuous lookout for signs of true religion, first and foremost in themselves but also, as is appropriate for a missionary, in their "people." Their church records show that there were few convincing experiences of this kind, a shortage suffered by evangelical missions everywhere. In 1831 the number of native church members stood at 550, although the hundreds of scattered native-run mission schools embraced more than fifty thousand "souls" exposed to the word of God (MH 29, 19–20). The missionaries complained that "with many of this people it is ignorance of themselves, and a certain dullness of perception, that induces them to suppose themselves religious, when totally ignorant of the nature of true religion" (MH 28, 220). Speaking of their station in Kailua on the island of Hawai'i, the reverend Asa Thurston and his younger colleague Artemas

Bishop found that, "here there is scarcely a family where morning and evening prayers are not regularly offered, and yet we have no hope that the majority of families live under any fear of God . . . They probably at first are sincere but ignorant, and in this way they continue for a long time, until they think it disreputable openly to turn back, and so at last they resort to direct deception to keep up the appearance until detected" (MH 28, 220). The way native congregations presented themselves gave rise to the style of penmanship that in later years would mark the mission with the stigma of outright ethnocentrism and contemptuousness of all things Hawaiian. In the language of evangelicalism, "nothing but cold formality" could be detected, with no real "change of heart" (MH 29, 60). Of course this is not all that the missionaries had to say; almost as often the members of their congregations showed "evidence of piety," some were "hopeful," and others "much affected" by the menacing, "plain" sermons. Still others were in an "interesting state." Nevertheless, it would be wrong to say that the missionaries were altogether so credulous and unperceptive in the face of their large congregations that they could not see the sudden rise of Christianity in its proper context of the Hawaiian social order. In fact, the missionaries were armed with a strong cultural motive to observe anything that might in their view represent a deviation from nature's course, or what they took to be the correct way to salvation and order. It is here that the political discourse of American republicanism meets the evangelical prescription for the soul.

In general, the framing of political representations among foreigners in Hawaii was founded on natural law premises, including popular sovereignty and freedom of opinion and conscience, which were best protected in a republic. But the evangelical missionaries were somewhat different from other republicans in their assessment of human condition. Although American Protestantism had diversified a great deal by the early decades of the nineteenth century, when the first generation of missionaries was recruited by the ABCFM, the adherents of the religion of the heart, or the evangelicals, all shared the view that the debased condition of humankind caused by Adam's fall could best be remedied through regeneration by God's grace. The main avenue to grace consisted of serious repentance of one's sins and surrendering unconditionally to God's will. The evangelicals had learned—without assuming Arminian doctrines here—that good deeds and Bible study were sometimes instrumental in advancing the convert's journey. In theological terms, the missionary movement tended toward Edwardian Calvinism. It took only moderate steps to fit the doctrine of complete depravity of man more closely to the demands that were set by missionization of ungodly people, and were promoted by some learned moderates like Dwight and Taylor. So, at least in the heartland of New

England where Congregationalists and Presbyterians dominated, the movement was at once both conservative and radical: on the one hand, it was a call to revive a lost spirituality of religion; on the other, it represented a shift toward a more humanistic view of grace. In bringing "true religion" to the masses, the evangelical movement was also potentially a radical challenge to the secularized and elitist standing order of New England, even in its renouncement of the decadence of the present and its search for a golden age of purity (Heimert 1966).

For evangelicals, the blooming capitalism of New England was a great scene of self-asserting and proud individualism, and hence a breeding ground for sin and disregard of "true religion." It was all too clear that such conduct in earthly affairs led people to disregard their inherited depravity and the required humility, and to eventually destroy the polity itself. The missionaries who labored among the "perishing" heathen of Hawaiian Islands were soon to find an analogy between their worldly New England countrymen, the great unchurched majority (Conkin 1995, 115), and the Hawaiian congregations. Religiously indifferent sailors and migrant beachcombers were a distressful sight, as described by the missionary Charles Stewart in an account published in the late 1820s: "These, and, I am sorry to say, too many others, who, from their birth and education in a Christian land, ought to be examples of rectitude and morality, are the greatest corrupters of this wretched people; and present the most formidable of obstacles to the moral influence of our teaching. Fancying themselves, in this remote part of the world, free from every restraint of God and man, instead of attempting to turn the heathen from their darkness, they encourage them in sin; even become pioneers in iniquity; and the instruments of doubly sealing them, as we fear, in the gloom of spiritual and eternal death" (Stewart 1970, 160).

Yet, in the view of the mission, the heathen congregations were even more affected by the most debasing element of human nature: the inflated trust in one's own efforts in the face of God. The American masses were indifferent, but the Hawaiians were posturing, witty, and deceitful. In the revivalist spirit of Jonathan Edwards, the reverend Jonathan Green lamented this in a letter to the mission board: "I have just concluded a series of discourses on the 'ten commandments.' This morning, I preached from Rom. iii, 19, and labored to show my poor people that they were under condemnation, and could by no means expect justification by the deeds of the law. I believe that no people on the face of the earth are more inclined to rest in their own doings, for justification before God, than the people of these islands. They are slow to perceive the spirituality and extent of the law of God, their deep guilt in having violated it, and their utter inability to obey it. Hence the few cases of deep, pungent conviction of sin" (dated Aug. 21, 1832, MH 29, 240). Green was anxious to see the radical change that he and his brethren had witnessed in New England revivals: the birth of Christian virtue through a profound experience of conversion. The adopted customs and manners of "civilized nations" could do no more than give an outward appearance of virtuous life, which conveyed but a false meaning of civilization, a kind of civility and restraint that was so notorious among the economic elite in Boston.

The same unhappy condition prevailed in the Hawaiian polity, as the missionaries saw it. And even worse, their disappointment with the refined although spiritually impoverished society of New England liberals turned into a cultural shock when they witnessed the carnivalesque displays of wealth by the Hawaiian chiefs, whose behavior only occasionally became a more subdued imitation of polite society. Their religious efforts were naturally the context for evaluating Hawaiian political order, but it should not lead us to think that the missionaries were engaged in mere theological speculation. They were articulating, in a comparative sense, a conception of virtuous citizenship that was already declining in the American states, but which strongly informed evangelicals in their attempt to set back the tide of liberal self-centeredness and the paraphernalia of secularized theory of social contract. They were fighting against a society founded on infidelity and immorality. The virtuous citizen conducted his and her affairs in a manner of self-government that rested in divine spirituality, a true sense of community, and a deep personal conviction that one's actions were in harmony with the order of the universe.

Because this was not supposed to be the situation among the heathen, the missionaries found a natural occasion to elaborate on this idea. Hiram Bingham remarked on this in his journal in 1821: "In all countries, but especially in countries which are uncivilized, the example of chief men goes very far. It is easy to see, that if the king of the islands [Liholiho] should attend diligently on the instructions of the missionaries, his subjects, to a great extent, would do so too. The truths of the Gospel, which always have been, and always will be mighty through God, would thus be brought to act upon them with great and increasing energy; and Woahoo [O'ahu] and Atooi [Kaua'i] might soon become like Taheite and Eimeo" (MH 18, 213). At the time of this journal entry, the great years of missionary influence were still to come, and the mission was struggling to capture the attention of Hawaiians. The missionaries were aware of and quick to adjust to the Hawaiian principle of chiefly hierarchy. The quote from Bingham tells us also that they were ready to accommodate the power of Hawaiian chiefs and the revivalist doctrine of regeneration. Following the moderate course of the orthodox party, Bingham maintained that a prolonged exposure to Christian teaching, even if initiated by chiefly authority, would make Hawaiians conscious of their sins and urge them to repent and be prepared for the acts of miraculous grace. In spite of this "prudence," the missionaries looked to the chiefly authority as a great evil because it prevented the rise of virtuous citizenship in Hawaii, and threatened the civilizing objective of the mission with failure.

The idea of virtuous citizenship hinges on the difference between covenant and contract. If evangelicalism can be taken as a defense of covenant society, then liberalism and the new individualism found culturally satisfactory expression in society based on contract. The contract represented the power of the individuals to judge whether it was beneficial to give up part of their perfect freedom in exchange for security. For evangelicals, this calculative citizenship was a Hobbesian perversion (see Heimert 1966, 18, 516); no citizenship could be founded on a legal scheme of contract. The road of social contract led to selfishness and sin, as the parties of the contract were not changed in their hearts, only in their appearances and manners. A good evangelical missionary could never be satisfied with mere outward restraints of behavior based on calculative reason. The idea of contract resembled an image of a great masquerade; behind the civilized masks lurk the true selves, the humanized wolves driven by the lowest urges and passions. The change of heart was a strong metaphor which informed also the evangelical theory of the good society, the covenant. Asa Thurston and Artemas Bishop, for example, enacted this imagery in their 1828 description of the sudden progress of Christianity on Hawai'i. Those who approached the mission in hopes of becoming church members appeared thoroughly changed: "Mutual love and confidence toward each other have succeeded to hatred and disgust. The furious savage has become the humble follower of the Lamb. The dishonest, the brutalized, the libidinous son of earth has now become the peaceful citizen and the zealous promoter of order, sobriety, and Christian morality" (MH 25, 316). Their account stands in contrast to those given in times of religious decline, but only insofar as it is here meant to convey an empirical truth, and in other times only a hope for its eventual realization. The importance of the imagery, however, comes from its use as an interpretive pattern.

It is interesting that Hawaiian chiefship, and in fact the whole social order, was in some ways interpreted in these same terms. Starting from the shortcomings of the heathen mind, the adherents of this pattern concluded that, in essence, the Hawaiian polity, like the ideas of contract society and legalism, lacked the spirit of communal responsibility. It therefore came natural for the mission to view Hawaiian polity as an artificial expression of the powers that be. From the first encounters onward, Hawaii was described as an absolute monarchy. The Hawaiian elite was often seen as having pursued political ends through their traditional religion and, later, through their embracing of Christianity. Describing the religious conviction of the first Kamehameha, the London Missionary Society deputation that visited Hawaii in 1822 concluded, after interviews with their American brethren, that "it was suspected that his religion was only a part of his policy" (Tyerman and Bennet 1831, 444). Earlier, the first company had alluded to the same by relativizing Kamehameha's relation to Hawaiian gods as being a matter of legitimating his sovereignty rather than any firm belief. That Kamehameha was "tenacious of his religion" was attributed to his use of religion "as an engine of government" (Bingham to Worcester, May 13, 1820, HP/HMCS). Thus the missionaries felt a great deal of ambivalence in their relations with the chiefs. We have seen that the mission was seriously co-opted by the Hawaiian standing order, but that the mission itself worked through the chiefs. Also, in allowing themselves to be co-opted, the missionaries were critical of the chiefly rule. From the first days in the field, the public sermons contained biblical references to proud kings and the hypocrisy of the powerful. "Be wise now, therefore, O ye kings, be instructed, ye judges of the earth," Hiram Bingham thundered, through an interpreter, in the morning service of the first Sabbath of February 1822 (MH 19, 182).

This kind of criticism was biblical in content, but beneath it lay also the cultural script of evangelical republicanism, which proscribed a social order founded on power and deference only, and called for communal unity through the miracle of grace. This is not to say that the missionaries were radical democrats willing to level everything. They did welcome hierarchy and all forms of social distinction, and in principle did not disapprove of the elevated position of the chiefs. The only thing they found wanting was a proper foundation of hierarchy, and this want made the whole Hawaiian polity a perversion of good order. In the correctly founded society, social distinctions would merely be functional, and would reciprocally contribute to the common good of all. The corresponding secretary of the ABCFM, Samuel Worcester, posthumously expressed this view in the instructions given to the second missionary company in November 1822:

> You will never give countenance to the popular error that men must be civilized before they can receive the Gospel. You are well aware, that an ignorant and heathen people never can be civilized without the Gospel. There has not been an instance, since the first promulgation of Christianity, of a barbarous nation brought into a state of well-regulated society, unless by the means and motives, which true religion alone can furnish. You may, indeed, easily prove to a heathen and a savage, that good laws, wholesome restraint, constant occupation, and a regular discharge of the domestic duties, are favorable to the enjoyment of this life; but when your proof is ended, what have you accomplished? "Alas, leviathan is not so tam'd" . . . If God should honor your instrumentality as preachers

of the Gospel, civilization, purity of morals, refinement of intellect and of manners, will follow of course (MH 19, 108–109).

Nowhere was this theory more evident than in the missionaries' frustration and disappointment in their attempt to turn Hawaiian Christianity from an orchestrated mass movement into a private matter of the proselyte. This was difficult to accomplish even among those natives who, on the basis of their religious erudition and exceptional moral advancement, had been given access to restricted meetings and the embryonic learned societies. In 1832, the reverends Dibble and Lyman reported from Hilo, Hawaiʻi: "You will perceive that the meetings of an exclusive character, open only to persons of certain moral qualifications, have been discontinued. Their influence, we found, was to foster pride and self-righteousness. We have reason to fear that many individuals in these associations have relied upon their membership, more than upon Jesus Christ, for the salvation of their souls" (MH 29, 237–238).

As I have said, the missionaries were not pursuing Christian commonwealth blindfolded, although their misapprehension often equaled the accuracy of their observations. In this case, the mission accumulated sufficient material on Hawaiian tactics of reaping the best of the new religion so that the mission board published, in 1833, an official statement of caution as to "the state of the islands and the progress of the mission." The board ended up describing Hawaii as a nominally Christian nation that possessed "the mere primary elements of Christian character." This statement is an important document because it gives a fine summary of the many observations made in different stations by missionaries, who interpreted their encounter with Hawaiians through the doctrines of covenant and evangelical republicanism. Their ideal was a society founded on mutual obligations, personal responsibility, and reciprocal harmony, all inspired by God's grace and the regeneration of the sinner. The competitive chiefs, the deep gulf that separated them from the common Hawaiians, and the exploitative nature of the Hawaiian polity contradicted this ideal. I shall quote the text at some length to give a good flavor of evangelically minded comparative political theory:

> It is necessary to understand the genius of the Sandwich Islands government. It is but a little while since the chiefs were regarded by the present generation as something more than mortal. A feeling the most despotic on the one hand, was met on the other, by the great body of the people, with a feeling the most abject and servile. This is still true to a very great extent, and is the natural result of the oppressive tyranny to which the islands have been subjected from time immemorial. It has hence come to pass, that the great body of the people perform most of the acts of their lives from a regard to the authority of the chiefs, and not in obedience to their own sense of fitness and propriety. It is

true, also, that it is most impossible for the chiefs to give their subjects what may properly be termed *advice*. Their *wishes*, when once known to the people, are in effect as absolute as their *will*, and their *advice* has all the force of *command*. This gives their *example*, too, prodigious influence upon the people. And this fact is one of great importance in estimating the real extent of the national changes, which have taken place in reference to religion. When the chiefs were moved by the Holy Ghost, as they doubtless were, to embrace the Christian religion, and advised the people to embrace it, their advice and example must have had the force of law. It would seem, too, that whenever the chiefs have exhorted the people to attend upon the instructions of the missionaries, their exhortations have come with authority. So when the chiefs call upon them to attend church, they attend; and to study the word of God in schools, they study it; and to purchase books, they purchase them; and to become religious, they put on the form of godliness. All this is not mentioned as of course an evil in the state of things at the Sandwich Islands. If the common people are such children as they are described to be, and as they doubtless are, it is desirable for them to be under authority, and to have this authority carried much beyond the bounds which would be desirable for people with mature minds. It is well for them to be commanded to attend school, and to attend church, and to study the Bible (MH 29, 454).

The missionaries had also noticed the growing appetite of the chiefs, and of the labor taxes that were ever more frequently levied on the populace. "Their Sandal-wood is gone, and their resources are now failing. This induces the chiefs to be more exorbitant in their demands of the common people; and we strongly feel that the interests of religion require a change in these respects" (MH 29, 268). Although the missionaries claimed to have encouraged the virtues of the covenant society—"justice and temperance in the rulers in the execution of law; and loyalty, order, and peace among the subjects in all the relations and duties of life" (MH 29, 165)—it seems that the chiefs showed no mildness in their rule, and that the subjects' loyalty was not of that disinterested and internalized type so much sought after by the mission.

Perhaps the most frequently used observation to support this theory was church attendance. Before the general acceptance of Christianity by the chiefs, the mission churches were not attended by the great masses, as became the norm after 1825. Instead, the chiefs were present, occupying the front seats, and the common people were typically gathered outside the church building. The missionaries soon recognized that the people came for the chiefs and not for the word. Even after the formal introduction of Christianity it was not uncommon that when a "pious" local chief died his or her people would forsake the church (MH 29, 237). For the missionaries, it was a minor puzzle when the services were attended by common people in the absence of the chiefs (MH 20, 112). The same pattern permeated almost every aspect of the mission's intercourse with common Hawaiians. This was not altogether unexpected, because the mission, although claiming independence, represented an extension of the intensified chiefly rule. Hence "indolence and apathy" dot the pages of missionary letters (this argument is more developed in Sahlins 1992).

There was a marked contrast between the judgment of the mission and some of the early accounts of Hawaiian chiefship. Although in the first recorded observations Hawaiian polity was taken as being a despotic system, the people in general appeared to be active and vigorous. For example, James Cook's second lieutenant, James King, saw in 1779 some functional features in the Hawaiians' continuous warfare: "but despotic as is the Nature of their Government, yet it is not of that worst sort, a dull uninterrupted sameness, for it appears that battles for some cause or other are very frequent, which of course will give weight & consequence to many lesser Chiefs" (Beaglehole 1967, 614). If King had visited Hawaii in 1820, his evaluation would have been different. Continuous warfare had ceased, and the chiefs continued their competition through other means, exploiting the land as they could to purchase foreign goods. In King's terminology, the worst kind of despotism, one that knew no rotating principle in the rulership, had become instead—and for the native population meant—"dull uninterrupted sameness."

In some ways the missionaries, who were equipped with a full-fledged theory of the human mind and society, shared this view with King. Their psychology started with the empiricist idea of the mind as filled with custom, hence subject to outside influence and change. The follies and whims of the human mind, perpetuated by custom, as Locke and the Enlightenment thinkers would say, are a result of insufficient use of reason due to social circumstances.[2] In order to perfect and guarantee the reasonableness of one's life, and that of society, one must be educated, for only mature reason may be usefully applied in the creation of political society or the consensual body politic. Indeed, there was in nature something for every human being to be discovered and learned: the divine—and, we should add, logical and thus rational—equality of people in natural society. This equality would irresistibly provoke a dilemma inherent in natural society, namely that each person, being the sole executioner of his (and perhaps her) freedom— a quality Laslett aptly calls "natural political virtue" (1988, 108)—finds it difficult to reconcile this freedom with an organized form of collective existence. The only way out of the dilemma seemed to have been to use part of this natural freedom, and give up part of it to the representatives of the collective, who would use that power to give universally binding laws.

Because the Hawaiians were seen to have spent their lives under the influence of superstitious beliefs and the divinely inspired absolutism of their chiefs "from time immemorial," it was only natural that these customs could not be wiped out but gradually. And for the time being, these customs seriously inhibited the progress toward republican civilization. First, the habits of the common people made them quite unfit for citizenship under covenant, because that required active participation in the affairs of the community, and a communal spirit that would connect the idea of being an active participant and the common good of all. To be obedient in such a system required a moral judgment that one's actions were for the good of others as well as for oneself. To allow the most sacred of all aspects of consciousness, religion, to be dictated by those in power, was for the evangelical missionaries fundamentally flawed. That Hawaiian society operated in this way revealed to them in plain terms that the structure of the society was without foundation. Under such a system, people could never learn to discover in themselves their true nature as moral beings. Second, the chiefs were also unfit members of the covenant society because of their insatiable appetite for the luxuries of this world, and their disregard of the will of their subjects. And yet the chiefs, even if they had wanted to change, were helpless because their word had such a power over people. In this respect, the chiefs were better candidates for the Christian commonwealth; in their actions voluntarism was the guiding principle, they willed and thus showed signs of personal responsibility. The common Hawaiians, however, were more difficult to deal with, and the mission resolved that it was better to have them forced to church, school, and their Bibles than to turn them adrift without the genuine voluntarism needed for membership in a covenant society.

Identities at Risk

As in any boundary situation, collective identity was possible only through the creation of contrast, in this case that which the missionaries created between themselves, the Hawaiians, and the traders and seamen. This was particularly important for them because of the co-opted nature of the mission, which was quite easily recognized by other foreigners. In this task they made use of the familiar theory of civilization upon which the whole mission was founded. Accordingly, customs and habits that did not conform to those of the civilized world constituted a descending realm of graded barbarism, which reached from a semi-rational being to total chaos. It was also very useful to mark out a special place for true believers also in relation to the representatives of the civilized world. The missionaries were attentive to what they called "conflicting elements of civilized life" (Andrews and Richards to Evarts, Sept. 30, 1828, HP/HMCS), behaviors that deviated from the course of life prescribed in the Bible, and more generally from the life ways of a New England country parish, far removed from the dangerous speculations of the Boston libertines and the ungodly mass. Among those groups in the civilized world who stood out for their taking little or no heed of the biblical backcountry code, seamen ranked high on the list.

The battle against evil was therefore fought on two fields: the Hawaiians would have to be saved not only from their own ignorance and their false notions of divinity and the law of nature, but also from the bad influence of foreigners, those who had, in their pride and disregard of their souls, forsaken God for the gratification of momentary and earthly pleasures. Taken together, the two fields formed a great perversion of human society, its constitution and endurance. In order to distinguish themselves in such an environment, the missionaries were encouraged to organize themselves according to the ideal principles typically held up in their political theology. This they did by identifying themselves as a *political* unit, which was established through divinely sanctioned human freedom. In other words, the missionaries, by becoming a mission, moved from a natural society to an artificial, political society, and gave themselves a distinctly political identity. This should not be confused with a partisan position, but rather taken as an expression of a culturally prescribed way of ordering their own existence.

In their instructions to the first group of missionaries, the mission board stated plainly that "the Kingdom of the Lord Jesus is a Kingdom of order. Missions for the advancement of this kingdom are to be maintained & conducted by a regular, though simple & free *polity*" (SIM 1819, my emphasis). A few pages later, the text adds that "like the members of other Missions, you will find it convenient & necessary to form your selves into a *body politic*, [illegible] rules & regulations of your own" (my emphasis). This was possible because they represented correctly—no matter how marginally—understood Christian civilization, what others have aptly called evangelical republicanism. In practice, the annual general meeting of the mission was usually the only manifestation of the missionary "polity" in which free equals were called together for deliberating on their common course. Between these annual sessions, each member dedicated his or her lonely labors to the good of all. This covenant mentality subjected the self of a missionary to the imagined political body. Although the mission was not a completely harmonious little society—the missionaries had lost their physician in 1820 during an internal schism (see Andrew 1976, 112–113)—the missionaries had good practical and ideological reasons to act as if unanimity would have prevailed. In general, nothing speaks against the missionaries' genuine dedication to mutual harmony, as instructed by the mission board (MH 19, 106–108).

This was also observed by the competitive and *ali'i*-seeking Hawaiians, received into their oral traditions, and put into writing in 1838 by a native scholar. It was repeated by the Reverend Sheldon Dibble in his 1839 book on the history of the mission: "Ho'okahi no ano o ka na misionali hana ana, aole ku e kekahi i kekahi" (The missionaries have but one aim in all that they do—there is no division among them) (Dibble 1839, 79; Kahananui gives a slightly different translation, see 1984, 239, 123).[3] Although the words fit well in the polished public image of the ABCFM missions, they most likely reflected a true sentiment among the Hawaiians, whose main source of ideas about foreigners were the "riotous" sailors and rivaling traders. Also, the Hawaiians apparently found little motive for cooperation even among themselves in the forced labor system already grown out of proportion in the 1820s. These—Hawaiians, traders, and seamen—were to a varying degree (at least in the eyes of the missionaries) unable to constitute among themselves a morally lasting political society. This was because of their ignorance or neglect of God, whose law, when fully internalized, would prescribe the proper duties for each member of society and bring disharmony to an end. The mission, in its constitution, was a microscopic facsimile of this ideal society (see Bingham 1849, 60).

In the context of 1825, the mission faced the problem of maintaining itself as a free and independent "body politic," and avoiding a total absorption into the chiefly structures.[4] The integrity of the missionary identity being at stake, the mission resorted—besides attempting to circumvent the chiefly monopoly of authorizing the distribution of *palapala* and organizing massive congregations—to the old evangelical strategy of controlling the behavior and the seriousness of the faith of those who claimed to profess Christianity. In this way, they could at least hope to retain some of their independence and initiative. They made it extremely difficult for anyone to become a member of the church, and, as if to guarantee that the congregation remained a community of free equals, echoing the evangelical version of republicanism, they admitted some common Hawaiians to church membership before allowing the same benefit to the chiefs (Bingham 1849, 252–253, 257–268, 277; Bradley 1968, 145). In realist terms, this was only a formality, and for many years the strategy simply failed, because the actual operation of the mission was so deeply steeped in the interests of the chiefs. The attempt to control behavior was more successful, but even here the chiefs were the driving force behind the deep sense of guilt and affecting emotions.

Hiram Bingham provided a striking example of the measures to which the missionaries sometimes resorted to fulfill their function as the source of moral rectitude. Soon after the death of Ka'ahumanu in 1832, Kauikeaouli decided to assume full control over Hawaiian affairs. In doing this, he ritually challenged all the basic codes of pious Christianity supported by Ka'ahumanu *mā*. A particular

instance of his challenge was excessive drinking, to which Kauikeaouli encouraged his immediate followers and also some others who were more renowned for
their churchgoing than their wine tasting. In February 1833, a granddaughter of
Kamehameha, Kekauʻōnohi, had participated in the drinking and as a result "absented herself from meeting on the Sabbath." The missionary investigation that
followed is a good testimony of the importance of behavior control on the one
hand, and the cooperation of the mission and the Kaʻahumanu *mā* in matters of
Christian tabus on the other. Before Bingham set out to question the culprits,
two prominent chiefs, Kīnaʻu and Kekāuluohi, had suggested that Kekauʻōnohi
confess her sin personally to Bingham, which she did "with apparent emotion."
Another concerned chief, Kaʻahumanu's ex-husband, Kealiʻiahonui, was also
present. After her confession, Bingham started the questioning, which was recalled by the mission accountant Levi Chamberlain:

> After she [Kekauʻōnohi] had finished the visit she went with Rebeka to the
> house of Kamau to eat. While there she was invited to drink spirit, but de-
> clined and asked for wine. Wine was brought forward and she and the company
> drank a bottle. Mr. B[ingham]. asked her why she did not come to meeting in
> the afternoon. She said she was afraid her breath would be smelled and the
> people would say she had been drinking. In relating her drinking on the Sab-
> bath she did not seem to think that in that particular she had sinned. Mr. B.
> was not fully satisfied with her acct. but wanted more evidence. He however
> advised her to go to the King and acknowledge that she had done wrong, and
> also to acknowledge her fault to Kinau & Auhea [Kekāuluohi], and moreover
> told her she ought by all means to go to Maui to see Mr. Richards. She said she
> wished to go; but the King wished her to stay.
>
> Yesterday some new light was thrown upon the subject of her drinking by
> a statement from Kaaiahua the wife of Aikanaka. She stated that she saw
> Kekauonohi at Kamau's and that she was *ona* [drunk]. Keliiahonui called to
> get her to go home but she declined and it was not till dark that he got her to
> consent to leave the place.
>
> To day Mr. Bingham has been sifting the stories & getting out the truth.
> He sent for Rebeka, Aiahua & Kekauonohi in order that he might converse
> with them all together. Kekauonohi refused to come. Dr. Judd however went
> after her & succeeded in getting her. The investigation proved that what was
> drunk was called wine; but was in reality either brandy or wine so mingled with
> brandy as to be very strong. Rebeka called it at the time brandy. It was very evi-
> dent from the smell & its effects that it was stronger than simple wine. Herein
> however Kekauonohi had a pretext for calling it wine it being called so by others
> in the room, the witnesses testifying to Mr. B. that it was so called at the time.
>
> Mr. B. having got at the truth of the story, he advised & urged Kekau-
> onohi to set out immediately for Lahaina. She seemed to be willing to go: but

the King wished her to stay having said if she went he should consider her as having *haalele*'d [forsaken] him. Mr. B. proposed going with her to the King: but she seemed rather inclined to go alone, he however wrote to the King. She went to the Kings [sic] house but he was absent and she concluded to go to Lahaina without an interview and embarked on board the *Waverly*.

Two days later there was a church service during which the subject of drinking was publicly taken up. "The service opened with singing and prayer. An address was made by Mr. Bingham after which and in connexion [sic] with conversation he called upon those who had violated their conscience in any way to state the act by which they had wounded their own souls and done the cause an injury . . . Rebeka who had been guilty of drinking what is supposed to have been brandy mingled with wine on the Sabbath and keeping away from meeting in violation of the day was called upon and she made confession of her sin. Kinimaka who had been guilty of drinking wine with the King and thus countenancing his conduct was called upon to make his statement which he did" (Journal of Levi Chamberlain, Feb. 21 and 23, 1833).

With this careful and unremitting scrutiny, the mission unwittingly worked against itself. In its own internal business the mission could retain its original covenant of free equals, the "fellow-citizens in Zion," but in their relations with the chiefs and the common Hawaiians the missionaries, simply by living up to the standards of their calling, joined their forces with those of the arbitrary powers, of the chiefs as the source of tabus. The more they occupied themselves in checking the behavioral details and secret thoughts of the Hawaiians, the more other foreigners saw them as agents of a theocratic system. They were thus drawn out of their ideal microcosm of free equals. To some extent, the missionaries knew that their "labors" might have been counterproductive, and they found themselves reflecting on the relationship between church and state. Some of the missionaries saw the two as having been fused during the sudden conversion of Hawaiians, and explained this as a theological necessity. Bingham had a curious, but typically evangelical, way to present the position of his program, by sanctifying the state yet keeping the church institutionally, if not ideologically, separate from the state:

> The ministry of religion and the ministry of the state each has its duties; but each in its own order and place, and both for the glory of the same Master, in accordance with the Divine will . . . The state, deriving all its powers from God, both rulers and subjects being bound to do God's will, and its chief magistrate being emphatically God's minister, ought to be, and in an important sense is, a religious institution. It is organized for self-protection, and for securing the enjoyment of certain rights which God grants to men, and the performance of

certain duties mutual among men, which God enjoins. Still the state, though in fact a religious institution, incapable of securing its proper ends without recognizing religious obligation, is not a church (Bingham 1849, 278; see also Ricord 1844, 59–60; Armstrong to Judd, Apr. 23, 1844, FOE).

Hence, "the divine will being the foundation of all human authority, it was not difficult to infer, nor unsafe to teach, that no lawgiver, legislator, or magistrate, had a right to contravene the will of Heaven by requiring or licensing that which God forbids in his Word" (Bingham 1849, 444).

If this led to a union of the church and the state, it was perhaps for the good after all. At times, Bingham was openly in favor of what could be called forced Christianity. In an exchange with the American merchant Henry A. Peirce, Bingham noted his conviction that "by *persuasion* [sic], and the force of *public opinion* I hope the Sabbath will be sustained" (Bingham to Peirce, Mar. 4, 1833, MSL). Persuasion, of course, referred to the chiefly system, which was thought necessary in holding the ignorant masses to the right path. Peirce, evoking the principles of social contract, answered wittily: "Keep down ecclesiastical tyrrany [sic]. Look at the United States; there the Sabbath is as 'religiously observed' as much or more as in any nation—yet it is done by public opinion solely . . . You must and do know that the force of law will never make *men* good and virtuous *Christians*" (Peirce to Bingham, Mar. 5, 1833, MSL).

Among the missionaries, only Sheldon Dibble, who arrived in 1831 at the height of the period of chiefly Christianity, explicitly stated that "such a union [of church and state] did exist to a very considerable extent, notwithstanding the constant endeavors of missionaries to prevent it" (1909, 78). Whereas Bingham and some others sought theological pretext, Dibble took a more ethnographic path. His explanation was based on the understanding of the constitution of the traditional Hawaiian *aupuni*, in which Dibble saw an "alliance between the civil power and heathen worship," which was then, according to Dibble, more or less faithfully applied to the reception of Christianity (78).

Of course this does not mean that Dibble was not against this perceived union; as he himself said the missionaries tried to prevent it. But since the missionaries propagated a moral code that had a biblical foundation, they were obviously fencing a very small pasture for themselves. Bingham might have been more prone to literal application of the biblical world than the missionaries in general, but the mission, it seems, was rather united in defending Christian morality against the interests and recommendations of the other foreigners, as well as the old customs of Hawaii. It was "the maxims of men, the policy of human government," to use Bingham's prose again, that was seen as the encroaching evil surrounding the Hawaiian rulers and pushing them away from "the principles of the Bible" (Bingham 1849, 444). Thus it was not altogether contradic-tory, disquieting though it was, to sustain the alliance with Kaʻahumanu *mā*, because through the instrumentality of the chiefs the Hawaiians might have a chance to experience a true rebirth of the heart. For the same reason, it was not contrary to the mission to introduce the Ten Commandments as the basis for the new laws, or to extend minute investigations into the personal lives of Hawaiians as if to superintend whether the laws against moral crimes were fully obeyed.

The disquiet caused by the missionaries' new status in the Hawaiian hier-archy resulted in attempts to clarify the particular circumstances in which they were so untenably placed. To alleviate their obvious feelings of anxiety and compromise (they had been explicitly instructed to "withhold . . . from all in-terference and intermeddling with the political affairs and party concerns of the [Hawaiian] nation" [SIM 1819]), the missionaries first seized upon the Hawai-ian principle of land tenure, according to which the chief could take back the granted land "at pleasure." They, too, were subject to this peculiar condition. Early on the mission complained about the heavy taxes levied on the land they occupied, so that only "little benefit" could be derived from it (Thaddeus Jour-nal, Nov. 13, 1820, Feb. 17, 1821). True as this probably was, diminution of their rather privileged position was also a practicable way to communicate back to the headquarters in Boston, and at the same time a temporary personal relief for this group of people locked between the requirements of their official policy and the necessity to conform to the structural order of Hawaiian society. Be-sides, they were also instructed to pay "all proper respect to the powers that be" and to render "to all their dues" (SIM 1819).

It was profoundly difficult for the mission to find a balanced place in the Hawaiian order. The missionaries were insiders who tried to stay aloof as much as practicable from the order, which they saw as a crystallized example of a falsely grounded political society, of "crooked" and "perverted" heathenism (SIM 1819). To avoid becoming accomplices in what they considered an oppres-sive system, the missionaries cautiously guarded against profit-making and other signs of material affluence, and felt that their mission was not so much a matter of direct wire-pulling but of indirect influence on government through a moral reform of the chiefs, mediated by the word of God. Most importantly, the mis-sionaries tried to restrict their authority to the moral behavior of church mem-bers and those who claimed to be Christians. Nonetheless, they obviously suffered in seeing how the chiefs cleared the way for the new religion as the mis-sionary printer Elisha Loomis recorded in his diary:

> Soon after we set out on our return [from the district of Wahiawā in central
> Oʻahu], we met a company of *Lunas* or king's officers—some armed with fire-

brands and some with swords. About 5 or 6 days since orders were given by the king to the people of this and other districts to go to the mountains and pro-cure timber for a new Chapel at Honoruru, the officers we passed were going thru the districts to see if the people had complied with the orders. If any men were found at home, their houses were instantly fired. The maimed, the blind, the aged and women and children alone were excepted. This is the custom of the people; and appears to be almost the only method of enforcing the orders of Government. (We passed 4 or 5 houses that were burning, while the fami-lies who had inhabited them were sitting around and bewailing their misfor-tune.) Some of them were heard to observe that their next house would be a hole in the side of the earth and wondered what method the chiefs would then take to destroy them; as they would not burn (Journal of Elisha Loomis, Sept. 22, 1825).

Observations such as this had to be rationalized as custom, ignorance, or prelude to a true, voluntary Christianity. At the root of finding acceptable rea-sons for allowing such excesses of power was the prescribed, although ambigu-ous, duty of the mission to keep church and state separate, and therefore not to raise their voices against the chiefs. On the other hand, by keeping themselves in relative poverty, the mission held up the ideal of independent churches. This constantly reappearing task also provided the foundation for the missionaries' identification of a political system in Hawaii. True, they had, before ever having put their feet on Hawaiian ground, contemplated the chiefly society in monar-chical terms, as had every Western navigator and visitor after Cook. However, the monarchical model, which was used to creating European equivalents or approximations for the Hawaiian rulers, was reinterpreted through the cultural theory of heathenism as soon as the missionaries became part of the regime, and their identity thereby became vulnerable. If the missionaries had not rational-ized their involvement in the chiefs' use of power as a necessity, the discourse of comparative politics might have remained undeveloped, with the simple transplanting of monarchical terms its dominant mode. It will be seen that the monarchical mode could not have given rise to any widely shared or more elabo-rate political discourse between the different parts of the foreign community. Such a discourse did arise, but only through a serious dispute over the proper form of religion, the limits of civil power, and the freedom of conscience. Once again, church and state were the concepts that largely organized this discourse.

CHAPTER 3

Culture in the Making
The Rise of Political Discourse

Things would have been less complex had only the Hawaiian conceptions of divinity been similar to those of the missionaries and other foreigners. If Hawaiians had difficulties in distinguishing the existence of their *aupuni* from their god, the foreigners were all the more anxious to call their attention to such a separation. These two modes of conceiving the institution of an organized society were particularly intricate, because the real means of communication across the cultural groups were so underdeveloped in comparison with the cultural profundity of the arguments. At the intersection of the two cultural systems—Hawaiian *aupuni* and Western theories of government—the missionaries came to a conceptual deadlock. However nonexistent the political motives of the mission were, they were nonetheless caught in a political structure, one that gave the missionaries little choice but to interfere with "political affairs." Quite independently of their intentions , the missionaries were already meddling with politics, as identified by themselves and other foreigners.

The chiefs in general were not interested in Jehovah as such until sometime in 1823, and yet the mission managed, during the first year of its stay, to shake up the ongoing tabu-free state of Hawaiian society (*noa* as opposed to *kapu*) to a degree that alarmed many. The mission's schools, which were organized within a few months after its arrival, became centers of ritual challenge. Thus, for example, when the few native students declined the order of the chiefs to practice their *hula* on the Sabbath or the tabu day, *ka lā kapu* (Bingham 1849, 129; cf. Gast and Conrad 1973, 248), some of the foreign residents, who had little sympathy for the evangelical moral code, found occasion to complain against the mission that the Sabbath interfered with "the affairs of the chiefs" and opposed "the orders or honors of the government" (Thaddeus Journal, Jan. 14, 1821).[1] *Hula* was already a significant manifestation of native as opposed to *haole* ways. Not only was the goddess of *hula*, Laka, retained in dancing (Thaddeus Journal, Feb. 20, 1821), in apparent defiance of the abolition of traditional worship, but also foreign clothing—otherwise in great demand—was strictly forbidden to the dancers (Bingham 1849, 123). Thus, it seems that the missionaries happened to strike, completely according to their own cultural logic, at the very center of Hawaiian practices that were transforming the traditional symbolic difference between natives and foreigners into concrete life.

This took place less than ten months after the mission was first allowed to land, and was, right from the start, a clear indication of the conflicts that would surround the mission. The two most prominent instances of these conflicts deserve particular attention: namely, church-building and prostitution. In the 1820s, and especially after 1825, the main extra-domestic activities of common Hawaiians consisted of cutting sandalwood for the chiefs, and attending schools and church services. It is evident that the combined effect of these activities resulted, even according to common Hawaiians (Kotzebue in Barratt 1988, 245–246), in neglect of cultivation. At the very least it redoubled the workload of the common people, who now had to cultivate their own means of subsistence in addition to attending religious instruction and fulfilling the work obligations they traditionally owed to the chiefs.

The foreigners, by generalizing their own local values, interpreted the new situation in two distinct ways. For the traders, the misery of the Hawaiian commoners was a particular result of using the corvée labor system for building still bigger churches and meeting houses, or schools and missionary residencies. These projects were seen by the traders as exemplified abuse of ecclesiastical powers, and symbolized all the extremities and vanity of a dogmatic religion. Traders considered the system only a means to prevent the Hawaiians from practicing fair trade, and an instrument in producing an atmosphere suitable for "building of churches instead of paying the Depts [sic]" (Reynolds 1989, 108). As could be expected, for the missionaries the hard work extracted from common Hawaiians in building projects was a laudable effort for the glory of God, and sandalwooding was the real cause of difficulties. Thus the interpretations of the commoner hardships were adapted to the goals and values of each group, irrespective of apparent logical contradictions. So, for example, Bingham denounced the Hawaiian chiefship for its "illiberality" and "arbitrariness," while at the same time procuring materials and manpower for his own massive building enterprises (Bingham 1849, 225; Bingham to Kuakini, FOE, 1834).

For the chiefs, who accumulated a considerable amount of cash and property from the sandalwood trade, the church building was an important symbolic means of reworking their power base in cooperation with the new god and its priesthood. Among the three groups, the chiefs were the most consistent in their dealings, because they had an equal interest in sandalwooding *and* church-building. Both kinds of labor were collective and oligopolicized, if not monopolized, and the entire active population of any particular area was engaged in one or the other at any one time. It was customary to let a local *konohiki* (headmen under chiefs, the middlemen between the island governors and the common people) assemble the common people, *maka'āinana*, of the place and impress upon them that the particular work would be their only employment until it was finished. When the first church was built in Kāne'ohe, O'ahu, in November 1834, the local *konohiki* called Amasa had a prosaic (and perhaps typical) way of making this known: "Aole a kakou hana e ae, ka kakou hana hookahi ko keia" (We do not have any other work, this is our sole work to do) (Amasa 1834, 22; cf. Kepelino 1932, 148).

The same rigor applied to moral legislation, which was implemented down to the smallest detail. Part of the new moral code was a prohibition against prostitution, which had been practiced for several years by common Hawaiian women. The building projects and prostitution were connected in that the new material landmarks of Christianity were signs against prostitution but also appropriate labor camps for those for whom the business of paid love was still more lucrative than *palapala*.[2]

It was this prohibition that finally launched the political discourse in public. The building projects had been a source of irritation and frustration mainly for the traders, who saw in them an effective threat to their own livelihood. But though they certainly conceptualized the situation in political terms, their discontent never materialized on a scale comparable to the violent outbursts of the seamen during the prostitution debate between 1825 and 1827, when the chiefs first experimented with the Decalogue. For more than three decades prostitution had served important functions in cultural exchange between Hawaiians and foreigners. For common Hawaiians, prostitution had been a means to obtain foreign goods, which for the most part were monopolized by the chiefs through their control of provisioning and sandalwood trade. But at the same time it was an institution of death, maintaining a steady level of venereal diseases among Hawaiians. For the visiting sailors, Hawaiian prostitution had become a recreational institution, which made more bearable the sailors' routine of criss-crossing the Pacific. In this convergence of Hawaiian consumerism, miserable death, and images of promiscuity, the missionaries saw only ungodliness and sin. To be exact, in missionary eyes, prostitution was but one example of the relaxed sexual attitude prevailing in the islands. According to Patricia

Grimshaw, "it was the conjunction of the Western male's sexual predacity and the Hawaiian's easiness about sexuality which most affronted missionaries' sense of propriety and drove a strong wedge between the mission and the rest of the foreign community" (Grimshaw 1989, 63). When the chiefs in 1825 moved forward to check the amorous trade that now stood between them and the kingdom of God, the mission took another step toward isolation.

Predictably, the new directions in conducting Hawaiian public affairs resulted not merely in missionary isolation but also in open conflict, especially between the missionaries and the transient sailor population. The conflict also involved a great many Hawaiians and some of the more stationary merchants. In other words, and quite like in the New England commercial centers, the rise of the evangelical mission stirred up a greater part of the island community, because their interventions cut across practically every established interest. Schematically speaking, the mission was fully occupied in Christianizing Hawaiians and eliminating the forces of darkness; the rank-conscious chiefs were moved by their apparent need to consolidate their power in the contact situation; the residents were concerned with the expected decline in profits as the new order could turn the chiefs away from gratifying recently created "artificial needs"; the sea captains busied themselves in providing for the sorts of appeasing entertainments their unstable crews required; and finally, the frustrated whaling crews saw the sudden collapse of a sexual paradise. Although several stakeholders reacted negatively to the new Christian measures, the whaling crews and a few captains formed the most virulent opposition, and were ultimately those whose violent actions forced missionaries to publicly reflect on "the political and party concerns of the nation" (MH 24, 104).

The first of these hostile encounters took place in October 1825, when the crew of the English whaling ship *Daniel IV* took up arms and marched to the mission house in Lahaina on the island of Maui.[3] They demanded the missionary William Richards to give orders to let the women come out to the ship. According to Elisha Loomis, the sailors were serious "in their determination to kill Mr. R[ichards]," unless he did not "comply with their request in regard to the females" (Journal of Elisha Loomis, Oct. 8, 1825). A few days later, Loomis, who was stationed in Honolulu, received more information from Maui, and on October 11 he added a host of details:

> The sailors landed in a body armed with knives and forming in order hoisted a red flag and marched in this imposing manner to the house of Mr. R[ichards]. A guard of unarmed natives had been stationed there, but of course could make no resistance against the mob that approached. The chiefs, however, were upon the lookout and had already taken measures unknown to

Mr. R[ichards] to punish any aggression that might be made. The critical moment had now arrived which was to determine the fate of our dear brother and sister. They were ready. They calmly left the house and presenting themselves before the bloodthirsty ruffians, said "If you are determined to take our lives, here we are—but our principles we will never give up. We came hither with our lives in our hands, and are ready to sacrifice them in the cause of religion." At this moment one of the sailors in attempting to force the gate, made a pass with his knife at the native who stood there. The chief who was watching observed it and instantly said, "The play is over, we must be serious now," and immediately gave orders for the people to arm. This was soon effected, and the cannon in the fort were loaded, and men with lighted matches placed near them. The appearance of a multitude armed with guns and swords convinced the sailors that it was necessary to cease from further operations and they accordingly retired to their boat. It was fortunate they did so, as the consequences might have been serious; for orders had been sent to all the people in the district to assemble, with the fixed determination of not only securing the sailors on shore, but of taking possession of the ship in case violence should be offered to Mr. and Mrs. Richards. All the canoes were put in readiness; and in a very short time Lahaina was filled with armed men. But the retreat of the sailors rendered it inexpedient to pursue any offensive measures. A guard of armed men were, however, placed about Mr. R[ichards] night and day; and even on the Sabbath he was escorted to the meeting house by several hundred men (Journal of Elisha Loomis, Oct. 11, 1825).

The missionary most directly involved, William Richards, described the first meeting with the sailors:

A little after sun set, two men from the Daniel called, and expressed a desire to converse with me alone. I unhesitatingly followed them to the door. They immediately introduced the subject of the new law [against prostitution] and said the law was an improper one, and that I was the means of its being passed. I entirely disclaimed having any thing to do in enacting this, or any other law of the nation, except, that, to the best of my ability, publicly and privately, I inculcated on the chiefs, and on the people, the principles of the scriptures, among which, I, of course, included the seventh commandment. They said, I could, if I pleased, procure a repeal of the law. I replied, that I could do it in no other way, than by telling the chiefs, that the law was inconsistent with the law of God, and that God would be angry with them, if they kept this law in force. I then appealed to them, whether, in speaking thus to the chiefs, I should be speaking the truth, or acting in the character of a Christian missionary (Richards' letter journal, Oct. 5, 1825, in MH 23:41).

This time, hostilities did not escalate into open violence, but the course of events made the majority of the chiefs more determined in securing their authority by more rigorous enforcement of what was commonly called the tabu on women. On October 19, the chiefs sat in council "to take more effectual measures to prevent females from visiting ships." A week later, Loomis noted in his journal that the new regulations and the general Christianized posture of the chiefs had completely changed the foreigners' attitude toward the mission. In his opinion, "when little or no attention was paid to our instructions, and crimes were committed with impunity, we were generally speaking treated with much politeness—now we are looked upon as enemies and every thing which malice can invent seems to be urged against us" (Journal of Elisha Loomis, Oct. 29, 1825).

While some foreigners became openly hostile toward the missionaries, the chiefs, as the patrons of the mission, took another step along the novel path. They began to systematize the will of the Christian god by introducing a code of restrictions, a method that squarely fit decontextualized biblical commands into their own conception of order. Setting cosmology aside, we need only know that the code, directly derived from the Decalogue, was not adopted without serious deliberation and conflict of opinion. In consequence, it took some years to implement the selection of the Ten Commandments, but for the foreign opposition their stance was clear from the beginning: the mission was operating outside its proper mandate and was seriously compromising its neutrality. In December, the chiefly establishment, leading missionaries, and a fair selection of foreign residents and sea captains, had a tense public meeting about the new restrictions:

> Yesterday at the close of divine service Karaimoku arose and requested that the chiefs and teachers [missionaries] would assemble on the ensuing morning to give their united advice to the people in regard to the Kanawai of Jehovah. The Kanawai (Commandments) were translated some time since, the most of the chiefs after giving them an attentive perusal expressed an earnest desire that they should be regarded by all the people. As the laws of God it was thought they were binding on every person, and the chiefs wished to give their united public testimony in favor of their being observed, and even to enjoin their people to obey them. With this view the meeting was called. We knew nothing of it, however, till Karaimoku rose in the meeting as before stated. Receiving from Karaimoku an invitation to be present, we went at the appointed hour, and were not a little surprised to find nearly all the resident foreigners present and 5 or 6 commanders of vessels. One of them, Capt. Ebbets, addressing Mr. B[ingham], said "We have come to oppose you." It appears that a report of the intended meeting early reached the foreigners, who, perhaps judging from the growing spirit of Christianity among the chiefs thought some greater restric-

tions on certain vices might be imposed, entered into a combination to oppose any new regulation that might be proposed. Karaimoku, Kaahumanu and other chiefs stated their desire is to have the laws of God binding on all the people. Boki replied it was his desire also, but he thought they had better wait till the return of Mr. Charlton [the British consul] from Tahiti before anything was formally done. Boki's objection was not unexpected. Several of the foreigners were known to have had interviews with him and it was not doubted on what subject they dwelt. Among the foreigners, Capt. C, Capt. M, Capt. Lauson and Capt. Adams and Messrs. Gowing and Reynolds distinguished themselves by their violent opposition to everything proposed by Karaimoku and Kaahumanu. In one instance they made a grand mistake which had it not been observed by Capt. ___ would have proven fatal to their cause. Mr. Gowing, their interpreter, said to the chiefs "You are the rulers of this land—you have a right to make laws—we have no objection to that—but we object to the Missionaries having anything to do with it." Mr. B[ingham] instantly replied "That is right—the Missionaries do not wish to interfere—let the chiefs do as they like". Capt. E perceived what was likely to be the effect and instantly commenced a speech and succeeded in turning the conversation to another point. Several of the foreigners encouraged Boki to oppose the object of the meeting—saying—he knew better than the others—he had been to England, and in the king's palace, &c. After listening to what the foreigners had to say, Karaimoku, Kaahumanu and others again expressed their desires to have the laws established. But Boki, whose feelings had by this time got raised to a high pitch, ventured to disclose to the king that if the laws were established he would not support him. Keriiahonui now rose and commenced a speech in which he was recommending David's resolution to serve the Lord, when Boki interrupted him by inquiring "Who?" "David" was the answer. "Was you there?" asked Boki. "No" replied Keriiahonui and would have continued, but Boki, who was a much higher chief, motioned him to be silent. This conduct of Boki excited feelings little less than of indignation in the breasts of the others and almost the instant he stopped Keriiahonui he was himself by Karaimoku directed to be silent. In this state of affairs the king said he was afraid, and proposed to adjourn, which was accordingly done. The principal chiefs are highly displeased with the part Boki took, and but for the influence of Christian instruction, would at once make an appeal to arms. That this would have been the case, at a former period we have the authority of the chiefs to say. But, as it is we do not anticipate any serious civil commotion. It is however, an unhappy circumstance; and brought about altogether as we believe by the interference of foreigners. They allege that they were invited by the chiefs; but we have inquired of the principal chiefs, who all say they did not wish to have them present, nor did they know of their design to attend. The foreigners also allege that they were informed that the penalty of death was to be annexed to each law in case of its being violated. Whether the chiefs had or had not a design to

annex a penalty to any one of the laws we do not know, but there is no proba-
bility that they could have thought of punishing with death, for the violation of
anyone, unless, the sixth. As far as I can learn, it seems to have been the design
of the chiefs simply to expose publicly their united voice in favor of the observance of the ten Commandments (Journal of Elisha Loomis, Dec. 12, 1825).

This was the first of the several public meetings on the subject of Christian
laws. Two conflict-ridden years would elapse until the new laws were formally
established (see Kuykendall 1989, 120–126). At this point, however, we need
not introduce more details. The conflict had clearly reached the mark where
the foreigners' concern about Christian regulations had found a sort of summary expression. No more were their remarks random and bitter lashes at the
mission. No more did they single out examples of what they regarded as absur-
dities and religious fanaticism, such as forbidding horse races, and kindling fires
on the Sabbath. No, the absurd measures reflected a deep missionary interference "in matters of government" (MH 23:204). By the end of 1826, the foreign
opposition to the missionaries had developed into a petition movement asking
the chiefs to deport the mission.

In other words, the debate took on more elaborate forms. While those who
first constituted the mass of participants—foreign sailors and Hawaiian prostitutes—were silenced by captains and chiefs, the documentary landscape was
also reshaped. Captains and chiefs, joined by traders and missionaries, shifted
the focus from the real relations in the field to general relations of principles. In
historical documents the expressions of anger and frustration became more abstract (but no less intense). The level of confusion experienced was reduced by
translating the events into the language of ready-made concepts. The missionary who was ready to die for his religion in Lahaina appears in another light a
few weeks later in Honolulu. He who denounced prostitution in the name of
Christ became a lawmaker, whose status was extremely dubious in the eyes of
"the commercial world." He who was first merely an obnoxious messenger of
Christian civilization turned into a sectarian politician, headed deliberately toward a fusion of church and state. In fact, the whole debate was heading toward
a transplantation of very recent American history, or a shared memory of it,
into a Polynesian society. What was first interpreted as prostitution now meant
a moment in a struggle to separate ecclesiastical powers from secular authority.

The second clash was just a few months ahead. In January 1826, the U.S.S.
Dolphin arrived at Honolulu, and in February several members of its crew, with
sailors from other ships, stormed the houses of Kalanimōkū and Bingham, again
in order to have women on board. This time the attacks were more severe, and
Kalanimōkū's men were ordered to quell the furious sailors. Although the de-

fenders of the tabu easily prevailed in the confrontation, Poki, the head chief of O'ahu and a wavering opponent of the Decalogue, finally allowed the women of Honolulu to continue their usual trade (Bingham 1849, 285–288). In the beginning of April the dangerous foreigners retreated, and the ban was enforced again. In the summer Ka'ahumanu and Bingham, with a retinue of some two hundred people, toured O'ahu propagating God's law, which had not yet taken firm root among the great masses (Journal of Levi Chamberlain, Apr. 1, 1826; Bingham 1849, 294–297; Levi Chamberlain to Evarts, July 26, 1826, HP/HMCS).

How is it, then, that prostitution marked the "beginning" of politics in the context of contrasting views of the human condition? This is a legitimate question because the Westerners had no great difficulties in identifying politics in the dealings of Hawaiian chiefs long before the first missionaries landed. One obvious reason for this was the very pronounced social hierarchy that was reflected in the deep rift separating the ruling chiefs from the common people and the conflictual nature of the chiefship. In the 1820s, Hawaiians and their wars were already part of the world literature, and the earliest documentation on Hawaiians tells us perhaps more about conflict than anything else (for sources, see Sahlins 1992, 36–45). But when it comes to prostitution as a political matter, the question is not just of representing Hawaiians in political language; there was nothing new in that. It is more important that the political representation of Hawaiians became a theme of talk in the somewhat disharmonious local community. Representing Hawaiians politically was no longer a literary matter engaged in by passing observers, or a part of the strategy discussed in the imperial map rooms; it became a social matter which gradually came to involve those being represented. The reason for this change was that the struggle over proper conduct of Hawaiian women was historically atypical. Culturally it was malleable, but it was sociologically unusual for the place because it directly involved a distinct group of foreigners who had a program for social change. Because the program pretended to represent a true civilization— a variety of evangelical Christianity—it had an unintended effect of bridging the categories of religion and politics through the events of prostitution. On a more elaborate conceptual level, this bridge was the essence of the conflict.

Strange as it may sound, politics in a genuinely comparative sense was first a matter of putting a stop to an established practice of carnal love being a commodity. It came as a challenge to a standing order of foreign exchange by the domestic advocates of that order itself. But because these advocates, namely certain Hawaiians of high birth with an eye to upward social mobility, had formed an alliance with a band of spirited missionaries from New England, this reversal came to involve a generous amount of argumentation. The presence of conflicting foreign parties—missionaries and sailors—produced a conflicting exchange of ideas, which were synthesized under the concept of politics. The events in the narrative illustrate how this unique conflict, launched by the sudden, mission-inspired curbing of Hawaiian prostitution, gave birth to conceptual distinctions which resulted in the creation of politics as an object for talk in and about Hawaii. The uniqueness of this talk was that it was for the first time taken inside Hawaiian society in a comparative sense. Besides contending over the proper place of politics in the scheme of civilization, the parties were also seeking signs of both legitimate and corrupt forms of politics in Hawaiian society. We can witness comparative politics being practiced long before it developed an aura of science.

These events made the missionaries highly conscious of the suspicions, accusations, and hatred that were being directed at them from other foreigners. The times were critical, especially because the network of *palapala* was beginning to take shape in massive dimensions as a result of the chiefly tours. Bingham recorded some twenty-five thousand students in the fall of 1826. Moreover, Kuakini's church project in Kailua, Hawai'i, occupied the time and labor of "some thousands" in the summer. When Kuakini's church was dedicated in September, the complex was filled with people, up to five thousand according to Bingham (1849, 298; SIM 1826a; cf. Reynolds 1989, 152, who gives a larger figure). In the early part of the year, several Hawaiian women were taken from their white lovers and cohabitating companions and ordered to bring stones for a church as punishment for their illicit relations. This caused much discussion among foreign residents on the subject of church and state (Reynolds 1989, 123–124). All this put the mission in an uncomfortable position, particularly as Ka'ahumanu *mā* had "publicly declared their determination to follow the precepts of Christianity in the government of the people" (Bingham 1849, 298).

To alleviate the likely protest against themselves, the missionaries, in their annual meeting, which they held in connection with the dedication of Kuakini's church, prepared a rule of conduct to be followed in their dealings with the chiefs. In this guideline, the idea of noninterference was once again put forth. The text began by recalling the critique of divine right: "Resolved, that we consider ourselves required by our instructions, as well as by nature of our office as Christian Missionaries, to abstain, like our Divine Master, from all intermeddling and interference with the political and party concerns of the nation" (SIM 1830, 37). The Divine Master was a great orchestrator of the laws of nature, but he left reasoning and the establishment of the proper social organization to mortals. Thus the mission excluded itself from several areas of life, for example, the choice of rulers, taxation, dividing of lands, general administration of the islands, and "the customs and usages of the country that are not in direct variance with the spirit and precepts of the Gospel" (sim 1830, 38). In the following paragraph the declaration informed the world that the mission was, nevertheless, allowed to teach the laws of the Bible "however opposed these prohibitions and requirements may be to the former customs and present practices of the people" (sim 1830, 38). In the next paragraph the missionaries went still further in qualifying their assumed neutrality, in that they thought it proper to give advice and information to the chiefs if they so requested and use their "influence to discountenance every vice and encourage every virtue" (sim 1830, 39). Here we can again detect the spirit of republic founded on virtue instead of unbounded freedom. The good political order would arise from this virtuous foundation; and the perceived lack of virtue gave the missionaries a great deal of confidence in defending their mandate, which appeared quite ambiguous to the outside world.

A missionary declaration (sim 1826b) based on the above principles was printed in the mission press and circulated among the resident traders and captains of the whaling fleet in the last week of October 1826. The declaration did nothing to counteract suspicions. On the contrary, in chartering the mission to continue its course, the declaration can be seen as a strategic error. But more importantly, it was a product of the collective effort of the missionaries to initiate a rationalized and organized form of political dialogue in public, although their primary motive was to deny any interference in the political affairs of the chiefs. One could even say that politics as a collectively and locally defined concept was a by product of this denial, which was deeply rooted in an un-avoidable cultural misapprehension.

The missionaries were anticipating a public hearing, which they were anxious to have in order to prove their point in an undisputed manner. The hearing was held in Honolulu on December 8, 1826, and chaired by Captain Jones of U.S.S. *Peacock*. Except for the outspoken English Consul, Richard Charlton, the foreign residents and sea captains turned out to be less eager to criticize the mission in a formal hearing than in their own private meetings. When even Charlton declined to provide any evidence against the mission in writing, as the missionaries demanded, Captain Jones ruled in favor of the missionaries and ended the hearing (Journal of Levi Chamberlain, Dec. 8, 1826; Reynolds 1989, 167; Bingham 1849, 301–303).

The whole episode ended half-heartedly, yet it had much wider, macroscopic consequences for the contact culture in Hawaii, because it created a social context for political discourse from the cultural elements the concerned individuals had brought together. Their motives might have been disjointed, but these were conceptualized in a uniform manner as a division of labor between church and state. For the missionaries the involvement of church was justified as raising the level of virtue among Hawaiians, particularly among the chiefs. The chiefs' idea of becoming virtuous by fiat was interpreted by other foreigners as religiously inspired tyranny and a violation of natural freedoms, those of the common Hawaiians as well as human beings in general. Chiefly Christianity was absorbed into Western political discourse that emphasized individual liberty, instead of social cohesion and conformity, as a universal value. The evangelical missionaries could never effectively defend themselves before the "commercial world," because for them virtue could not be generated out of license. The juxtaposition of license and virtue objectified Hawaiian society, producing the first concepts that had clear comparative value, concepts that would determine for years to come how foreigners and foreign residents saw the Hawaiian polity. Now there was a socially codified way of seeing church, state, and politics in the Hawaiian society, that had come about mainly through changed attitudes toward the missionaries. In other words, politics as a cultural signification—that is, the distinction between church and state—was posted in the harbors of Honolulu and Lahaina because the mission wanted explicitly to change Hawaiian society, and the great majority of the traders and sailors were much less inclined toward any such project. Threatened by one group, the other enacted its cultural theory of government.[4]

The hostilities culminated in October 1827, when the English whaler *John Palmer* fired five cannon balls toward the mission houses in Lahaina, and William Richards was called to another public hearing, this time accused of libel. The canons were fired in an effort to free the ship's captain, a certain Clark, who had been detained in the Lahaina fort for not letting ashore several Hawaiian women who had broken the tabu against prostitution. The ship's mate, having gone after his captain, was given orders to open fire. The captain was released on the promise of taking the women ashore, but before he could reach his ship the mate had already discharged the guns. However, the women were not returned and the ship sailed off to Honolulu, where the news had broken out that Richards had published an article in *The Missionary Herald*, portraying Captain John Buckle, the commander of the whale ship *Daniel*, in a very negative light. In the article Richards had related the particulars of incidents in October 1825, involving Buckle's crew, and Buckle himself, buying a Hawaiian woman. Buckle and Clark, united with the English Consul, created so much trouble and public excitement that Ka'ahumanu called together all the chiefs to have the skirmish settled. Richards was called to attend the council for an explanation, but again the hearing ended before Richards ever had a chance to confront the captains in public. Ka'ahumanu, after consulting with David Malo, made her ruling in favor of Richards and the meeting was closed (Reynolds 1989, 201,

204–209; Dibble 1909, 195–199; Bingham 1849, 313–319; Kamakau 1992a, 281–283).

The discourse of politics was becoming most tangible, different people uniting to pursue the same cause, public hearings being organized, circulars printed, petitions drawn up, and open violence flaming in the ports. The presence of politics was soon felt among the greater part of foreigners in Honolulu and Lahaina. Political language, however, was not as manifest as moral language, including religious arguments, ridicule, and backbiting. In the actual battles politics was much more abstract and less tangible than were the tabu against prostitution, or revenge. Nevertheless, all of these emotional outbursts and practical efforts were translated, or rather channeled into political language via the cultural fluency of the participants. Forming a perfect consensus, the foreign community placed politics at the top of their conceptual hierarchy, so that it appeared every time the strained relations between the mission and other foreigners were brought up through organized and public avenues. For instance, when the commander of the U.S.S. *Dolphin*, Lieutenant John Percival, addressed a public letter to other ship masters and warned them against allowing too many men to leave ships lest there would be more fighting, he formulated the brutally concrete recent events in a language that gave them a universal formula among the foreigners: "The excitement of the seamen toward Mr. Bingham, and from the recent outrage committed by them from the belief that he had *interfered with some of the civil regulations* of this place, and thereby deprived them of an enjoyment they have always been in the participation of when they visit this island, I have to request you will let but a small portion of your crew come on shore on Sunday; by complying with this request you will aid my wishes in preventing anxiety to the missionary family" (quoted in Bingham 1849, 288, my emphasis). The more fundamental cultural categories, which were shared by the missionaries, traders, and sailors alike, allowed these foreigners not only to make sense of each other's motives and arguments, but also to produce a familiar context in a strange environment, that is, a political system in which the church and the state were the essential, fixed points for the generation of arguments.

Of course the Hawaiian chiefs were part of the constructed context. Yet they appeared to be less concerned with the infiltration of a form of worship into their governing practices. Their cultural motivations were perhaps more different than the missionaries first hoped for, but Christianity and the new tabus were, once again, their conscious, although not unchallenged, choice. The violent outbreaks against the tabus were more likely interpreted as a threat to their authority. As Kaʻahumanu said to Lieutenant Percival, who demanded the women to be set free for prostitution, "it is for *us* to give directions respecting our women—it is for *us* to establish tabus—it is for *us* to bind, to liberate, to impose fines" (quoted in Bingham 1849, 286). Thus, in a traditional way, the foreigners' behavior was taken, quite correctly indeed, as a threat to *aupuni*, which was standing because of the tabus. Finally, the Hawaiian women had the role of supporting either of the competing theories of society (yet, for the most part, the chiefs manipulated the situation by regularly removing the women to the mountains inland).

In brief, this resulted in a cultural differentiation of the subjects of the debate in a more systematic way—missionaries, traders, captains, chiefs, and common Hawaiians—which caused politics as a concept to be reserved for the foreigners. We shall see whether at this point there developed any conceptual bridging across the cultural groups, despite the profound differences in perceiving the world.

Context and Translation

The differentiation, which was already developed in 1826, only intensified in the years that followed. As Bradley and Grimshaw have observed, the mission was increasingly isolated from other foreigners after the incidents between 1825 and 1827 (Bradley 1968, 171–175; Grimshaw 1989, 62–65). This was perhaps best symbolized in William Richards being escorted to his church by several hundred Hawaiian guards on October 9, 1825 (Journal of Elisha Loomis, Oct. 11, 1825). The immediate result of the isolation was the strengthening of the alliance between the mission and the chiefs, to which we should add, as an amplifying factor, the generally reserved attitude of the chiefs toward the traders, whose occupation was rather disgraceful for the Hawaiians (Vancouver 1984, 854–855; Kotzebue in Barratt 1988, 155; Kamakau 1992b, 123; Kepelino 1977, 42). The attachment of the Hawaiians in general to the missionaries seemed also to have deepened, as the mission printer Loomis observed: "The change of feelings in the natives toward us since the time of our arrival and first years residence is very remarkable. Then they were exceedingly jealous of us, and not very forward to assist. Now, they have the utmost confidence in us and we have every reason to believe, would think it a great calamity to be deprived of our instructions. They appear as ready to defend us as their own persons. The guards who now patrol the streets with loaded muskets, amount to several hundred" (Journal of Elisha Loomis, Oct. 28, 1825). While the missionaries, as a result of the reinforced alliance, became more and more involved as interpreters for the chiefs (Judd to Anderson, Apr. 19, 1842, quoted in Judd 1960, 108), they also identified themselves more strongly with the objects of their work, the Hawaiians.

For the development of comparative political expressions, this meant primarily that the conceptual tools of the foreigners' world were translated by using ready-made Hawaiian concepts, and little regard being paid to cultural or conceptual differences. The outside world came to be known in concepts entirely Hawaiian. This was, in fact, only a continuation of pre-missionary practice. The trusted Europeans and Americans who had translated for the chiefs before the missionaries came were, like everyone else, very much dependent on the chiefs' favors and in every other respect found a situation that encouraged them to adapt themselves to Hawaiian conditions of life, rather than the reverse (e.g., Campbell 1967, 118–120; Chamisso in Barratt 1988, 175; Cox 1957, 30–35; Freycinet 1978, 19–20; Golovnin 1974, 40, 46–47). Besides technically advising the chiefs, it seems that they did little to formalize cross-cultural concepts, which would have required more systematic methods such as teaching and dictionaries. We have little or no evidence to suggest anything beyond mere technical interpreting.

For example, when Don Francisco de Paula Marín, a resident since the mid-1790s, translated Kalanimōkū's account of the acceptance of Christianity for Kotzebue in January 1825—likely using French—he found it necessary to render *aupuni* as "state" (Kalanimōkū's Hawaiian is not given but *aupuni* is the only probable choice). Kalanimōkū was almost certain that after his death the present *aupuni* would fall apart, as the chiefs, after Liholiho's departure, were openly considering war. Linking the difficulties in establishing the worship of Jehovah among the common people with the possibility of revolt, he said that "the *state*, which I have with difficulty held back from ruin, may fall apart after my death" (Kotzebue in Barratt 1988, 189, my emphasis). If this suggested a union of the church and the state, it was a signification between Marín and Kotzebue; for Kalanimōkū, the condition of Hawaiian society was still conceptualized through his native *aupuni*. Thus a technical interpreting is not sufficient evidence that there evolved any mutual understanding of each other's cultural systems. Here we aim deeper than, say, learning the different modes of saluting, as the Hawaiians surely did without having anyone to explain the meaning of these customs: "Encountering Europeans they bow and shake hands according to our customs, but among themselves they observe their own custom of rubbing noses and holding arms" (Golovnin 1974, 53).[5]

The culturally subordinate position of the mission became even more evident when the Decalogue and Jehovah were challenged by some high-ranking Hawaiians. Some narration is needed to make the point. During the two years preceding the publication of the first Puritan laws, in December 14, 1827, the younger brother of Kalanimōkū, Poki Kamaʻuleʻule, had several times opposed the adaptation of biblical laws and openly defied Kaʻahumanu's authority (Journal of Levi Chamberlain, Dec. 12, 1825; Journal of Elisha Loomis, Dec. 12,

1825; Levi Chamberlain to Evarts, Feb. 22, 1827, HP/HMCS). In March 1828, when the three laws against killing, theft, and adultery were to take effect, Poki, the high chief Kauikeaouli, and their retinue sailed to Hawai'i, where Poki gave the lands of Hilo to Kauikeaouli for redistribution among his favorites. Poki, who apparently did this to maintain his dignity, because the reception in Hilo had been substandard, drifted into a conflict with Ka'ahumanu over the extent of each other's authority. Poki being the guardian *(kahu)* of the future ruler Kauikeaouli, he thought he had at least as much to say in the affairs of the islands as did Ka'ahumanu, Kauikeaouli's foster mother. Poki's behavior at Hilo displeased Ka'ahumanu and her closest chiefs, who decided not to include Poki's debts to the foreign traders in the collective debt of all other chiefs, a decision that was a great source of dishonor for Poki. Offended, Poki and his followers prepared to take arms against Ka'ahumanu. The process was halted by a bold but successful mediation effort of Kekūanaō'a, husband of Kīna'u, Kamehameha's daughter by Kaheiheimālie.

Poki gave up his military plans for the time being, and in March 2, 1829, two more laws, against intoxication and prostitution, were proclaimed (Reynolds 1989, 255). But early in the next month it was again rumored that a rebellion against Ka'ahumanu was being planned. Whether Poki was the real culprit is uncertain; he was spreading a rumor that a conspiracy existed to kill all the white people on O'ahu and to put Kīna'u in Ka'ahumanu's place and make Kīna'u's son by Kekūanaō'a the heir to the paramountcy. A few days earlier Poki had "a long talk" with Kekūanaō'a and Ka'upena, the wife of Manuia, Poki's close associate, for their "quarreling in his absence." Stephen Reynolds heard that Poki was angry with them because they had talked about killing the white people. At the time, Kauikeaouli was in Lahaina and, according to Poki, would not come to Honolulu until he had received a clearance from him. The clearance was given, and on April 8 Kauikeaouli arrived at Honolulu. Poki met his "son" on board the ship, which was considered quite exceptional and added to the already tense atmosphere. Reynolds thought "it was the first time, any chief ever visited him on board, before he landed" (Reynolds 1989, 258–259), the sea being normally *kapu* during the approach of the highest chiefs.[6]

The next day, Bingham went to meet Poki and Kauikeaouli in Poki's *Blond Hotel*, where a reconciliatory air prevailed. In the evening Poki, Kauikeaouli, and Ka'ahumanu got together at the Binghams' for a cup of tea and a few psalms. As a result of these meetings, Kauikeaouli promised to return to school, from which he had been absent for some time, and Poki "proposed to attend again to instruction." In addition, Poki and Kauikeaouli asked Bingham for 190 books to be distributed to their attendants and, as Bingham recalled, "concurred with Kaahumanu and the people connected with my station in the erection of a church." The new church in Honolulu was dedicated to Jehovah on July 3, 1829, and Kauikeaouli, once again quite spontaneously as in the council of chiefs in June 1825, dedicated also his *aupuni* to Jehovah (Bingham 1849, 343–346). In October, the chiefs could proclaim with much confidence that all people, foreigners included, should obey the laws that forbade "Murder, Theft, Adultery, Fornication, Retailing Ardent Spirits at houses for selling spirits, Amusements on the Sabbath day, Gambling and betting on the Sabbath day and at all times" (Proclamation, FOE, Oct. 7, 1829).

In December Poki, his pride hurt, went sandalwood hunting with two ships, and never returned. Poki's wife Liliha assumed his vacant position, but she also clashed with Ka'ahumanu over the guardianship of Kauikeaouli. Liliha's rebellion was short-lived, and she was dispossessed of her lands and the guardianship in April 1831. The chiefship of O'ahu was then given to Kuakini, who took prompt action to enforce the Christian tabus, as he had previously done on Hawai'i island.

The story suggests that the context the foreigners had created for the Hawaiian political system (including the difficult relationship of church and state) was such that the outsiders' discourse of politics and morals was always translated in view of the chiefs' interests, because the motives of Ka'ahumanu *mā* in maintaining the integrity of the present *aupuni* were culturally so strong. The chiefs carefully watched over the foreigners and took the foreigners' god as the emblem of their rule. Thus, for instance, when Bingham arbitrated between Poki and Ka'ahumanu, in April 1829, the whole issue seemed to revolve around certain rituals of the native church. The arbitration culminated the following summer with the dedication ceremonies of the Honolulu church, which all points to the need to secure *aupuni*. In this respect, it is only logical that while the foreign community talked politics explicitly, using it in the sense of civil power, the secluded missionaries and the chiefs closed a deal set in more cosmic terms. When Bingham reasoned with Kauikeaouli about matters of practical government, the usefulness of the tabus were the main point he advocated. "It is very difficult to govern men who are drunken," he said in Hawaiian, and added nothing that would have indicated that there was, even in his own culturally informed theory, a fundamental difference between a law and a tabu (Letter of Hiram Bingham to an unknown recipient, 1832, MSL). If he ever did, it was always explained as God's law.

Instead of being a genuine mediator, Bingham accommodated his moral views to the needs of the chiefs, the same views that were interpreted by other foreigners in political terms. While morality, or the tabus, and the chiefs' interest in preserving their *aupuni* were the unifying factors in the discursive alignment between the mission and the chiefs, the concepts of church and state mediated the intercourse between the mission and the foreign mercantile community. There was not only a physical and social split in the community; the divide was also conceptual, ultimately materializing in words and their cultural significations.

As we have already seen, the missionaries were in a difficult position as regards the confrontation of the way they conceptualized Hawaiian politics (a lack of virtue), the Hawaiian understanding of *aupuni*, and the foreigners' accusations. This is not at all surprising considering the reception of the Christian god by the chiefs, who, according to a venerable priest of the old type, lived "in fear of an uprising supporting the idolatrous worship of the old pagan gods" (Duhaut-Cilly 1983, 33), or the servants of the Devil, as the Christians would have it. Thus the Hawaiian powers that be, Ka'ahumanu *mā*, decidedly chose to advance the worship of their new god with sweeping measures. For them, the new God, Jehovah, was a means to the traditionally desired social stability and permanence, which the Hawaiian concepts of *aupuni* and *malu* convey. Or as they collectively stated it in 1829, "the great thing by which we shall promote peace" (oia ka mea nui a makou e hoomalu ai). For that reason all who remained in the islands should have obeyed the laws of God (Proclamation, FOE, Oct. 7, 1829).

The missionaries knew the hazards of this kind of authorizing, but were nevertheless conditioned by the Hawaiian language and concepts through which they were communicating the word of God to Hawaiians. Every time they had to refer to God and government in the same sentence, they were—perhaps unintentionally—affirming the old Hawaiian structures. A good example is an 1835 exhortatory article published by Artemas Bishop in a native Christian paper: "If they [the chiefs] will praise God, he will bless them and perpetuate their *aupuni*. But if not, he can overthrow their rule. The rule of the chiefs in this world is from God. And chiefs who conducted their *aupuni* according to the laws of God would be preserved by God so that their reign is blessed" (Bishop 1835, 113, my translation).

Here, the ideal of the virtuous republic is still recognizable, but elements of Hawaiian chiefship have been added. Without a single foreign concept to provoke a sense of difference, the person of a chief is made a direct object of divine mediation, functionally just as in the *hono* rite. We can conclude with some certainty that from the point of view of the missionaries, the whole interpretative context was prestructured in an unrewarding way. As their actions were passing through the cultural categories of both Hawaiians and foreigners, they were doubly bound to the requirements of their environment.

The missionaries were in a structured situation in which some key actors (foreign residents, the mission board) had already brought politics to their attention and placed some expectations before them regarding the reality of politics in the Hawaiian Islands. To find a relatively comfortable place in this field, where they had lost much of their independence, the missionaries were forced to develop arguments and practical theories concerning their own mission relative to, on the one hand, the demands set by foreign residents and the mission board, and on the other, their place within the Hawaiian social order. Their overall position was one of balancing between the hostile merchants, who jealously guarded their customary enjoyments of freeman life, and Hawaiians, who after 1825 increasingly demanded the services of the mission. For the zealous missionaries, the balancing was frequently made difficult by their own unshaken faith in the divine legitimacy of the mission, and the well-known consequences of conflict.

There is no direct evidence that the missionaries would have propagated a systematic political theory for the Hawaiians and for this reason the missionaries were hardly cultural mediators in the full sense of the term, much beyond their own specialty. Of course, it is a completely different matter that other foreigners saw politics where the missionaries saw religious instruction. Politics was, of course, recognized in Hawaii from the first contacts (which resulted in an international folklore of absolutism), but it was, in the debate between the mission and the foreign residents, recalled to life in a more elaborate form soon after the arrival of the missionaries. It seems that as the missionaries were put in a defensive position they stuck to the idea of religion as distinct from politics and constructed an image of Hawaiian society in which the chiefs' affairs could be divided into politics and religion. While realizing that the two spheres were melding (reflecting what they called heathen worship) the missionaries increased their efforts to show that the "true religion" cannot be politicized without turning biblical truths upside down. This only amplified their cultural disposition to see everything in moral terms, and to reject any share in authority that was founded on secular motives. They revealed a commitment to an evangelical republic in which all political activity was subordinated to virtuous conduct. This greatly inhibited or at least considerably slowed cultural mediation of political ideas. Instead, the missionaries constructed comparative conceptual equivalents that were rather neutral, or camouflaged as ideas that were *moral* ideas, and therefore proper to teachers of religion. Often this meant communicating things to Hawaiians in their own terms, and to foreigners in theirs. One of the most important Hawaiian concepts that was frequently used across cultural groups was indeed *aupuni*, the word used for the Hawaiian government, and, as we saw in the rituals of the establishment of a chiefdom, one pregnant with mythology (see chapter 1). We need to examine how this word was commonly translated by the missionaries and other foreigners during the early period of chiefly Christianity (1825–1832), and to what extent it served to shed light on each others' polities.

The Missing Concept

Something interesting to observe from this period is the complete lack of any recorded translation of the concept of politics. Instead, when foreigners referred to native polity the notions of kingdom and government were frequently used. The word that denoted these meanings was, as said, *aupuni*, which the Hawaiians likewise used when they talked about foreigners' polities. In the pre-missionary period, the practical nature of cross-cultural contacts, the highly personalized relations between the chiefs and foreigners, and the widely shared image of Hawaii as an absolute monarchy made it less likely that the two cultures would be spanned by a more varied political terminology. During the missionary period, the likelihood that such a terminology would emerge was considerably increased because the mission's relationship to the chiefs was defined in political terms by the foreign community, and because the mission was there to profoundly change the Hawaiian way of life. Nevertheless, the terminology remained thin, most likely because the missionaries felt it urgent to pose the mission as a neutral moral agency, and avoid involvements that could be used against it. And yet, this does not mean that the missionaries were not perceptive enough to see that the Hawaiian *aupuni* was more than a mere organization of graded nobility. However, because the missionaries thought it showcased a perverse foundation of human society, they found it pointless to include all its "heathenish" aspects in their vocabularies and dictionaries, which were, after all, by-products of Bible translations.

Although the native Hawaiian imagery of governing is varied—ranging from surrounding, shadowing, and protecting to residing above, breathing, standing erect, setting in order, eating, and consuming—*aupuni* displayed a marked uniformity in translations. As a dictionary entry, *aupuni* appeared first when William Ellis in 1825 included it in his brief vocabulary, which was appended to his popular *Journal of a Tour around Hawaii*. In early vocabularies "government" was not given as a translation of *aupuni*, but "kingdom" was universally offered. Ellis, an unusually keen observer, added more of the native flavor to his rendition of *aupuni* as "kingdom, state of peace, undisturbed state of a nation" (Ellis 1825, 245). It seems that Ellis, who was well advanced in studying Polynesian languages, had inferred something from his conversations with Hawaiian *ali'i* and his Tahitian apostles. The "state of peace" and the "undisturbed state of a nation" have strong elements of the chief-centered theory of society, as expressed, for example, in the rite of *hono*. They remind one of the sensitive balance that prevailed in Hawaii as the chiefs were consolidating the new order, the new *aupuni* that would guarantee order through worship. The other early translations are less informative, although they are significant in their own right as expressions of the state of cross-cultural communication of politics. An English visitor recorded *aupuni* as "king's reign" in 1825, when the young Kauikeaouli was made "king" (Bloxam 1825). The missionary Artemas Bishop, whose earlier vocabulary was the basis for Ellis' appendix, in a manuscript vocabulary also used the word "kingdom" (Bishop 1828). In Hiram Bingham's vocabulary, "kingdom" was also used with no hint of the native idea of social order (Bingham 1832, 12).

Here a word of caution is in order regarding the drawing of any definitive conclusions from these word lists, because they can hardly give us an approximation of the daily translation work that was being carried on by the missionaries. Nonetheless, they are useful because they support the impression given by other sources that the moral kernel of the mission seriously downplayed more thorough political theorizing. Besides, it was difficult to find God's government in the Bible, where the "kingdom of God" was the favored expression. We must look to the post-Ka'ahumanu era to find another appearance of the native theory in translation. Lorrin Andrews was the missionary who took the study of Hawaiian language most seriously, producing the first two dictionaries in 1836 and 1865. In his first dictionary, Andrews summarized the previous translation history of *aupuni*: "to be in an undisturbed state, to be in a state of peace and quiet, as a kingdom," and "a kingdom, dominion, jurisdiction of a king" (1836, 5–6). Andrews clearly echoes Ellis, and it seems difficult to assign single authorship to any of these early translations. For example, the Frenchman Mosblech followed the example and gave three meanings to *aupuni*: "kingdom," "reign," and "to be in peace" (1843, 9).

Seeking "government" as a translation of *aupuni* we must move further forward in time. In 1845, the Reverends John Emerson and Artemas Bishop used the word *aupuni* to translate both "kingdom" and "government" (Emerson and Bishop 1845, 65, 84). They also made a clear distinction between the two. "Kingdom" was translated simply as *aupuni* (65), but "government" required more Hawaiian explanations, because Emerson and Bishop wanted to impart the abstract understanding of the notion (i.e., the legal framework of governing, and the directing of a kingdom's affairs) without reference to a physical body of people with executive authority: "na kanawai hoomalu" (the governing laws) or "ka hoomalu ana i ke aupuni" (governing the kingdom) (84). By that time, the Hawaiian chiefship had been transformed into a constitutional monarchy and the missionaries, together with a great many foreigners, could finally say that the "civil institutions" were now in place. Hawaii was assuming social order that was seen as far less deformed than previously—as a non-arbitrary entity, Hawaii could have a regulated government. All this comes down to Emerson and Bishop's attempt to render "government" in Hawaiian, because now Hawaiians were thought to have some institutional prerequisites for understanding the functions of government, and for making the distinction between the rulers and the abstract body of government.

"Government" and *aupuni* were finally made full equivalents in the 1854 *Hawaiian Phrase Book* (Bishop 1854, 20), although the actual event might have taken place years earlier. Perhaps reflecting this development, French visitor Jules Remy translated both "government" and "kingdom" using the same word, *aupuni*, making no distinction between them (Remy 1852–1855). Of course, this does not mean that the gloss "kingdom" would have been replaced; Hawaii was indeed a constitutional monarchy from 1840 to 1893. However, at some point a new epithet for "kingdom," *aupuni mōʻī*, was invented, and in 1887 was recorded in Hitchcock's *English-Hawaiian Dictionary* (122). The expression utilizes the apparent neologism for king, *mōʻī* (see chapter 5, note 17), to distinguish *aupuni* as government (97) from *aupuni* as kingdom.

The fullest account of the word *aupuni* was given by Andrews in his 1865 dictionary: "A region or country governed by a chief or king. Originally the word did not imply a large country, as there were formerly several aupuni on one island. At present, the word is used to signify a kingdom; the dominion and jurisdiction of a king." Other meanings he gave were: "To be in an undisturbed state, to be in a state of peace and quietness, as a kingdom," "to become a kingdom," and, while introducing the word "government," "relating to the kingdom or government" (1865, 34). The preeminence of "government" as a translation of *aupuni* became evident at least after the overthrow of the Hawaiian monarchy in 1893. In the revised edition of Andrews' dictionary, the sentence "[a]t present, the word is used to signify" does not end with "kingdom," as in the 1865 edition, but with "government." In the same vein, the revisor Henry H. Parker added the word "republic" after the word "kingdom" in the sentence "to become a kingdom" (Andrews 1922, 73).

We can form a better idea of the missionaries' understanding of the indigenous imagery of *aupuni* by refocusing on its literal translations, some of which can be found already in the period before Kaʻahumanu's death in 1832. The word is a composition of two words: *au*, meaning "place" or "territory, compounded with other words"; and *puni*, meaning "around," "around on every side" (Andrews 1865, 34; Bingham 1832, 9, 268). In his early vocabulary, Bishop added the meaning "to surround for protection" (1828), again indicating the life-giving attributes of a chief. Thus the literal meaning of *aupuni* would be a safe, surrounded territory. Besides protection, the word *puni* carries connotations of completion and control (Pukui and Elbert 1986, 355), and this easily places the origin of the word *aupuni* in the traditional Hawaiian warfare between chiefdoms, and the establishing of *aupuni* after settlements of the feuds. This is implied by the antonym of *aupuni*—*auhuli*—which Bingham and Andrews translated as "to overturn a kingdom" (Bingham 1832, 10; Andrews, *Vocabulary*, n.d.). The word *huli* signifies a sense of reversal, which, in the case of *aupuni*, would indicate undoing the protective surrounding and upsetting the peace. *Auhuli* has also served as the root for translations of "revolution" *(ka hoʻāuhuli ʻana)*.

I have talked about the traditional Hawaiian conception of *aupuni* at some length. Although the early translations are on their surface quite silent about the divine nature of *aupuni*, a closer look at the Hawaiian supplementary vocabulary surrounding the notion of *aupuni* brings forth a different and richer imagery, one which underscores the chief's person as the peculiar condition of *aupuni*. Accordingly, *aupuni* is a result of some serious efforts by the prominent *aliʻi* to make things firm and stable so that he could dwell *(noho)* or stand *(kū)* at the head of *aupuni*, and provide life *(ea)* and protection *(malu)* for his people, become the source of life, retired in divine passivity. Further, the stability was not possible without a proper and satisfactory performance of the division of the lands, and the corresponding nomination of chiefs to these allotments of land *(hoʻoponopono)*. These chiefs could then go on with their daily lives of being above the common people *(kaʻamaluna)* and consuming the appropriated land *(ʻai)*, sometimes abusing the powers of their high position and overburdening the people *(hoʻohaku)*. In sum, the native theory of "government," as reconstructed from historical sources, presents a dimension of intensity from the protective *malu*, to the oppressive *hoʻohaku*, through the more neutral *aupuni* and *hoʻoponopono*, reminding us of the chiefly dualism of blessedness and danger.

In the long process of translation, the continuities between the various expressions and their cosmological context is greatly underrepresented. Further, the more we advance in time the more underrepresented these become. This comes as no surprise if we appreciate the driving force behind the translations. The goal was not only for them to make sense, but for them to make sense in order to create a system of equivalences that would correspond to a set of real social relations. In other words, the mission produced a minimal vocabulary of politics. The language of morals and evangelical republicanism was much richer, and we must turn to those vocabularies to approximate how politics was mediated across the two cultures.

Again, *aupuni* is the significant concept here. It was, along with *aliʻi*, the first formally translated concept that had some bearing on the rise of political discourse in 1825. Besides appearing in the early Hawaiian treatises with foreign countries and other business connections, it was also used to inform Hawaiians about the countries whose peoples they were dealing with in their daily lives. *Aupuni* brings together the missionaries' moral discourse and the prototype of comparative politics. In this sense, one of the earliest, if not the first systematic attempts to present a comparative account of foreign countries to Hawaiians was an 1832 geography book. A central feature of the book, following the practice of teaching geography and history together (see "Notes on Teaching" n.d.), is a review of each country's governmental form in historical terms. The reviews, compiled and embellished by the missionaries Samuel Whitney and William Richards, generally resemble the genre of traditional Hawaiian storytelling, in which the scene is usually divided between the chiefs and the common people. This division also forms a dramatic tension that animates the geographical comparisons. For example, the French Revolution is covered as follows:

> In the old days, only the nobles *[ali'i]* had a say in the affairs of the land, they decided what was right and what was wrong. They did not think much of the benefits of the people, who lived only according to the consent of the nobles. During the reign of kind nobles people were blessed and prosperous, because they were comforted; until *aupuni* went to other nobles, who were pompous and burdened the common people, who grew angry and rebelled. The land was not at all peaceful *[malu]*. At this time, the word of God was treated with contempt, that was the cause of the wrongdoings. The Sabbath was not observed, there was no prayer, the people did not listen to the words so as to be righteous, they were not afraid of God and death; therefore, people died because of their wrongdoings, the nobles died, too, and *aupuni* was divided into factions. The people rebelled and killed the king *[ali'i nui]* who controlled *aupuni* . . . (*He hoikehonua* 1832, 49–50, my translation).

To understand how much the missionaries were conditioned by Hawaiian conceptualizations, compare the style and thematic structure of this with the following David Malo account of the ancient high chief Waia: "In the tradition of the old Hawaiians, Waia's *aupuni* was full of faults. Because he went after merrymaking, he forsook the charge of his father to pray to gods and take good care of *aupuni* in view of taking care of the common people, so that his country[7] would be righteous . . . The people under him said that he did not worship gods, he did not have priests or readers of omens, he could not manage *aupuni* . . . An epidemic arrived at Hawaii and a great many was killed by it. Only twenty-six people survived . . ." (Malo 1987, 159–160, my translation).

In this same style, with a liberal touch of enthusiastic patriotism, the history and the political system of the United States are explained. Again, in a remarkable likeness of the two worlds, as they appear conceptually in the text, only Hawaiian words are used (excluding some proper nouns, and the Senate and the House of Representatives, which are retained in a slightly Hawaiian-ized forms). This is not to say that by using Hawaiian words the missionaries would have been unable to establish the difference that prevailed in the functional principles of the two societies; it is rather to emphasize that all of these countries were reduced to a set of comparable units, on an obvious moral scale, and that the comparisons sprang from the Hawaiian universe. In other words, Hawaii was the standard of comparison. It may have been that the missionaries intended to rank the United States highest on the scale, and indeed this is quite apparent in the text, but the cultural-linguistic circumstances allowed only a compromise in which the superiority of the democratic America was conveyed as in any evaluative Hawaiian story of a chief's reign. The next quote will illustrate the compromise. Once more, I concentrate on the use of the word *aupuni*.

> The leaders of the nation [*ali'i*] straightened up the land in the proper way. This is how they take care of the land.
>
> There is one principal leader [*ali'i nui*, meaning the President] above all the states [*moku*, traditionally a major land unit]; he was not born as a leader [*ali'i*]. He ruled because he was chosen by people. They had become an enlightened and benevolent people and skillful in the affairs of *aupuni*, and he [the President] was made the leader [*ali'i*] above all the lands. His rule lasts four years. When the four years have passed and if he is not chosen again, he will rule no more; he will become a true commoner [*kanaka maoli*, cf. Campbell 1967, 122], as he was before.
>
> The laws of the land are not in the hands of the principal leader [*ali'i nui*] alone. Under him there are two groups of leaders [*po'e kanaka ali'i*]. They are chosen by people (*He hoikehonua* 1832, 127, my translation).[8]

The geography book of 1832 is all the more important as an instance of cultural translation because it was written first in Hawaiian and only later translated into English for private use, possibly by Lorrin Andrews. For example, in the English translation, *nā kākā'ōlelo*, or the hereditary advisors of the chiefs were rendered as "political advisers" (NDOC 193). The context was the French universities, which were, among other things, described as educational centers for "political advisers." Thus the missionary writers had a familiar context in mind when they wrote the book, yet they were sufficiently satisfied with the expressive power of the Hawaiian language (cf. Andrews 1864), so that, in what they identified as the political realm in Hawaii, they opted for indigenous concepts instead of inventing neologisms or borrowing from English.

Although, due to the lack of documentation, we cannot know to what extent the English concepts were received by Hawaiians, we can be sure that by

1832 Hawaiians were well-versed in comparing different nations in Hawaiian terms. The missionaries' choice of the moral language they used to render Western political and religious history for Hawaiians fit with native ideas about legitimate rule. This correspondence did not go undetected by foreign residents, who cited it in their grumblings against the mission for having assumed a political agenda. When a number of foreign residents protested against the severe persecution of native Catholics in Hawaii in 1840, they quoted the geography book—"a standard work at the schools"—and tried to show that the Protestant mission presented a seriously distorted idea of the nature of Catholicism, and thereby induced the chiefs to restrict freedom of conscience. The geography depicted Catholic priests as "lying teachers," who repented other people's sins for money. The priests were said to have "exalted themselves above the word of God." The Pope was close to the Antichrist: "He lives in great pomp, believing himself to be equal to God." In Catholic countries the Protestants were persecuted: "very many have been murdered there, the number is countless" (Suppliment [sic] to the *Sandwich Island Mirror* 1840, 88–89, translation in the original). The Hawaiian *aupuni* was certainly taken as a theocracy by the foreign residents, who made it a public affair to wonder how such illiberality was possible "in this enlightened age."

Conceptually, this astonishment was restricted to foreign circles. Indeed, the intelligibility and communicability of these ideas, like the word of God, had to be based first on concepts already known to Hawaiians. Thus, Catholicism, for example, was seen by the chiefs as a threat to their *aupuni* and less as a matter of freedom of conscience, although this concern was brought to their attention several times. For a small group of advanced Hawaiian scholars things changed in the mid-1840s when the mission experimented for a few years with the teaching of English (cf. Emerson and Bishop 1845) at the Lahainaluna High School. Again, we have no detailed information on the manner of teaching, or the dissemination of the language among Hawaiians, but we can assume that the knowledge received in English was reticulated in Hawaiian.

In the view of the present study, the most important result of this New England reaction was the appearance of political discourse in the island public sphere. However, this small arena was split into two debates, one operating in the English language, the other in the Hawaiian. The two debates met hardly at all, and this inhibited the construction of Hawaiian equivalents for the Western political concepts. The debates were also socially distinct: the early days of the English debate took place between the mission and the foreign residents, and the Hawaiian between the mission and the chiefs. Later, a bilingual arena evolved, in which various mediating efforts linked the two language groups. But little is known of this process.

It is true that the specific representations of Hawaiian politics either as heathen deformation (missionaries) or uncivilized illiberality (foreign residents) developed through interaction of the concerned parties, and were constructions based on a blend of ideas and historical events. However, all comparative and systematic accounts that appeared at the time were more or less monocultural, as in the case of *aupuni*, or sporadic and contingent and developed in social circumstances that hardly presented any systematic manner of approaching cultural differences and their accommodation. A few examples of the latter will suffice. When Lord Russell of the British Navy, in November 1836, was forcing a treaty between the Hawaiian chiefs and England, he was questioned by Kīna'u—who had inherited Ka'ahumanu's place as the active arm of Kauikeaouli—about the origin of the proposed text of the treaty. Levi Chamberlain recalls Kīna'u's inquiry as follows: "Kinau asked the question whether the Document presented by Lord Russel [sic] was drawn up by Kalaimoku (which upon explanation I found to mean the Prime Minister of Great Britain" (Journal of Levi Chamberlain, Nov. 12, 1836). Kalanimōkū, who died in 1827 and whom the foreigners used to call "prime minister" (Campbell 1967, 122; Bingham to Jackson, Feb. 14, 1821, KC/AH) was the likely source of this confusion. At some point, Kalanimōkū, perhaps by some foreigners' suggestion, took the name Billy (William) Pitt, the English prime minister who died in 1806. For Hawaiians, there was nothing unusual in taking a new name of whatever origin, but it bears testimony that both Hawaiians and foreigners had means to view each others' societies through common practical instances, in this case the name Billy Pitt.[9] The Hawaiians knew that in England there was a high-ranking person who ran the affairs of the English *aupuni*; the foreigners knew that there was an equally high-ranking person in Hawaii who also took care of the practical affairs of the islands and was the next man from the high chief or king. As Kalanimōkū (or Kālaimoku), who was thus called Billy Pitt, held the office of *kālaimoku*, there developed a practice of calling the foreign prime ministers—those second in rank—by the same Hawaiian word (*kālaimoku*).

In this the Hawaiians had an advantage in disadvantage. They did not have access to the complete contexts of the foreign cultures, but in making sense of the contingent events they translated the foreign ways into Hawaiian conceptual schemes. In a similar ad hoc manner, Poki, upon his return from England in 1825, made sense of the English order of things. According to Kamakau, "Boki [Poki] assured the chiefs that of all the information he had gained in England as to how affairs were operated in that famous nation, the things that impressed him most were the great importance given to the word of God as expressed in the cathedrals and churches of London, of which Saint

Paul's seemed to him 'to my mind the foundation on which was built her fame'; and the fact that those who were educated and learned in letters were the important people of the country, compared to whom the common people were like dust under their feet. The king of England [he said] lived in a way similar to the tabu chiefs of old" (Kamakau 1992a, 273).[10]

Besides being a perceptive account, this testimony is a good example of cultural comparison, which, in the absence of thorough knowledge of the foreign culture, filters off the noise and selects a few themes by projecting central categories of the culture of the person doing the comparison. In Poki's case, the categories were the building of temples as connected to creation of *aupuni*, social hierarchy, and the traditional seclusion and strict court etiquette of the highest chiefs. In a manner of speaking, this could have been the beginning of seeing Hawaii as a monarchy by Hawaiians, as the Hawaiian chiefship was compared to the courts of England and France and included into the same general category of monarchies. This comparison was carried on in native oral traditions, and occasionally recorded as likeness of the old Hawaiian court etiquette to that of the great European monarchies (Kepelino 1932, 140).

Of course the foreigners did the same by generalizing their own cultural categories. Thus the missionary Lorrin Andrews, who translated David Malo's essay on the Hawaiian depopulation in 1839, characterized Malo "as a politician," who "is considered by the chiefs as rather *ultra* and is so treated at the present time" (Malo 1839, 121). Andrews was alluding to the less commonly celebrated fact that Malo had incurred the chiefs' disfavor and had his lands taken away. Andrews' identification of Malo "as a politician" reflected Malo's position as a non-*ali'i* adviser for the chiefs. According to Andrews, Malo "was called to advice in the councils of the nation, and from his standing, as he does, between the chiefs and the common people, he may be supposed to be informed as to the things of which he speaks" (121). The reason for the chiefs' displeasure with Malo was his aggressive manner of advocating reforms. Andrews wrote that Malo was urging "improvements which the King and chiefs do not yet see to be necessary" (121). An opponent of the mission (perhaps the American Consul John C. Jones) put it in a slightly different way. According to him, Malo was stripped of his possessions because of his "unwarranted [sic] liberties, assumed importance, and dictatorial impudence when near the persons of the chiefs" (*Sandwich Island Mirror*, Sept. 15, 1839; cf. Malo to the Church of Northampton, Dec. 2, 1836, HP/HMCS). But even for this writer, Malo was a politician, a mediator of interests, who was forced to take a step toward that personal independence seen to be at the foundation of a healthy republicanism, even though he was a mission-trained sectarian and suitably at variance with the code of etiquette of the chiefly hierarchy.

For the missionaries and other foreigners, these sporadic events accumulated into a political identity of Hawaiian society. At the same time, both sides developed an understanding of the other that validated some of their preconceived values, whether evangelical or liberal. In the next chapter I shall take a more detailed look at the substantial issues of the constructed political identity of Hawaiian society. As the missionaries were instructed to exclude themselves from political matters, they had to resort to indirect forms of theorizing, in which politics in general was seen as an integral part of civilization, and a certain *type* of politics as a sign of a progressive civilization. Thus Hawaiian society was conceived of in holistic terms, and its political existence and survival were made dependent on all other aspects of life, but particularly on the freedom to appropriate what the foreigners called "natural resources."

CHAPTER 4

Political Economy

So far, we know that in the province of political knowledge the two cultures did approach each other. Yet the translation was not completed, because the comparisons were established in two distinct conceptual systems. A mutual understanding was certainly facilitated by frequent intercourse, but this did not allow the systems to converge or even to communicate so that a fair amount of cross-cultural learning could take place, and social distribution of such knowledge was limited. In other words, while focusing on the interactive scheme of the missionaries' identity maintenance, and the clashes of the mission and the mercantile community, we learned that the discourse of politics that developed from the conflict was conceptually quite independent of the Hawaiian community, although it was structurally tied to the chiefs' proselytizing efforts. I now wish to focus on more systematic attempts to facilitate cultural learning, to turn representations into practice, as they were framed by the using of political concepts in the 1830s and 1840s.

In tracking down the historical events that took place within the chiefly establishment, we can detect a change in the general atmosphere after the death of Ka'ahumanu on June 5, 1832. Just prior to her death, it had been rumored that she was considering a restructuring of *aupuni*, inspired by the advice of a certain General William Miller (Bingham to Evarts, Dec. 30, 1831, HP/HMCS; Bingham to Evarts, Feb. 6, 1832, MSL; Journal of Betsey Lyons, June 5, 1832; see Kamakau 1992a, 306–308). Miller, who would later become the English consul in Honolulu, had a series of discussions with missionaries in Honolulu in 1831 (Bingham to unknown recipient, Dec. 13, 1831, MSL) and, after Bingham's solicitation, he put his ideas in writing (Miller 1831). Bingham later delivered this "Memorandum" to the chiefs, but it is not known how it was received.[1]

In its general character Miller's proposal was typical of the foreign community and the occasional visitors of the time, but in other ways he had uncommon sympathy for the mission and managed to carry on a peaceful conversation with Bingham.[2] According to Miller, the chiefs should have established "some defined form of government," which should have included measures to guarantee "security for property." For him, as for other foreigners, the manifest reason for discontent was the "capricious and arbitrary measures of the native rulers" and the "oppressive measures made known by a town crier" (Miller 1831, 1). It was noted by foreigners that this was possible because land management, or "ownership," was concentrated in the hands of the highest chief, from whom the other chiefs held their lands, and so on down to the smallest farmer. In Miller's words, this was "indeed the root of all evil" (p. 2). As Miller appreciated the evangelical program of the Hawaiian mission, he also was sympathetic toward the common Hawaiians, whom he thought should have been transformed gradually into petty landowners.

Miller also furnished the chiefs with some concrete measures for implementing these ideas. However, here I am more interested in the fundamental social theory that Miller was applying in his reform proposals. After outlining the major defects of Hawaiian society and suggesting the best remedies for them, Miller turned to theorizing about an ideal society, and rehearsed the familiar understanding of the elementary dynamics of society, the contract: "At all events it [the allotting of permanent land grants to common Hawaiians] would be the means of creating a middle class of society composed of free men whose fidelity might be depended upon, since it would be to their interest to support the govt. that protected them" (Miller 1831, 3). This view was generally appreciated by the mission, and a few years later it undertook a bolder strategy in civilizing Hawaiians.

On the question of liberty, though, Miller departed from the idea of basing the social bond on individual virtue, as in the evangelical republicanism, and here he was much closer to the views of foreign residents of Honolulu than the mission. Again the context is important. Kuakini's appointment to the head of O'ahu after Liliha's downfall in April 1831 caused much alarm in the foreign community. Kuakini was known for his rather independent and sweeping measures to enforce Christian tabus, and for a period of two years on O'ahu he greatly upset the town of Honolulu. "There was quietness and peace in those days," as a missionary historian says (Dibble 1909, 216). Bingham was more specific: "We can say that *the horses rest in Honolulu on the Sabbath*" (Bingham to Evarts, Nov. 23, 1831, MSL). General Miller happened to arrive just in time to witness the early days of Kuakini's policing, and this was reflected in his proposals: "The late attempts to prevent foreign residents from drinking wine & spirituous liquors at their own table, to close the billiard room and to take away the horses of those who should ride out on a Sunday for innocent recreation, appear to me despotic & vexatious and to emanate rather from sectarian enthusiasm, not to say intolerance, than from justice and sound policy . . . it is, I think, to be regretted that their [the missionaries'] evangelical zeal sometimes carries them to extremes by exacting, or by their influence causing to be enacted, certain restrictions on society which I conceive ought to be attributed rather to overrighteous opinions peculiar to their sect than to true religion" (Miller 1831, 4–5). It is likely that Kuakini's measures did not receive an unambiguous blessing of the mission, as indicated by the debate on the alleged persecution of native Catholics (Bingham, Green, and Whitney to Anderson, June 23, 1832; Clark to Anderson, Mar. 30, 1833, both in MSL; FOE, Aug. 1840; Jarves 1843, 292).[3] It seems, rather, that what lay behind the mission's inactivity was that it had continued to operate in a subservient position in relation to the chiefs, which was not always understood by the foreign residents, or visitors like Miller.

Neither was this perfectly clear to the missionaries themselves until the native reaction against Christianity after Kaʻahumanu's death. For the mission this reaction had a great disillusioning effect as to the results of their work and the nature of Hawaiian society. It is true that even before 1832 some individual missionaries had written home letters filled with pessimism about the future, lamenting especially on conversion experiences among the natives (e.g., Chamberlain to Evarts, July 26, 1826; Chamberlain to Anderson, Feb. 13, 1827; Andrews and Richards to Evarts, Sept. 30, 1828, all in MSL), but the events following the death of Kaʻahumanu finally forced the mission to reconsider its strategy. It will be argued that the disillusionment contributed to the formation of a missionary theory of Hawaiian despotism, and to a sense of urgency regarding the need for relations of church and state to be finally put on the right footing and the foundations of society corrected. Paradoxically, in the course of living the theory, the mission assumed a more worldly look.

The issues of despotism, the absence of liberty and industry, and—to say it all—the arbitrariness of the Hawaiian society were mostly perceived through the school system, in which all of these issues manifested themselves in their indigenous forms. That is, for the mission the schools were the concrete instances in which the political system became visible and easily objectifiable. This perception was generated by a crisis, in which earlier missionary stereotypes were joined by new cultural learning through what can fairly be called alienation.

The process of alienation was not as abrupt as Kaʻahumanu's death. Some time before her death, the mission had concluded from their experience of school inspections and teacher evaluations that they were fast running out of means to both deepen and widen the substance of *palapala* (Andrews to Anderson, Nov. 3, 1829; Andrews to Anderson, Oct. 1, 1834, both in MSL; General Letter of SIM to ABCFM, July 7, 1836, HP/HMCS). Given that religious teaching had formed the core of the curriculum, other areas of knowledge had necessarily received much less attention. Besides, because the word of God was faithfully committed to memory in the native schools throughout the islands, the system had become a daily routine of dull and ritualistic repetition. As far as the Hawaiians were concerned, the schools were firmly established, *pa'a loa*, and served the intended purpose well enough; but for the missionaries, reviewing the Tahitian experience, this meant the beginning of decadence.

This fear of an education standstill resulted in the founding of the Lahainaluna High School, or the mission seminary, in 1831 (Dibble 1909, 250). Lorrin Andrews, the first principal of the school, had several occasions to reflect on the system of education. Even before Dibble (see Dibble 1909, 216–222), he put into writing his unpleasant suspicion that the schools had primarily served as organizational elements in the Hawaiian *aupuni*. According to Andrews, the native schools' "existence during these few years past has supplied a vacuum in the civil & religious affairs of this government which to all human appearance nothing else could have filled" (Andrews to Anderson, June 13, 1832, MSL). Further, the schools were only for the adult population, which the mission board in Boston found to be "not the most natural method." To this Andrews could only answer, referring to the chiefly-run organization of the schools, that "necessity compelled us to it, or rather the providence of God seemed to say that it was duty" (Andrews to ABCFM, Nov. 24, 1835, MSL).

This sentiment was not completely new among the missionaries. They were not blind to the decisive chiefly impetus, as observed in 1825 by Levi Chamberlain, the secular agent of the mission: "If the Chiefs did not favor instruction & religion, it would be almost impossible to get the attention of the common people" (Chamberlain to Anderson, Aug. 17, 1825; also Chamberlain to Anderson, Feb. 13, 1827, both in MSL). As the missionaries conceptualized the Hawaiian chiefship against the backdrop of European history and the struggle between civil rulers and ecclesiastics, the system of Hawaiian schools and religious instruction received the same rationalizing treatment. Later, in 1843, Sheldon Dibble would retrospectively inform his readers that, "it probably would have been utterly impossible, in those early times, to have restricted the power of the chiefs to civil matters. They had never known any such restriction. It has taken the civilized world a long time to learn the province of civil government, as distinct from the province of religious obligation. The chiefs at the

Sandwich Islands could not distinguish at once, and they do not distinguish very clearly even now" (1909, 210).

In fact, the missionaries arrived in Hawaii with their minds filled with similar ideas, according to which religion was indeed seen "as an engine of government," as Bingham put it (Bingham to Worcester, May 13, 1820, HP/HMCS; also Bingham 1849, 77; Ellis 1979, xvii; Tyerman and Bennet 1831, I, 444, 458). Not even the most liberal-minded missionary could attribute much value to this heathenish combination. The English missionary William Ellis, always more sympathetic to Hawaiians than were his American colleagues, did conclude from his experience of Hawaii in the early 1820s that the Hawaiians had been "an organized community for many generations." But again, even in its antiquity, the organization was false and but little advanced "in the art of good government" (1979, 309). The Americans, on the other hand, saw no trace of light: "The laws of society . . . are yet to be formed" (SIM to Evarts, Feb. 1, 1822, MSL).

It is clear that, in the main, the personal experiences of the missionaries only confirmed the stereotypical ideas they held of the political organization of a pagan society. But it seems that as long as the system of schools was holding together, talk of this apparent perversion in the foundation of Hawaiian society did not often surface in the missionary discourse. I have already argued that during the 1820s the missionaries were forced to consider their own position in terms of church and state. However, this was a much more mission-centered discourse and only secondary attention was paid to the Hawaiian system. By contrast, the post-Kaʻahumanu discourse was oriented toward Hawaiians, mainly for two reasons. First, after the events of 1827, the mission was quite excluded from the rest of the foreign community, and second, the major threat to *palapala* came at this time from inside the Hawaiian community. We should also mention that the missionaries were quite certain that Hawaiians, at least officially, had discarded their former religion and freed themselves from "the odious and abhorred superstitions" and were therefore ready to receive "the Gospel" (MH 19, 206). For this reason alone, very little attention had been paid to a possible continuation of "heathenism" in a Christian disguise. This heathenism, when it did become apparent, was seen as a totality, comprising beliefs as well as the earthly powers of the chiefs, whereas the earlier notion of heathenism had been mainly concerned with pagan religion.

Following Kaʻahumanu's death, a general theory of Hawaiian political organization was created that affirmed the longevity of Hawaiian traditions. Six months after the funeral, Artemas Bishop, realizing that the number of scholars and churchgoers was in decline, wrote to the board that the universal attention of common people to *palapala* had been greatly aided by "a governmental influence" (Bishop to Anderson, Nov. 5, 1832, MSL). A few days later, the disil-lusioned Sheldon Dibble told the board about his conviction that the success of the mission had almost completely rested on the shoulders of the chiefs and the hierarchical functioning of Hawaiian society, with its "union between church and state." Interestingly enough, he was writing in Hilo, which was Kaʻahu-manu's land: "A chief commands, or *advises*, (if you prefer the term without the meaning) the people obey. If it be to attend church, they attend; to study the word of God in schools, they study it; to purchase books, they purchase them; to become religious, they put on the 'form of godliness.'—If he neglects to com-mand, they sit in indifference & inactivity. Such has been the condition of this people & such in a great measure it continues to be . . . There can be no doubt that much of the appearance of religion has been & still continues to be of a spe-cious kind; in some cases a mere servile obedience to rulers, in other cases a sy-cophantic crouching for favor" (Dibble to Anderson, Nov. 9, 1932, MSL).

If Kaʻahumanu's death marked a decline of the school system, then Kauikeaouli's rise to the head of *aupuni* practically destroyed the entire system, or as Dibble put it, the system "crumbled at once into ruins" (1909, 249). The falling off from the schools was indeed significant. The data from the Protestant missionary records show a decrease of well over 80 percent in the school popu-lation between December 1831 and June 1838. Between June 1832 and June 1834, the number of readers dropped from twenty-three thousand to sixteen thousand, or about 56 percent (Schmitt 1977, 211). In the twenty-two station schools, which were taught and supervised by the missionaries themselves and mainly survived the crisis, there were only 535 adult students in 1836. Outside of the mission stations there was practically no teaching at all, because the anti-Christian revolt had largely deprived the missionaries of their native teaching staff (Coan, Emerson, and Thurston to Anderson, July 7, 1836, HP/HMCS).[4] There was also a significant plunge in church admittance. In 1832, 235 Hawai-ians were admitted to the Protestant church. The next year, when Kaui-keaouli's rebellion was full-blown, the number was only 72. The year 1834 showed an upward curve again, with 124 admitted (Sahlins 1992, 124).

Kauikeaouli's heathen rebellion began around January 1833 and gradually waned toward the end of 1834, although there were occasional bursts of anti-tabu acts throughout the 1830s. His method of restoring the *aliʻi*-ship to himself as the legitimate heir of Kamehameha consisted primarily of reviving traditional pas-times associated with the closing of temples during *makahiki*, such as *hula* and vari-ous games and sports, as well as sexual license and free drinking. According to a contemporary historian, violence, plunder, and burning of churches also occurred (Jarves 1843, 300). Kauikeaouli also formally declared void all the previously established Christian laws, except those prohibiting killing and theft, and a few days later he publicly took the reins of *aupuni*. Yet he made Christian Kīna'u, who had inherited Ka'ahumanu's position, his effective co-ruler, the so-called *kuhina nui* (Journal of Levi Chamberlain, Mar. 9, 15, 1833; FOE, Mar. 14, 1833). Kauike-aouli's and Kīna'u's unholy alliance was an effective check of the anti-tabu movement, to the extent that it prevented Kauikeaouli from completely dismissing the new ways. It was also a proof of the strength of the Christian party, to which most of the Ka'ahumanu (now Kīna'u) chiefs still belonged.

Among the lesser chiefs and common Hawaiians Kauikeaouli's rebellion was a welcome event. For, as Sahlins says, "the truly Hawaiian sovereignty was now represented by the suspension of tabu, that is, by outrages against the Protestant restrictions." Kauikeaouli was leading "the second historic declaration of the abolition of the tabus" (Sahlins 1992, 121, 123), which was a logical inversion of the rise of Ka'ahumanu *mā*. Just as the departure and death of Liholiho in 1824 had opened the scene for the new tabus, Ka'ahumanu's death cleared the way for restoring the tabu-free state and Kauikeaouli's honor.

After some serious confrontations between the heathen party and the Christian party, Kauikeaouli realized that Kīna'u and her associates were too firmly committed to their cause for him ever to prevail alone on the top. His reasons for giving up are not entirely clear, but in the latter part of 1834 he allowed Kīna'u and Hoapili to stop the un-Christian commotion. There followed some resolute destruction of distilleries (Kamakau 1992a, 339–340), and the following January, as a sign of truce, the island of O'ahu, which had been the primary locus of the rebellion, was given to Kīna'u (Journal of Levi Chamberlain, Jan. 5, 1835). Nevertheless, it is evident that the school system did not recover until years later, even though all the islands were now under Christian chiefs.

The final blow against the enemies of Jehovah came on December 30, 1836, when Kauikeaouli's sister Nāhi'ena'ena died at the age of twenty-one. She had joined her brother in the rebellion by mating with him in the presence of their followers in Honolulu, and she maintained her anti-Christian stance until her death. This was followed soon after by the death of Komi, Kauikeaouli's closest favorite, male lover, and instigator. In Dibble's words, Kauikeaouli "began to reflect and to change in a measure his course of conduct" (1909, 254). After that, Kauikeaouli moved to Lahaina, away from the temptations of Honolulu.[5]

The Missionary Theory of Oppression

The turbulent years, as these were called, involved a number of complex issues, ranging from tabu enforcement and intensified corvée labor to incest and succession. Despite this, the events of 1832 to 1837 had such a Hawaiian stamp on them that missionaries could easily, despite the great number of issues and their complexity, frame them according to their own progressivist social theory as signs of heathenism and ungodliness or, in milder cases, ignorance and stupidity. But for the missionaries the essence of these "disgraceful" events was still the lingering question of making human society stand distinct from nature, without introducing elements that would contravene natural reason. In concrete terms, Lord's Supper and prayer meetings no longer sufficed, particularly if the voluntary devotion had been only an illusion. The mission had to pay more attention to the molding of the social atom, the only true element of society, natural or political: the individual. "We have been making great calculation on seeing a nation grow up like a forest, & perfect itself as it grew, with the extraneous aid . . . of only a blow here & there to clip some ugly or unprofitable branch. God has of late been showing us that this is not the way; but that instead of trying to convert a nation, we should labor to save the individuals of which that nation is composed. We have had but little to do with individuals except the chiefs, & too much with the people en masse" (Emerson to Anderson, Apr. 8, 1835, MSL).

The necessary voluntarism was indeed a hoax. Suddenly only a handful of devotees clung to the mission church, and the masses of people who formerly filled school rooms and spacious chapels were now seen as having sunk to a level where there was no willingness, so badly needed in forming a society of equals. It has already been suggested that almost certainly for these Hawaiians Kauikeaouli's rebellion brought a welcome change in their lives (see Sahlins 1992, 122), anticipation of better times with more food and less toil, and an end to unnatural suppression of all things desirable. An interesting episode of antimissionary feeling among the common people was reported on Maui during Kauikeaouli's rebellion. According to Lorrin Andrews, "a rumor had been circulated that the missionaries were growing rich at the expense of the people—that those who worked for the missionaries ought to be better paid—that the missionaries had more property than the chiefs &c. . . . This manifested itself in several cases of disobedience and a general coldness to me . . . For about three weeks in Oct. [1833] I was obliged to carry up on my own shoulders all the fuel we used for cooking, ironing &c from Lahaina a distance of two miles or pay a price equal to the original cost of the fuel . . ." (Andrews to Anderson, Oct. 1, 1834, MSL).

The mission physician on Maui, Alonzo Chapin, made similar remarks in October 1833, and suggested that the missionaries should give up the lands they held from the chiefs (and common Hawaiians as their workforce) in order to prove the disinterested cause of the mission (Chapin to Anderson, Oct. 6, 1833, MSL). But since this mode of subsistence was the only workable option, the mission took the risk of being portrayed, at least partially, as having placed itself on the side of the chiefs and the increased burdens of the labor system. Paradoxically, had the common people been in closer contact with the missionaries, they might have agreed with the missionary way of thinking that forced collectivism and its corollary effect, ritualism, has a tendency to produce ineffectiveness and falsehoods, and lead to oligarchic and unwanted situations. Not that the common people would have possessed the individualistic traits so much valued by the missionaries, even had the chiefs let them decide themselves. They would nonetheless have been able to say that the pretended godliness, forced congregations, and protracted church-building were burdens which should have been replaced by another kind of collectivism, one supported by reciprocity between themselves and the chiefs.

It is true, however, that commoners found ways of surviving and even taking advantage of the new collective situation. In an afterthought, Sheldon Dibble found empirical proof for such stratagems, conditioned by the persisting chiefly structures but locally improvised by the common people: "A member of my congregation (Hilo) gave evidence of true conversion, and was admitted to the church. The following week I observed that almost all who came to converse with me used nearly the same language—there seemed to be a stereotype thought for the whole; and on examination I found that it was the substance of the last conversation which the newly admitted member had with me just previous to her entering the church. She had communicated it to others as a thought of some prevalency [sic], and therefore each adopted it as his own" (1839, 148).

This collective "insensitivity" to evangelical doctrine had some important consequences for the conceptualization of Hawaii as a political society. Although in the missionary sources common Hawaiians usually remain anonymous, the missionaries did learn something by observing the ritualistic and often calculating church-going, which rarely displayed the adorned qualities of a profound change of heart. Watching and listening to common natives helped the missionaries understand the sociology of the schools and churches, and guided their perceptions of what they called a political system. For them, ritualism on such a massive scale betrayed the rotten quality of people's principles of sociality and moral virtue, which were the building blocks of a sound political society. The missionaries saw the whole operation to be chief-driven, and its main features revealed intense tabu enforcement and massive and geometrically organized population movements, without the least intelligible suggestion of genuine voluntarism on the part of the common people. They therefore conceptualized the system as despotism—a word that was already on James King's lips when he put together the experiences of the Cook expedition (Cook and King 1784, 158).

The hierarchic nature of the Hawaiian society was well-known to the missionaries (e.g., Bishop to Evarts, June 1, 1825; Levi Chamberlain to Evarts, July 26, 1826, both in MSL). But earlier, from 1825 to 1832, the apparent success of the mission and a somewhat naive trust in the prospects of change directed missionary attentions less to Hawaiian social organization than to the substance of their own work and the disturbing elements from outside—the mercantile community and ungodly sailors. But things changed after Ka'ahumanu's death. The heightened sense of hierarchy after 1832 is nicely reflected in a letter, again from Dibble: "You have frequently been informed of the abject servitude not only of body, but also of mind in which this people are held to their formerly deified & still despotic chiefs; but it is difficult for the subjects of an enlightened & free government to form a just conception of the deep degradation & low vassallage [sic] in which a heathen intellect is held to the will of a despotic chieftain" (Dibble to Anderson, Oct. 14, 1833, MSL).

Another missionary, Dwight Baldwin of Waimea, Hawai'i, wrote to the same effect some weeks before Kauikeaouli's rebellion had lost most of its edge: "This people have been greatly proven to trust in a round of mere external observances, often perhaps in a mere attendance on public worship, thinking it constituted them servants of God, while the heart was wholly neglected. Our efforts were therefore more directed to break up these false views, which stood in the way of the sinner's coming Christ" (Baldwin to ABCFM, Nov. 3, 1834, MSL).[6]

The false views were indeed breaking up, as the bubble had burst against the faces of all concerned parties. The missionaries began to revise their strategy, and the common Hawaiians, who had been offered a more attractive alternative, forsook *palapala*. The chiefs, although still professed Christians, showed signs of easing their previously insistent demands for school and church attendance (Green to Anderson, Nov. 16, 1836, MSL). As the disillusioned missionaries attempted to organize new and independent schools and churches, they were forced to turn to the chiefs for donations, which never really materialized (*The Polynesian*, Dec. 28, 1844). Therefore, to a significant degree, the mission was forced to rely in their reorganization efforts on commoner contributions, and the results were necessarily modest since circulating money and labor were still tightly under chiefly control.

These reforms were clearly heading toward a more conscious realization of a system with a considerable Western genius. Yet the structural features of Hawaiian society made it practically impossible to remove common Hawaiians from their traditional positions in the system of chiefship, or to establish effective and independent local units cut off from the pyramidic hierarchy. If, as a missionary observed, "the policy of the chiefs is to monopolize all the talent &

influence of the nation for the purpose of maintaining their own power" (anonymous member of the mission to Anderson, Oct. 13, 1835, HP/HMCS), then to establish schools independent of the chiefs and their interests was indeed difficult. The monopolizing practices of the chiefs were particularly threatening in view of Lahainaluna High School, which was set up primarily to educate qualified native teachers for local primary schools.

As a result, one issue surfaced above all others, that of land and labor. After the collapse of the school system, the new focus became Hawaiians as individuals, and their structurally conditioned lack of initiative. This lead directly to the mission taking up issues of land and labor. Lowell Smith, the missionary who was forced by Kīna'u in 1834 to take a station in 'Ewa, O'ahu, in an apparent move to check un-Christian acts, began his missionary career amidst these new concerns. His journal entries from the mid-1830s show traces of personal hopelessness, but they also characterize problems that were now occupying the minds of all of the missionaries:

> Such is the state of government among the Hawaiians that I almost despair of their ever becoming a working, industrious people, a people to be compared with Americans. When the present offensive form of government shall be done away, and another which shall render to all their due shall be substituted, then we may hope for a reformation in every department of society, and not till then (Journal of Lowell Smith, Aug. 4, 1833).

> If the shackles were burst from this oppressed people and they had an opportunity to rise from the dust, degradation and ignorance, I think they would put forth one united, persevering and successful effort (Sept. 17, 1833).

> It is very lonely about here these days the laboring part of community all being gone to Moanalua, making salt for the chiefs. They have been absent about three weeks. The taxes of the chiefs are intolerable! O that there might be a revolution in the government of these Islands. We can have no schools—but no schools house or meeting house for want of aid. All paa i ka hana no na 'lii [busy with the work for the chiefs] (Oct. 15, 1835).

For the evangelicals as covenant thinkers, it was a matter of some importance to become fully aware not only of the functioning of the chiefs' power but also of the position that it had offered for the mission. The position was surely questionable from the missionary point of view. Thus the missionaries' gloom grew as a result of their increased self-understanding of the part played by them in a society that was a reversed image of their own ideal. In Hawaii everything radiated from the chiefs, worship as well as subsistence, which was a strong indicator that individual freedom was suppressed and the enactment of political society clearly erratic.

This view was only confirmed by the extinction of sandalwood about the time of Ka'ahumanu's death (Thrum 1904, 67). As this source of wealth was gradually lost, the insatiable chiefs, already grown to appreciate foreign luxuries, reorganized the neglected production of staple food for the provisioning of whale ships, but this time with previously unknown intensity and coercion (Sahlins 1992, 108). The Hawaiian traditional system of labor was again needed to produce revenue for the ritual economy of the chiefs. It was thus obvious that the same force that had driven the masses to attend *palapala* was also preventing them from attaining the level of individuality prescribed by civilization. The collapse of the school system and the simultaneous decline of the sandalwood trade made this defect all the more visible.[7] Another new missionary, Harvey Hitchcock, was quite upset after being two years in the field on the island of Moloka'i:

> As to the political condition of these islands it is in no enviable state. It is true that as it regards those oppressions which their ancient religion imposed on the people the times are now much better, but those coerced upon them by the cupidity of the chiefs are perhaps more untolerable [sic] than ever. The lands are all owned by the high chiefs, and given out by them to the lower ones, and by these distributed to the people who are to cultivate them & whose only freedom is to submit unconditionally to the exactions of their landlords or to leave their lands and do worse. Even dilatoriness to pay an enormous demand is sometimes followed by the ejectment of the whole population of the district who when thus ejected have no right to a morcel [sic] of food on the land, and would be treated as thieves [sic] were they to satisfy their hunger out of the fruits of their own labors. There are indeed a few individuals who are honorable exceptions to the above oppressive character. But the fact that these remarks apply to the most of those in authority will give you [end of page, words missing?] to their character as Christians without farther comment (Journal of Harvey Hitchcock, Nov. 1, 1834, copy of a letter).

It is not likely that the missionaries merely projected their prejudices and created a distorted or ideological image of the chiefship, either to better serve their own project or out of sheer ignorance and unwillingness to see any value in the Hawaiian way of life. Besides other accounts that give similar details (e.g., Newburgh 1835; writing six months after Hitchcock), there is a more speculative reason not to dismiss missionary material in this way. By merely describing relations of land ownership and intensified corvée labor, the missionaries were privately engaging in a sort of criticism that would have otherwise seriously compromised their rapport with the chiefs. Furthermore, an analysis of the chiefship's practices provided the missionaries with the elementary knowledge they needed in their future attempts to alter it. If a missionary wrote about idleness and poverty as "the only defensive means" the common people had at their disposal to "avoid many heavy exactions which would otherwise be laid on them" (Bishop 1838, 57), we may well assume that besides the voice of the missionary we also hear that of the common Hawaiian.[8]

The missionaries had previously conceptualized the chiefship by using typically Western tools: church and state. The would-be editor of the government newspaper *The Polynesian*, James Jackson Jarves, who was well versed in the missionary sentiments, testified to the missionaries' motives in keeping the two separate. As the *aupuni* was a totality of centralized order, the chiefs' edicts, no matter how minor (they were never insignificant), also carried in them a more universal meaning than the foreigners were used to thinking in terms of. The same universal dimension was entangled in the moral laws and work orders, in soil as well as people. When this was understood, the mission "was to widen these distinctions [church and state], and enlarge the liberty of the subject" (Jarves 1843, 250). Accordingly, a corrupted relation between church and state can amount to a sort of divine dictatorship, which is extremely destructive of all individual liberties, enterprises, and vital preconditions of civilization. Because the most penetrating of all Hawaiian institutions, the corvée labor system, was seen to function on such a basis, it was quite inevitable that the missionary representations of Hawaiian politics took a turn toward economic discourse.

In conclusion, the theory of oppression, through which the Hawaiian *aupuni* was viewed by the missionaries (and others) as a system of abuses, combined observations and social theory. The theory, when communicated and translated, was an important mediating force in later changes of the chiefship. The perversion of the chiefship was seen as the basic hindrance to the advancement of civilization, natural society, and economic ontology. All the negative qualifiers that were attached to the chiefship—arbitrariness, oppression, and despotism—and gave it new coherence in the foreigners' thinking, coexisted with the great disillusionment suffered by the mission. Without the latter, the excesses of the chiefship might have received much less attention, and the social theory might have remained silent. For the development of political comparisons, it was essential for the missionaries to realize how closely they had been united with the chiefs, and how much they had helped the chiefs legitimize their arbitrary power. The missionaries now saw themselves in the position of the native priests of the traditional era, and therefore as being "an inseparate and integral part of the political government" (Dibble 1909, 77). Because it was felt that such a union should be avoided in the future, more attention was to be paid to the power of the chiefs, the terms of ownership and land rights, and the overblown labor system.

God of Commerce, and Applied Theology

Hawaiian despotism was represented by missionaries in a language resembling, or actually duplicating, the idea of the birth of human culture as property. The beginning of culture as property was also the beginning of laws and government, that is, of politics. Thus Hawaiian despotism was really a grave mistake of a very old type, likened to original sin but now transposed to political life. This perspective was marshaled to guide the missionary project of converting the Hawaiian state of nature, or natural society, into political society without perverting and endangering the law of nature concerning property rights. As the chiefs' claims of corvée services were increasing, the nightmarish scene of nature's extinction was revealed to the missionaries in all its horrors. In Hawaii there was no private property in the Western sense, and so there was no proper foundation for enacting naturally based political society. The appropriation of nature, or natural resources, was concentrated in the hands of the chiefs, and as such it represented an incompatible breach of nature because God's law made natural resources equally available to all humans. Although missionaries could not approve of the legalistic premises of the theory of social contract, they did share some of its ideas, for example the naturalness of private property as everyone's relation to nature, and its divinely sanctioned protection.

Thus it was not an easy task for a true believer to witness his hosts, on whom his own project fundamentally depended, serving the Christian God while grabbing everything of value for themselves (Levi Chamberlain to Anderson, Dec. 11, 1832, MSL). Making matters even worse was the chiefs' habit of accumulating huge quantities of goods, which they occasionally distributed among their favorites but more often kept behind closed doors. Thus not even their amassment showed signs of rational behavior; it was all ruthless exploitation and jealousy, manifested in storehouses full of rotting goods and incidental piles of Chinese silk floating in the coastal waters.

As the Hawaiian logic of chiefly consumption was geared more toward competitive display than subsistence use, not to mention investment for profit (see Sahlins 1991), this was only to be expected. But there were more difficulties to come, as Hawaii became an object of foreign capitalistic plans in the mid-1830s. While the constantly diminishing number of common people grumbled under their lords, dragging their feet as possible, the foreign chiefs were on the rise, more powerful than Kūali'i or Kamehameha had ever been. Tough competition among the merchants induced several foreigners to turn to agriculture and seek leases from Kauikeaouli. He was at first decidedly against the commitments they asked for. His stance was conservative and consistent with the traditional prerogatives of the paramount chief. In 1834, he had this to say to

Kaikio'ewa, the head of Kaua'i, who was considering a *haole* lease: "And if we wish to discharge the foreigners, we can take the land back. Do not give land away permanently *(A i manao no kakou e hemo no ia alaila no lawe mai. Mai haawi lilo loa oe i ka aina)*" (Kauikeaouli to Kaikio'ewa, Oct. 24, 1834, M-59/AH).

Under the pressure of the so-called government, the debts to foreign merchants accrued by the chiefs in the sandalwood trade, and the insatiable hunger of the competitive chiefs to display their wealth, the Hawaiian *aupuni* was facing a serious liquidity crisis. As a partial solution to the cash problem, Kauikeaouli altered the lease policy in 1835, and gradually foreigners began to lease tracts of land. The foreigners would have liked permanent titles, but for the time being Kauikeaouli decided to remain "the life here on earth." Realizing what a dangerous species the American capitalist was, the missionaries were unwilling to recommend any outright sale of land: "The system of government, as you are already aware, is a most defective, and at the same time, a very oppressive one. How it can be altered is a great question. It would be unsafe to offer the lands for sale, & yet it is very desirable that those who cultivate the soil should own it. I think however that the greatest evil that exists is in the irregularity or instability of the government" (Richards to Anderson, Aug. 7, 1835, HP/HMCS).

The firm that set the leasing trend, Ladd and Company, had a benevolent if not pious reputation, mostly through Peter Brinsmade, who was a former student of Andover Theological Seminary and Yale Divinity School. He also served as the United States commercial agent in Hawaii from 1838 to 1846. With the help of Brinsmade's known interest in religion and reform, the young owners succeeded in securing missionary support for contracting a lease from Kauikeaouli. Even though the lease was "a special privilege," as Bradley says (1968, 239), it was also a positive signal for the prospective agriculturalists, mostly sugar growers, who had felt the trade slump of the late 1830s and were looking for new ways to prosperity.

The declining trade in Hawaii was an overseas reflection of the serious recession of 1837. In Hawaii, whaling fleets had been shrinking almost continuously from 1833. This development culminated in 1838, when the tide of recession reached Hawaiian harbors (*The Friend*, June 1, 1844; Bradley 1968, 216–220). For the chiefs, the recession and the declining whaling industry meant an accompanying decline in their revenue as the number of visiting ships dropped. Missionary and other contemporary accounts tell that the ultimate sufferers were the common Hawaiians, who had to labor twice as much to compensate for the declining wealth of the chiefs. The mission was generally quiet on the intensity of the commoner discontent, yet we do find Lowell Smith's opinion from late 1837 that the people in his parishes, and perhaps elsewhere, were extremely distressed and unwilling to support the labor system (Smith to Anderson, Nov. 20, 1837, MSL).

The difficulties that Peter Brinsmade, William Hooper, and William Ladd encountered in getting their sugar business started in Kaua'i were most certainly noted also by the missionaries, to whom the events at the Kōloa plantation must have been another signal of the despotic powers of the chiefly system. In an apparent bid to prevent their white competitors from enriching themselves too much and too fast, the Kaua'i chiefs imposed several tabus on wild cane, firewood, water, and plantation workers. The new entrepreneurs also had to deal with native work habits, which quite faithfully duplicated the patterns of resistance they practiced when working for the chiefs. In 1836, Hooper summarized the difficulties in his diary, remembering to mention the plantation's higher cause: "I have had more annoyance from the chiefs and difficulties with the natives . . . than I ever thought it possible for a white man to bear. Nevertheless, I have succeeded in bringing about a plan, which, if followed up . . . will eventually emancipate the natives from the miserable system of cheap labor, which has ever existed at these islands" (quoted in Alexander 1937, 6).

James Jarves, who visited Kōloa in 1837, wrote that the native workers were "the envy of the whole island," mainly because of their salaries. He also reported that paid work created a lucrative alternative to the chiefs' workdays, thus forming a serious threat to chiefly honor. Jarves was buoyed by what he saw at Kōloa, to the extent that he could predict the eventual downfall of "the present despotic system of government," as the natives "are beginning to comprehend their own rights and importance in the scale of political economy." As a sort of prelude to future events, Jarves quoted a native worker: "He [the worker] has got by his industry, plenty of *waiwai*, (property;) now if the chiefs do not take it away from him, we will try to accumulate some also" (Jarves 1838, 71–74).

David Malo, the most outspoken Hawaiian critic of the time, reflected the commoners' distress in launching what were by far the harshest native words against the chiefs' growing hunger for wealth (his essay was published in English). In Hawaiian terms, Malo aimed at a painful spot for the chiefship, the mutual harmony and care, the famous *aloha*, that ideally should have existed between chiefs and their people. According to Malo, the taxing and fining chiefs, deeply indebted to foreign merchants, "seem to have left caring for the people." As a result of their illegitimate use of chiefly powers, "some of the people are losing their attachment to the land of their birth" (Malo 1839, 126–127; see Belcher 1970, I, 269–270). For a Hawaiian, these were serious words. The missionary translator of Malo's essay, who generally agreed with Malo, remarked in a footnote that while the people were diminishing in number, "the wants of the chiefs were increasing; so that besides supporting the chiefs as formerly, the people must now pay the extra expenses which have been incurred, in consequence of a change of habits in the chiefs" (Malo 1839, 126, fn.).

The mission therefore had to meet two old enemies, and the tasks ahead look more complex than those before. First, there were the patrons of the mission— the hungry chiefs. While in nineteenth-century Europe private property was protected against the people, as Polanyi says (1957, 225), in Hawaii the direction of defense was reversed. Property was to be protected against the rulers, which again, adding to the missionaries' sense of reliving their own cultural past, reminds us of the situation in England before the revolution. More precisely, private property was to be invented for the common Hawaiians, and then protected. Second, to accomplish anything for the people, they had to be protected against another enemy, the foreigners, some of whom entertained the possibility of large-scale agricultural production if not an outright colonization. Whenever a warship was in the Hawaiian waters some trouble would ensue, usually to the disadvantage of the chiefs, whose business methods were rarely appreciated by the foreigners.

Commoner discontent and its corollary inefficient labor (see Sahlins 1992, esp. 114, 149), foreign agricultural designs, visits of warships, worldwide recession—these structural constraints all formed the context in which the mission operated during the latter half of the 1830s, trying to revive their glory days, but this time without directly serving the needs of the chiefship. Apparently there was much talk about advising the chiefs, who were losing the support of their own people and were being harassed by foreign naval forces. But the missionaries made no systematic effort to set political society on its prescribed course until 1836, when the mission composed a long statement to the Boston board suggesting various reforms. These were mainly intended to encourage change in the chiefship, as laid down in the tenets of classical political economy, embellished with divine sanctions. The statement interpreted the structural context of their apparent failure to control their own work as if the issue of land and labor was merely a matter of education:

> But the improvements in the civil policy of the government, and in the science of political economy, have by no means kept pace with the progress of Christianity . . . The reception of Gospel by the majority of the royal family did not abrogate their hereditary title to the soil; and though the Bible inculcates justice in rulers, it does not show the *modus operandi*;—it does not prescribe the form of government, nor direct the specific methods of administration . . . They need competent instruction immediately in the science of government, in order to promote industry, to secure ample means of support,

and to protect the just rights of all . . . The sentiment seems to be of ancient date, that "the sovereign cannot govern chieftains whose lands are not at his control, and that hereditary chiefs cannot easily govern *independent* landholders under them." This principle is not eradicated by the introduction of the Gospel, and it will probably yield only to the progress of moral and intellectual improvement (SIM 1836a).

This was a bold statement given that the missionaries had been instructed to observe the boundaries of politics and to not cross the line. The statement was drawn in July, and in August the mission solicited the approval of the impoverished chiefs to proceed with the scheme. Already in August the chiefs dictated their will and approval to William Richards, who had been selected in June to visit the congregations at home and present there the views of the mission and to procure the desired teachers (Journal of Reuben Tinker, June 28 and 30, 1836). Among the various artisans the chiefs requested to be sent to Hawaii was a teacher of land matters ("he kumu ao i na 'lii ma na mea o ka aina") (Hawaiian chiefs 1836).[9]

Richards left Hawaii in early December and returned some fifteen months later without the requested teachers. On June 6, 1837, he had presented the memorandum to the mission board in Boston, but without success (William Richards, *Journal of Travels*, June 6, 1837). After that, he toured several eastern states, but again without being able to promote his cause.[10] While Richards was away, the chiefs asked Lorrin Andrews to become their teacher, but after several weeks of meditation he declined, and returned to the principalship of Lahainaluna (Journal of Reuben Tinker, June 5, Sept. 18, 1837; Journal of Lowell Smith, Aug. 19, 1837). When Richards returned, it became evident that he would himself assume the position of teacher for the chiefs. This was first discussed with the chiefs in Kailua, Hawai'i, in May 1838, and was confirmed by the delegate meeting of the mission in June. Richards related the details in a long letter to the mission board:

But before the mission can be fully supported by the nation, the chiefs and people must have more instruction on the means of *Production*. This subject, or rather the general subject of Political Economy is every day increasing in importance, and the time has arrived when the rulers of the nation must have instruction on that subject. There is but one feeling in the mission in relation to it. How to provide that instruction has at length become a desideratum in our minds. The king & chiefs are fully impressed with a sense of the importance of this subject and have said much to us about it. They waited my return with anxiety & when they found their request sent by me to the U.S.A. was not complied with they immediate [sic] requested *me* to become their teacher, and offered to support me if I would do it. Indeed it was suggested to me by the brethren on my arrival that they were designing to do it. When the request was made, I laid the subject before the brethren and their views were alike. They considered the subject of vast importance and wished to see a man devoted to it, but did not consider it as embraced *directly* in the objects of the Board. They therefore left me to my own discretion. After considering the subject thoroughly with the king & chiefs, I at length accepted the appointment and now act as "chaplain teacher and Translator" for the king. He has engaged to give me six hundred dollars a year, but I am not to be removed from Lahaina. I continue to preach three times a week, but do not act as the pastor of the church. I consider the king & those directly connected with him, as my special charge. I completed my agreement with the king on the 3rd of July, and immediately commenced translating Wayland's Political Economy, or rather compiling a work on Political Economy of which Wayland's is the basis. I prepare the work in the form of *Lectures* & spend two hours every day with the king & chiefs in reading these lectures and in conversation on practical subjects naturally introduced by the lectures. They also expect from me free suggestions on every subject connected with government and on their duties as rulers of the nation, and in all important cases I am to be not only translator, but must act as interpreter for the king. These things you will perceive do now, and will continue to occupy all my time except on the Sabbath and that limited proportion devoted to preparation for the pulpit. It has been considerably trying to my feelings to turn aside in so great a degree from what is the more common and appropriate business of the missionary. But I am satisfied that the *spiritual* as well as the temporal good of the nation requires it, or at least require, that some one should be devoted to the business in which I am now engaged. The nation can not long exist without it. The people can not support the gospel without it. There can not be a nation of consistent Christians without industry, and for the encouragement of that there must be plans laid . . .

You therefore perceive the reasons why I am pursuing this new course. The king & chiefs fixed their eye on me while I was in America and my brethren to some extent did the same. The prospect of actually effecting something for the good of the nation is at present flattering. If this course is not successful, we know not what can be done. I have thus particular in order that you may see whether I am violating the principles of the Board or the instructions given to their missionaries (Richards to Anderson, Aug. 1, 1838, HP/HMCS; see also Richards 1943).

It is interesting to observe that in this early letter Richards framed his undertakings as being a prelude to independent native churches, since they would be supported from privately owned property of common Hawaiians, and not supplied by the chiefly network. In a joint letter, the mission echoed this idea, giving much importance to independent churches as small-scale model societies: "The Chiefs are disposed to allow and encourage the people to give their services, their productions, and their money too to the cause of the gospel. In this the acknowledgment of the right of the people to do what they will with their own earnings has an important bearing in other respects besides encouraging benevolent efforts" (SIM to ABCFM, June 20, 1838, HP/HMCS). In other words, church and state would be finally separated by means of introducing *a universal class of landed proprietors*. In practice, however, it was difficult to see the difference so far as reforms were articulated in religious language, the only means of communication really available to the missionaries. For them, even this phase continued to be a matter of civilizing Hawaiians through the gospel. Consequently, there had to be a way to introduce Western government so as to approach the affairs of the world as natural counterparts of God's commands. In accordance with their own cosmology, the missionaries thought that the political was secondary to the primordial elements of human life. Thus they repeated the old maxim: "we are not politicians; and if we were, the work to be done does not come into the appropriate sphere of a missionary" (SIM to ABCFM, June 20, 1838, HP/HMCS).[11]

By this time the Christian Hawaiians themselves had learned to connect the liberalizing reforms and the word of God, so that political economy did indeed appear to be resting on divine shoulders. While the chiefs and Richards were holding their conference in Kailua, Thomas Hōpū, one of the original native helpers of the mission, wrote to Kauikeaouli, criticizing the chiefs' oppressive course—just as Malo would a year later—and made it quite clear that God disapproved of the system of forced labor. Besides some advice on taxation, the letter was otherwise filled with biblical images of sin and destruction. Amidst the pleas for relaxing the intense demands of work, Hōpū, with a touch of a less-than-discreet diplomacy, portrayed a future state in which the chiefs might go without followers, in which people would rather leave their homes than continue under their chiefs. As God had apparently heard the complaints of the common Hawaiians, there was indeed no time to be wasted, for the wrath of God was strong enough to sink "these islands into the depth of Gehenna" (Hōpū to Kauikeaouli, May 21, 1838, IDM/AH, Box 1).[12]

If the chiefs were less concerned with the idea of Hell than were the truly converted native intellectuals, they were more likely to be alarmed by their declining popularity and diminishing wealth. Sahlins has proposed that the so-called Great Awakening, the massive religious revival between 1837 and 1839, was not simply a religious event but more precisely a protest movement through which the common people snatched the Christian god from the chiefs (Sahlins

1992, 127–129). It is possible to understand—in lack of explicit documentation—the interest in changing the form of chiefship in such a light, as popular resistance. Dwight Baldwin, the missionary in Lahaina, Maui, gave the following description of the common people's religious interests in August 1838: "During the week of the meetings, all business was, as if by instinct, suspended. Even the work of preparing food, to which hunger prompts, was not attended to. It was observed that no fires for cooking were kindled in all the place—a change which even positive orders from their chiefs would hardly have effected at any other time. The whole population seemed during this week, to view the time as a Sabbath" (quoted in Alexander 1953, 89). Considering that the chiefs' labor dues were also disrupted, and that the common people generally thought of it as the "time of turning to the *pono*" (Baldwin in Alexander 1953, 95), we get an idea of what the common people might have meant by referring to *pono* as a general epithet for Christianity. At the very least, the revival coincided with the intensification of forced labor and plans to alter the chiefly rule. At the height of the revival and fiscal slump, William Richards began his work of crafting political economy, the Bible, and Hawaiian traditional practices into a single continuum leading toward prosperity and civilization.[13]

The ambiguous task of teaching Hawaiian chiefs to rule their dominions according to the principles used in powerful foreign lands was the most systematic attempt of this period to establish ways to talk about politics in a cross-culturally meaningful manner. Before delving into historical events, let me review the formal translation history of "politics" in which the missionaries were again the main agents. Relative to the many meanings of governing, the translation and cultural codification of politics was quite focussed. Here, the underlying Hawaiian imagery is more straightforward. Instead of surrounding, shadowing and protecting, residing above, breathing, standing erect, setting in order, eating and consuming, the Hawaiian image of "politics" consists of cutting and slicing.

As a dictionary entry the word "political" appeared first in Lorrin Andrews' dictionary in 1865. This date makes this review rather misplaced in the historical chronology, although, as will be seen, the translation itself is about three decades older than this.[14] The Hawaiian word used by Andrews was *kālai'āina* (Andrews spelled it without diacritical markers), to which he gave three meanings: first, "to manage or direct the affairs of the land, i.e., the resources." Second, "the name of the office of the Minister of Interior." And third, "political economy" (Andrews 1865, 250). In the Western sense, and corresponding to the Hawaiian historical situation of the time, all three meanings were closely connected. The direction of the use of resources was conceptualized as the function of the ministry of interior, which, in turn, relied on the homespun doctrine of political economy. At least these were the functional relations in the nineteenth century. Andrews did not place much emphasis on the word and accordingly excluded it from the English-Hawaiian finding list, which he had reluctantly added to his dictionary.[15]

The word is a composition of the verb *kālai*, which basically means to carve, hew, or cut, and *'āina*, land, producing a literal meaning of land carving. Andrews went beyond previous vocabularies by adding the sense of "carving out" to the verb *kālai*. According to him, this could also be understood in the sense of "dividing out as one's portion." Thus, by expanding the image of carving out, *kālai'āina* signified the action of dividing out the land in portions. If we look beyond the missionary period we find that Henry H. Parker, in his revision of Andrews' dictionary, brought the meaning of *kālai* closer to what was understood by political economy as a branch of governmental knowledge. Perhaps because Andrews had already defined *kālai'āina* as a category of land management, Parker thought it best to add similar meanings to the root *kālai*. Accordingly, the verbs to direct, to conduct or regulate, and to manage were added (Andrews 1922, 251).

Kālai is unquestionably a word with a long indigenous history and it can be found in all major Polynesian languages (Hale 1968, 477). How much the word was manipulated by the early translators is difficult to say, but it is certain that it acquired new meanings in the process of translation. This culminates in Pukui and Elbert's dictionary with an expansion of meaning toward mental activity of planning and plotting, as, for example, in the expression *kālai'ino* (to plot evil, concoct mischief, contrive secretly to destroy by witchcraft or treachery, lit. carve evil), and a more modern concept, *"ke kālai 'ana o ke kuke"* (tariff policy) (Pukui and Elbert 1986, 121). Without indulging in a discussion of the scientific progress of linguistic research, it is enough to say that the acquisition of new meanings, whether through misunderstanding, manipulation, or accumulation of knowledge, can be important as such, as a social phenomenon contributing to the changing interface between cultures.

Taking the verb *kālai* as an opening for probing into Hawaiian culture, its meaning seems to have changed by 1865, when Andrews added the meanings "to divide" and "to manage resources." There is no sign of this management dimension in Andrews' vocabulary of 1836, or in the earlier vocabularies. In his vocabulary of synonyms from the 1840s, Samuel Mānaiakalani Kamakau, the only native Hawaiian lexicographer, was equally silent about management, and mentioned nothing implying political economy. Instead, he listed three synonyms, *"kūpā," "kalakalai"* and *"'oki,"* which are all applied to carving, hewing, or cutting (Kamakau, Quotations, n.d.).[16]

Setting the dictionaries aside, it seems that the word *kālai'āina* was rarely used in the Hawaiian language texts written by native Hawaiians in the nine-teenth century. Among the most noted authors, only Kamakau appears to have used the word in recording oral history and commenting on contemporary mat-ters. Kamakau left the impression that he associated *kālai'āina* with the valued skills of anyone seeking a high-ranking *ali'i* who could give the skillful person a place in his or her household. For example:

> O Namaka kekahi kanaka kaulana i ke Au o Kalaniopuu, he kanaka akeaka-mai—Ua olelo oia, "A loaa kona haku, alaila, hoike oia i kana mau hana aka-mai oia hoi ke *kalaiaina*, ke kakaolelo, ke kuauhau, ka lonomakaihe, ke kuhikuhi puuone, ka lua, ka lele a me ke kino." Ua ao ia oia i na oihana ike i Kauai, a akamai loa, alaila, hele mai oia i ka imi haku, a o Kalaniopuu no nae kona haku i makemake ai (Kamakau 1867a, my emphasis).

A mid-twentieth-century translation gives the following text:

> Na-maka was one of the noted men of Ka-lani-'opu'u's time. He was a man skilled in *politics*, oratory, genealogies, spear-throwing, the conformation of the earth's surface, bone-breaking, cliff-leaping, and the interpretation of omens, all accomplishments which he had learned on Kauai. Then he set out to find a haku (lord) to whom he might impart all his learning, and Ka-lani-'opu'u was the haku whom he selected (Kamakau 1992a, 111, my emphasis).

Two years earlier, in 1865, commenting on the preservation of native Ha-waiian traditions, he had used the term in a similar (perhaps identical) sense:

> Aka, o ka poe i ao i ka moolelo, a mookuauhau me ka naauao a me ke akamai i kela mea keia mea, ke kakaolelo me ke *kalaiaina*, oia ka poe i kapaia he poe akeakamai io. A ua naauao io lakou e like me Kauakahikahaola a me Kalaiku-ahulu (Kamakau 1865b, my emphasis).

> But, the people who teach traditions and genealogies with knowledge and skill in various things, like oratory and land matters, those are the people called true scholars.[17] And they are truly enlightened like Kauakahikahaola and Kalaikuahulu (my translation).[18]

Another interesting but rare example of this use of *kālai'āina* is a certain Z. Kaumaea, who in 1845 wrote a petition to Kauikeaouli proposing an alternative model for government reform than that which had just been initiated by the chiefs and their foreign advisors. Kaumaea suggested that the Hawaiian govern-ment should be divided into five departments, the first of which he named *kālai'āina*. The interesting aspect of Kaumaea's proposal was his simultaneous use of *kālai'āina* both in the sense of a Western-style government ministry, and also to mean the native expertise in the genealogies and deeds of the chiefs. To quote from his text: "The ministry of Kalaiaina; there we know the genealogy of this and that chief, and the birth of this and that chief, and the listing of the chiefly line of succession; and how the chiefs were related to each other. And the ruling of this and that chief, and the warring of this and that chief. The victories of this and that chief, and the defeats of this and that chief. The proper living together of this chief with his people and that chief with his people. The proper living of the people under their chiefs, and the people opposing their chiefs . . . There are innumerable things belonging to Kalaiaina, and they will not be shown here. Because it concerns the chiefs and the common people. And the legends of the chiefs and this skill and that skill" (my translation, original IDM/AH, Box 2, Nov. 1845).

As said, in the surviving sources this exposition of *kālai'āina* is rare. Generally the native writers, when referring to dividing of lands among chiefs, preferred the words *mahele* (e.g., Elbert 1982, 101, 143, 147; Ii 1869a, 1869d; Kamakau 1867b, 1870), *'oki* (e.g., Pogue 1858, 51), *'oki'oki* (e.g., Ii 1869b; Kahananui 1984, 60; Kamakau 1867b,c,d, 1868; Pogue 1858, 42), *ka'awale* (e.g., Elbert 1982, 171; Ii 1869c; Kamakau 1867c; Malo 1987, 130), or *pu'unaue* (e.g., Ii 1869d), which all carry the implication of cutting and setting aside as a separate portion. On the other hand, when emphasizing the management of lands and people, the native writers used terms such as *ho'oponopono* (e.g., Elbert 1982, 173; Ii 1869c; Kahananui 1984, 67; Kamakau 1867e; Malo 1987, 38, 121), *ho'omalu* (e.g., Malo 1987, 43), *mālama* (e.g., Kahananui 1984, 69), *kuapapanui* (e.g., Elbert 1982, 175), or *kālaimoku* (e.g., Malo 1987, 133). Sometimes land was simply given away (*hā'awi*), or figuratively given for adoption (*hānai*). Many times it was conquered (*na'i*), which meant that the land went (*lilo*) from one chief to another, or, when land was reconquered, it reverted (*ho'iho'i*) to the conquering chief (this also took place at the death of the subordinate landholder). When land was divided, it was all fixed and settled (*pau ka 'āina i ka 'oki'oki*).

This all makes it very intriguing that the earliest recorded use of the word *kālai'āina* was William Richards' 1839 translation of "political economy" into Hawaiian (Richards 1839). Before that date the word is simply missing from the recorded sources. It is very likely that no foreigner at the time saw a connection between *kālai'āina* and politics. For example, in early November 1837, the ship *Europe* arrived at Honolulu bringing in a few Chileans, who immediately upon landing applied for political asylum in Hawaii. They addressed a letter to the chiefs and expressed their desire in their native Spanish, which was first translated into English and then into Hawaiian. In English the statement began as follows: "We the subscribers, Citizens of the Republic of Chile have the honor to show to you that political difficulties of state have obliged us to flee from our country" (FOE, Nov. 2, 1837). The Spanish *politicos* was of course translated as *political*, but in the Hawaiian version the concept is completely missing—or no attempt was ever made to invent a simple equivalent. Instead, "political difficulties of state" was expressed as "ka pilikia o ka noho ana mamuli o na alii o ka aina," or, the trouble of living in accordance with the rulers of the land. Substantially, the translation was quite correct, but the conceptual shift in it is still worthy of note, particularly since we know that in Honolulu there was a continuous debate in which the English concept of politics loomed large.

The more commonly used and etymologically closer word was *kālaimoku*. David Malo's use of *kālaimoku* in the manuscripts of 1830s and 1840s is sure evidence of its wide applicability. For one thing, it is a term for the person who lends his experience and advice to the high chief in important decisions, as in warfare or land apportioning. Second, it is the verb denoting this activity, and third, the name of the general category of the variety of activities belonging to *kālaimoku* (Malo 1987, 121–133; 1991, 187–204). The early vocabularies do identify *kālaimoku*, but only as a person. According to Andrews and his missionary colleague Artemas Bishop, *kālaimoku* was a councillor or a minister of state (Andrews, *Vocabulary*, n.d.; Bishop 1828). For some reason Andrews omitted the word in his first printed vocabulary (Andrews 1836), but later added it to his dictionary, defining it as "one who is concerned in managing the affairs of the moku, i.e., island [district, sometimes the whole island]" or "one whose advice is valued in managing a people" (Andrews 1865, 250). He then added a quote from Malo's manuscript on Hawaiian history and traditions. In that manuscript, which was probably written about 1840, Malo gives the following definition: "O ka mea akamai i ke kakaolelo no ke aupuni, he kalaimoku ia" (Malo 1987, 44). When Malo's manuscript was finally translated and published in 1903, the definition was rendered as: "a counsellor, skilled in state-craft, was called *kalai-moku* (*kalai* to hew; *moku*, island)" (Malo 1991, 59). In his revision of Andrews' dictionary, Parker translated the same definition as "the person skilled as a counsellor for the government is a kalaimoku" (Andrews 1922, 251). Only Pukui and Elbert (1957, 112) were careful enough to add the corresponding verb, to perform such office.

Besides sharing the same root, *kālai*, the words *kālaiʻāina* and *kālaimoku* have as their object a land unit, *ʻāina*, the general name for land, being less specific than *moku*. But, notwithstanding Kamakau's and Kaumaea's passing insinuations (Kamakau 1865b, 1867a; IDM/AH, Box 2, Nov. 1845), there appears to be no native Hawaiian source for *kālaiʻāina* as clearly corresponding to Andrews' emphasis on management and direction of affairs or resources of the land. Kamakau used the word a quarter of a century after it had been introduced as the translation for "political economy" by Richards, who, for his part, might have encountered the word during his discussions with high-ranking chiefs in Lahaina (especially Kamehameha's sacred daughter Nāhiʻenaʻena, and Kamehameha's close adviser Hoapili, who was also at the head of the island of Maui until his death in 1840). Kaumaeaʻs use of the word coincided with the restructuring of the native *aupuni*, and can be taken as an attempt to reinterpret the ministerial structure by using together old native ideas and the new name given to the interior department. To draw any definitive conclusions is risky, if only because missionaries were in the habit of using native constructions in translating foreign concepts. Thus *kālaiʻāina*, although surely a composition of native Hawaiian words, may equally well be a Hawaiian neologism invented by Richards, possibly in cooperation with his Hawaiian co-workers such as David Malo (although his own attempts to redefine the word would hint to the contrary [see Richards 1839, 18]). Whichever the case, the word is of some major importance, because it mediated the doctrine of political economy into the Hawaiian language and into the organization of the Hawaiian state during the early 1840s.

As the result of these state-building efforts, there are plenty of sources that use the term in the latter two senses, namely, "political economy," and the "name of the office of the Minister of the Interior" (Andrews 1865, 250; see IDL/AH, Letter Book 1). As already noted, in the sense of "political economy" the word was first used by William Richards, who in his capacity as an advisor to the Hawaiian chiefs translated Francis Wayland's *Elements of Political Economy* (1837) into Hawaiian and used the book to base his lectures on the same subject to the chiefs in the years 1838 and 1839 (Richards 1943). He entitled the translation *No ke kalaiaina* (Richards 1839). It was in this sense that the word was later used by Kamakau when he chronicled the role of William Richards in the institutional changes that took place soon after he had assumed the position as the advisor of the chiefs (Kamakau 1869a, 1869b). From 1845 *kālaiʻāina* was used to designate the office of the Minister of the Interior (Kuhina Kalaiaina) and the corresponding duties (*ʻoihana kālaiʻāina*).

To be quite specific, Andrews (or Richards) did not translate *kālaiʻāina* as "politics," or "political," but "political economy," thus particularly referring to the branch of governmental knowledge. However, by 1887 the translation had become less closely tied to the meaning of political economy. In his *English-Hawaiian Dictionary*, Harvey R. Hitchcock, the son of the missionary by the same name, defined the word political as "pili i ka oihana aupuni" (relating or belonging to the activity of government). The Hawaiian word corresponding to this definition was *kālaiʻāina*. He also translated political economy as *kālaiʻāina*, as if to emphasize the intimate relation of governing and political economy (Hitchcock

1887, 156). In an earlier English-Hawaiian dictionary, the missionary John S. Emerson defined political in the similar manner ("pili ana i na mea o ke aupuni," relating or belonging to the matters of government) but without giving the word *kālaiʻāina* (Emerson and Bishop 1845, 117).

Still, in 1945, one hundred years later, *kālaiʻāina* was translated as "political economy" by Judd, Pukui, and Stokes, who added to its ambiguity by rendering it "politics" in the English-Hawaiian section, thus ignoring their emphasis on political economy in the Hawaiian-English section (Judd, Pukui, and Stokes 1945, 147, 251). A few years earlier, in the vocabulary to his elementary book of the Hawaiian language, the same Judd translated *kālaiʻāina* as "political party, politics" (1939, 99). The decision to clarify this confusion was finally made by Pukui and Elbert when they, in the 1964 English-Hawaiian dictionary, renamed political economy *ʻike kālaiʻāina*, *ʻike* being a term for knowledge and learning (Pukui and Elbert 1964, 117). They did not add the corresponding Hawaiian entry, but nevertheless marked the separation of political economy and politics, and political in general, which was, of course, already a common practice among Hawaiian speakers. It should not, however, be forgotten that from the beginning of the codification process the hierarchy of Hawaiian society was woven into the translations, which were, after all, supposed to serve some functional purpose in facilitating reform. The emphasis was on directing the affairs of government, not on party politics or politics "from below." This management orientation was in constant use throughout the nineteenth century. For example, when Princess Kaʻiulani died in 1899, the Hawaiian Political Association (Hui Kalaiaina) sent a condolence to her husband, admiring the Princess' educational career in what they called "ike kalaiaina" (Ahahui Kalaiaina, c. 1899).[19]

The formal history of the word "politics" somewhat overlaps with that of "political," but the dates of codification are generally more recent and we have to satisfy ourselves by looking at modern sources. *Kālaiʻāina* as a term for politics was first recorded by Judd in 1939 (see above). It was picked up by Pukui and Elbert, who used it in the first edition of their dictionary (1957, 112). In 1964 Pukui and Elbert added *hana kālaiʻāina* to the English-Hawaiian section of their dictionary (117). The phrase has a literal meaning of "political activity," and thus "politics" (equal to *hana politika*). We might also recall the translation of Kamakau's use of the word *kālaiʻāina*, which was rendered (presumably by Pukui) as "politics" and published in 1961 (Kamakau 1992a, 111). The loan words *polokika* and *polotika* were also recorded in the first edition of Pukui and Elbert's dictionary (1957, 313).

Recalling Hitchcock's translations, it appears that *kālaiʻāina* was still in 1887 used in the sense of political economy or as the adjective "political." At least

Hitchcock did not use the word to translate "politics." Instead, he felt, for some unknown reason, obligated to explain the term by defining it as the knowledge pertaining to the duties or functions of the government ("ka ike e pili ana i ka oihana aupuni") (1887, 156). Forty years earlier, Emerson had tackled the same problem and solved it by using a definition instead of a direct translation: "ka oihana o na luna" (the business of the officials) (Emerson and Bishop 1845, 117).

In conclusion, the translation history of the words "political" and "politics" speaks in favor of a meaning shift of the word *kālai'āina*, from political economy to an understanding that puts the emphasis on modern party politics and the running of the state affairs. This development betrays a movement toward a more extensive application of the word as an expression of the intention to define a people politically. At the same time, the possible indigenous meaning of *kālai'āina* as the customary institution of land apportioning is increasingly put aside, not only by the Western translators by also by native Hawaiians. I cannot but speculate whether the word is a neologism. To reconstruct the historical events that led to its first recorded use is nevertheless informative, and helps us recognize its important place in making comparative statements of Hawaiian chiefly politics.

CHAPTER 5

Natural Rights, Virtuous Wealth

Richards began his lecturing by pointing out the fundamentals of human culture as he, as a native of New England, knew them.[1] His first difficulty was to make the chiefs understand that they were essentially not different from the common Hawaiians in regards to the appropriation of nature. In order to achieve this, Richards outlined what could be termed a political theory of desire. He set out to define—or, as he thought, to redefine—the meaning of wealth (*waiwai*). For Richards, wealth consisted not merely of those things that were necessary for subsistence but of all things that people desired, providing that they were beneficial to a morally sound life (Richards 1839, 18). The next step was to deduce that because wealth requires human agency—as gratification of human desire transforms the pure elements of nature into wealth—it is reasonable to assume that all humans are entitled to an equal opportunity to produce wealth for their own use: "Things that merely exist by themselves are not wealth . . . When they are taken by human hand, then they become wealth; they are not wealth during the time they just lie by themselves [i.e., in the state of nature]. If they are not taken by human hand, the desire is not fulfilled; it is not satisfied. When the object is obtained, the person's desire is fulfilled; he is satisfied; he is also wealthy" (Richards 1839, 19, my translation).

The chiefs were seen to have exploded the latent capacities of individualist appropriation in full force, in a way that resembled the rise of commercial capitalism in New England, with a corollary decline of spiritualism in social relations. Richards called instead for an evangelized version of natural law thinking. Human progress was not to be a showcase for unlimited willpower but, rather, of deliberate, rationalized, and highly conscious selection in developing and elevating society to a level of redemption. It would be a process of drawing the right conclusions from the fundamental freedom and obligation of individuals to take hold of nature's gifts and to govern themselves. Richards, appropriately, used theology in founding the basics of human existence. At the time of the creation, there were only the things that God had made, and hence there was no wealth. But as people multiplied and their knowledge grew, they also began to appropriate the nature that God had given to them. Wherever the human hand was found to have united with the God-given resources, there was wealth (1839, 35–36). A theory such as this could not function properly if the wealth produced by the great majority was expropriated by rulers. Therefore, Richards transformed his theological ontology into a political theology, one which combined appropriation of nature with self-governance, equality, and virtuous living. Thus, "God did not create people to work for the chiefs and to enrich the chiefs. God gave the office of the chief as to bless the common people and also to benefit the land" (1839, 64, my translation).

In his use of words Richards was approaching the language of native intellectuals, who reminded the chiefs of their traditional obligations to reciprocity. Richards could not be too open in his critique of the abuses of the traditional rule without endangering his own position and bringing the experiment to an end. However, some native church members did take the risk of displeasing their chiefs. I have already mentioned Thomas Hōpū, who in the spring of 1838 addressed his *ali'i* (i.e., Kauikeaouli, who was residing in Kailua, where Hōpū also lived under governor Kuakini) with words that quite matched Malo in sharpness of critique. Writing from the annual meeting of the mission, Hōpū combined biblical analogies, mission-inspired reform, and Hawaiian custom to compare the chiefs' iniquity to the cruel conduct of the Pharaohs of Egypt, who faced the wrath of the Old Testament God. In the spirit of the Hawaiianized Wayland, Hōpū reproduced the chiefly duty for redistribution as a prototype capitalism, with the right to the products of one's own labor, and he imagined the chiefs being returned to their traditional passivity, their urge for foreign goods replaced by virtuous living.

> If all the tasks of the land were put together [and given] for the people and if everybody went to do his own [private] work, the land and the government [*aupuni*] would benefit and be in just order. Therefore the land of the chief and all the people will become prosperous. Let the chiefs not think that the wealth would be gone. Certainly not, that is a truly ignorant thought. The idea comes from the Devil, not from learning. [It is] from indifference. If the working people are not satisfied with the burdensome laws and all the oppressive work, the government [*aupuni*] will be embarrassed [lit. yellowish color will

rise upon the cheeks of the government, signifying blushing]. Do not think of overburdening the common people lest their number will end from fleeing away and they will abandon the government [*aupuni*] and the land and they will go to other governments [*aupuni ē aku*] of the earth. Listen my beloved chief as the common people cry under the burdens and the weariness of having no property, everything in their hands will go to another. They are really the oxen and mules in the oppressive work for all the chiefs in this realm. God in Heaven has taken notice of the crying of the weary people and the very oppressive labor in their neck [i.e., a heavy load on their backs]. Isn't this a very great work for God? Isn't this the millstone on the necks of the Pharaoh's people, drowned in the sea of Hell? Yes indeed. Doesn't this sin concern us? Wouldn't it become a millstone on our necks, and we shall be drowned under the Pacific Ocean?

This sin indeed pertains to us here. Because of it God can capsize these islands into the sea of Hell, and [we shall] completely disappear into the darkness of eternal death . . . Let us shut our eyes from paying attention to the foreign money . . . Here are indeed the truly correct, agreeable, and right laws for the high chief's government in these islands. The high chief who has the government and all the other chiefs [should] enrich everybody else [the common people], too. For them [the common people] are all the good duties of the earth, the dirty work and the improper work if done by the chiefs are not for the chiefs or the chief who has the government [*aupuni*]. Upright, correct, and mild conduct without overburdening the native government [*aupuni kanaka* refers to the totality of indigenous people as opposed to foreigners] is the high chief's duty, to truly restore all the people to [their] work (Hōpū to Kauikeaouli, May 21, 1838, IDM/AH, Box 1, my translation).[2]

Although Hōpū was certainly not the originator of these reformist ideas, or even the first native to have supported them, his letter is a fine sample of the native discourse on the nature and condition of their *aupuni* in a comparative sense, and testimony to the creative longevity of culture. As a trusted associate of the mission, Hōpū connected the new ways with Protestant God, and with superior knowledge of the West, but the substance of virtuous living still had a Hawaiian base as the principles of ruling were revealed through worship. It would be inappropriate to read this as an expression of evangelical republicanism modeled after missionary thinking. Hōpū was indeed a devout Christian, but he never wanted to abolish chiefly rule or dishonor the chiefs. In an interesting manner, Hōpū implied that the chiefs' Christianity was not internalized, and for that reason they held erroneous views about securing their status by not allowing the common people the right to the products of their labor. The chiefs were accused of being indifferent (*naaupalaka*) in their worship, and therefore of failing in their obligations toward their people. In Hōpū's thinking, the chiefs' status was something to be protected through evangelical faith.

Hōpū also referred to a serious source of embarrassment which was a direct result of the chiefs' indifference to the word of God. Hawaiians were leaving the islands because the chiefs were increasingly unable to protect and care for them. As Malo would do publicly a year later (Malo 1839), Hōpū also found the Hawaiian *aupuni* to be an *aupuni* among other *aupunis* of the world, although one that caused embarrassment to its holders. The virtue of a chief that was considered traditional in 1838 consisted of the chief's capacity to provide for the people, who in their turn supported the chief. A chief who was seriously indebted, as were the chiefs of the 1830s, was an anomaly in this scheme, because an indebted chief was not the ultimate source of all wealth. Malo was more explicit than Hōpū on this point, in that Hōpū merely insinuates that the chiefs should pay less attention to foreign money, that is, cease exploiting the land in order to get foreign goods. According to Malo: "The people have been burdened in seeking sandal wood to pay the debts of the chiefs—many have died in the mountains; this continued until the sandal wood was exhausted, but the debts remain unpaid. Even at this present time the chiefs are in debt, and the people are generally seeking for money to pay the chief's debt" (1839, 126–127). This was an embarrassment for the people, too, because their lives were extensions of their chiefs' lives, and they partook the chiefs' honor as well as dishonor. As Malo said, the people were trying to find money to pay the debts. This was also in Hōpū's mind.

Toward the end of his long letter, Hōpū says that the ongoing practices of the unrighteous rulers would be considered shameful "in the enlightened countries." According to Hōpū, the Hawaiian *aupuni* was a great disease *(he mea maʻi loa)* with which the foreigners were uncomfortable *(aole lakou e oluolu malaila)*. For the foreigners, inequality was another name for the disease, but for the Hawaiians it was a matter of correctly balanced hierarchy, or as Hōpū said: "Let us look for the means to enrich all the people so that they could help the high chief's government" *(e imi kakou i mea e waiwai ai kela kanaka keia kanaka, i hiki ia lakou e [sic] kokua i ke aupuni o keʻLii nui)*. Although Hōpū thought that God was the only head of all governments, his God was not the great leveler, but rather promised a way to more harmonious living. When the people were relatively equal in terms of wealth, the *aupuni* itself would become morally sound and correspond to the expectations that the common people had for their chiefs: *"Ina o ka pono ana o kela kanaka a me ka oluolu ana o keia kanaka a me ka waiwai ana o kela a me keia mea, o ka pono ana no ia o ke aupuni o ke ʻLii"* (when the people are virtuous, comfortable, and have property, the chief's government will also become virtuous).

It is likely that it was these ideas that were most strongly felt by Richards' high-ranking students, because in them the means to return to peacefulness and prosperity were spelled out, in a context that formed a link to the long-lost past rather than a radical break with it. Richards brilliantly made use of legendary figures, such as George Washington (Kanaloaahokana in Hawaiian), whose words, as he rendered them, echoed exactly those sentiments that we find in the writings of commoner spokesmen, such as Malo or Hōpū. For example, "Here are the words of Washington. 'The righteousness of God and the righteousness of ruling, those are the only supports that will fill the land with blessing . . . Let us not think that it is possible to adjust the ruling if God's will is not faithfully observed' (Richards 1839, 122, my translation).

We might think that Richards was infantilizing Hawaiians by relating obvious facts as if they were not already known, for instance, that the wealthiest countries were also Christian. But this is only possible through an anachronistic reading. As I suggested earlier, Richards, in his lecturing and translating, was largely conditioned by Hawaiian concepts which had a cultural link to a larger historical context (despite attempts at redefinition), and which could not be eliminated from the scene of communication. Consider, for example, the following: "Protection and peace (*malu*) and the unified rule will not be endured if the right duties (*pono*) are not observed. The duties of the chiefs and the duties of the common people are the only source of making the laws and government (*aupuni*) permanent. The wrongdoings are like the polluted wind and the polluted water which will make people sick. It will also make the government (*aupuni*) sick. The good wind and the good water will strengthen people. Such is the proper conduct when it is observed. By this the government (*aupuni*) will be strengthened and will endure" (Richards 1839, 123, my translation).

Furthermore, infantilizing receded into the background as soon as Richards turned to the heart of the problem—the common people's growing discontent. This he never put directly into writing in the form of a critical attack, yet he did bring out the effects caused by the lack of motivation among the common people. "The pertinence of these words to the people of this land is known. People cannot make big and excellent taro patches, because they are afraid that the produce will go to another and the land will be taken away and the work will be in vain" (Richards 1839, 136, my translation).[3]

This type of political economy, however, was not based on the efficacy of the invisible hand or the public benefits of private vices. Rather, the profit motive was made an extension of a form of worship, well understood by the Hawaiians familiar with life under a prosperous *aupuni*. And because the profit motive was itself made an intimate part of a lasting *aupuni*, the intelligibility of Richards' narration was more than apparent. So much so that we risk nothing in suggesting that he, as a specialist in the affairs of the foreign lands, was restoring Hawaiian society to its original and culturally superior condition, the history of which reached back generations beyond Richards' students. This was true both for the chiefs and the missionaries, for they all, in their own separate ways, shared an understanding of human history as a mythical totality, in which there was a beginning, a loss, and a recovery. To regain the original human condition as an appropriating animal, nothing less than true godliness was required, as Richards clearly recommended: "Here is the most important thing that will protect wealth, thinking of God and of those things that are shown in the word of God. If the chiefs are considering the seeking of means to protect wealth and land, they should seek the means to turn the people to the right [*pono*, meaning the Christian moral code]. If the people will truly turn to God, then, mischievousness and the things that cause harm will be at end and wealth will be really protected. If all the people are in the wrong [*hewa*, meaning contrary to Christian morals], then, the laws are in vain" (Richards 1839, 137, my translation).

This was the ultimate object of the system of practices Richards called *kālai'āina*. In the beginning of his lectures, Richards defined the word as "the adjustment of land in order to enrich" (*o ka hooponopono ana i na aina, i mea e waiwai ai*), referring to "*na kakaolelo kahiko*," or the old-time counselors. In turn land was defined as "various things that will enrich the multitude of people" (*O kela mea keia mea e waiwai ai na kanaka he nui*) (1839, 18, my translation). In order to produce a logically hermetic system, Richards harnessed *kālai'āina* to the service of God and the fulfillment of God's laws (1839, 146), so that nothing of what went by the name "political economy" in the West was in fact directly translated. Wayland's original text was completely transformed, and Richards at least partially addressed the crisis of legitimation of the Hawaiian nobility, and used Wayland's mixture of morality and capitalist principles for this task.[4]

The modification was extended even to elections and principles of democratic government. As an introduction to the theory of elections, Richards made a reference to one of the laws of God, namely, that knowledge universally precedes wealth (1839, 157). And because this was true by nature, no one ill-versed in *palapala* should be given a say in the matters of government: "As to those who do not know how to read and write it is proper to deny them the right to have a say in the affairs of government (*aupuni*). In the righteous lands some people are genuinely chosen by the people to become crafted chiefs (*ali'i ku'i*). These chosen people have a say in the affairs of government (*aupuni*). They can decide on taxing. But, it is not proper for those who do not know how to read and write to choose. It is proper only for those who know. If this is the method of conducting these affairs, all the people will want to learn so that they will have a say in the affairs of government *(aupuni)"* (Richards 1839, 162, my translation).[5]

This was not only an attempt to explain the democratic fundamentals of political society, but also an indication that God made his presence known through acquisition of knowledge as means to prosperity. Similarly, notwithstanding the eventual climax of history, progress in this world was not independent of human action. In the evangelical spirit, it was made conditional of the right choices (Conkin 1968, 13). So it was with civil liberty and political institutions, which could be elevated to a higher level only by a virtuous people reborn in Christ, who could rationally employ their freedom for the common cause. The same was substantially true in other respects. The principles of ownership, land rent, capital investment, paper money, interest, wages, and the like were first poured into a theological system and then, by way of a detour in the traditional values of chiefship, they were reinserted into the present state of *palapala*, in which the chiefs were rapidly losing their leading role as the worshipers for the people.

The radicalism of Richards' teaching—the republican spirit—was less pronounced but not completely hidden. For him and his colleagues, an enlightened government required participation of the common people, a principle which the chiefs probably dismissed at the time as fatal for their status (see note 4, above). Because the greatness of a chief was a function of his or her capacity to redistribute land, food, and valuables, a republican form of government would leave very little to redistribute—the will of the people would form an effective check and eventually an essential condition for the distributive function. And that would have been utterly at variance with the idea of the Hawaiian *aupuni*, which was in fact just another name for the chiefly function of ultimate distributor. Although by 1839 the chiefs were more famous for self-aggrandizement than generosity toward the common people, the ideal state of *aupuni* was, as will be seen, used to evaluate the contemporary malice as well as any reform. In this sense, we can easily understand the reluctance of the chiefs to step back, and also the common people's unwillingness to bring down their chiefs.

In any case, Richards' school of political economy was by far the most systematic attempt to initiate a cross-cultural project in bringing the conceptual spheres of Hawaiians and foreigners to a common level of understanding. Yet the adoption by the leading chiefs of the laws of Jehovah, and Richards' own profession as a missionary, prevented him from diverting too much away from the universalizing myth of the values of Kahiki, and thus de-Hawaiianizing Christianity. These values had for years encompassed his own idea of conversion as a return to good life, which now faced Hawaiian conceptions of good rule as the condition of good life. It was principally for this reason that the fundamental focus was again on *aupuni* and its sacred foundations. This time it was not on human sacrifice, which belonged to the period of fall from the grace of God, but rather on the ownership of land and the correctly sanctioned appropriation of nature, which were the last hidden resources of the foreigners' god. We saw that even democratic elections were not presented simply as a mechanism of sharing power, but more properly as a way to obey God's law. In a comparative sense, as we shall see in chapter six, *aupuni*—and government—remained the bases for conceptualizations of political discourse that were taking shape as the chiefship was systematically being transformed into a constitutional monarchy of the European type.

Kingship and "Body Politic": The Prevalence of *Aupuni*

The constitutional monarchy that sprang up from the discussions at Richards' school—with the help of some graduates of Lahainaluna seminary (see Richards 1943, 67, fn. 4; *Constitution and Laws* 1842, 3–4; Kuykendall 1989, 157–159, 167–169; Kamakau 1992a, 370)—also incorporated the biblical idea of the origin of human culture. The first laws of the new type were published in June 1839. On the opening page the divinely sanctioned method of turning nature into wealth was clearly established, and the law book itself was titled "The law of adjusting wealth" *(ke kanawai hooponopono waiwai)*.[6] The first page was dedicated to an American-inspired "Declaration of rights," which proclaimed the sacred inviolability of the elements of the liberal state: life, limb, and liberty. More concretely, it was aimed at securing the products of each person's labor—the appropriation of nature—to the laboring person. "The office of the chiefs and ruling for the peace are indeed also from God; but in drafting laws for the land, it is not proper to make laws that will protect *(ho'omalu)* the chiefs only and not the common people. It is also improper to enact laws that will enrich the chiefs only and not the common people. After this, there will be no laws that are in opposition to what is said above, no mere taxing, no enslaving, no making people to work contrary to these words" (He kumukanawai 1939, 3, my translation).

The concept of *kālai'āina*, which was now crafted into the mythical history of its main proponents, was also incorporated into the textual body of the new laws. It was made a duty for the governors *(kia'āina)* and *konohiki* under them to read the new laws to the common people during the prescribed days for laboring for the king and the chiefs. It was emphasized that the landlords should inculcate the virtues of industry and hard labor in the minds of their people, with the notable difference that labor was no longer thought to be arbitrary or oppressive. For now there was a biblical theory behind it, making Hawaiian society a rudimentary image of the commonwealth, established by equals in a rational act of agreement.

In adjusting the various things of their land (*kona*), let the people work patiently with their minds turned to their own bodies, as it is said in the writings
of political economy (*kālai'āina*), "The living of the person who does not work
is not at all comfortable. He will not get the good things if he will not strive for
work. The person will not become enlightened if he will not strive for learning.
There will not be things that comfort the body and the living, if there is no effort. If the people intend to become wealthy, it will happen only if they are diligent in work. That is how the government (*aupuni*) was gotten by the chiefs,
with energy and effort." This is what God taught to our first ancestors. "In the
sweat of thy face thou shalt eat bread." That is the task of the people spoken
of in this law. Consider carefully the meaning of the words said in this law (*He
kumukanawai* 1839, 13–14, my translation).[7]

Although Richards and his mentor Wayland were keen on supporting a rudimentary labor theory of property, they departed from the political tradition an-
chored in Locke and other contract theorists, who took the initial individualism
much further into the political realm. What Richards and Wayland shared with
this tradition was their belief that social order existed already in the natural society, without the exercise of political power. In the Lockean version, political society was established in accordance with the very same natural principles, the
logical outcome of which was a public authority based on explicit consent of the
people bound by this authority. In harmony with contract theorists, Richards and
Wayland were interested in defining the limits of government by developing a
theory of contractual enactment of political society, which would be morally and
logically binding and acceptable to all its members. But this is where Richards
and Wayland left off, because they did not believe in the instrumentalist idea of
the social contract.

A form of a covenanted society was a more typical evangelical answer to the
problem of social order, one that would provide deeper meaning for the contract.
This was particularly clear in another important book by Wayland, *The Elements
of Moral Science*, which was also used by the mission, although it was translated
in a different spirit, more literally rather than allowing the Hawaiian idiom to
blend into the text.[8] The most striking feature overarching the whole work is
Wayland's evangelical understanding of the moral fiber that is made to penetrate
an otherwise liberal theory of the state. It is also a nice tribute to the covenant
heritage of the fundamental division of natural and political societies and their
divine nature. Thus, Wayland argued that civil freedom and stability of political
society cannot be sustained merely by a formal agreement or enforcement of
laws. The whole idea must be internalized as part of everyday life, otherwise the
theory will surely fail in practice. Therefore, in Wayland's evangelical system, a

whole way of life rested on the degree of virtue prevailing among a people: "There is no self-sustaining power in any form of social organization. The only self-sustaining power is in individual virtue. And the form of a government will always adjust itself to the moral condition of a people" (1963, 328).

The rejection of contract theory was quite widespread in the evangelical circles. Locke, for instance, the foremost of contract theorists, was received with much suspicion by the evangelical clergy (Heimert 1966), and while he was often referred to in public writings and political oratory, his status was elevated mostly among those who espoused the rising individualism. This thinking was more clearly associated with those who paid little attention to citizenship based on Christian virtue. John Pocock has raised the same issue in arguing that the emerging liberalism fundamentally changed the relationship people had maintained with their polities. Commercial liberalism destroyed the form of (elitist) life whose very rationale was an undivided dedication to the public good. In the liberal state the political virtue was leveled, so to speak, and only partially present in any one individual. As commercial transactions of naturally free members of the society multiplied, less and less time was allocated to public affairs, and they were more often left for hired specialists (Pocock 1985). It is true that the Lockean natural law theory was valued, especially in higher education, from about the 1740s onward (Robson 1985, 17, 66), and Locke's works were used both as regular reading in classes and in preparation of oral and written presentations. However, in the collegiate curricula the Lockean political program was much overshadowed by his ethical theory (Robson 1985, 83). In the denominational colleges of Congregationalist and Presbyterian origin, Lockean contractualism was read with moral emphasis and through the lens of the covenant idea and in defense of political virtue. In fact, the political theory of this type was seen more as a part of social and personal ethics than as a calculus of national or personal gain. To follow Alan Ryan's (1989, 311) suggestion, Lockean political theory was thought to be primarily about justification of a whole system, not about a license to self-fulfillment. Although the individualistic elements inherent in the theory of the social contract were of course important, they did not dominate the theoretical mood of the revivalist era, except the thinking of the Unitarian rationalists who had grown strong in the urban area of Boston and Cambridge.

Now, as if to crown his system, Wayland borrowed from the covenant idea that the required amount of civic virtue is best guaranteed by a proper revelation of natural rights, which are best supported through religion, "in its purest form." Thus, there was in Wayland's social theory a causal relation, if not an equation, between Christian godliness and civil liberty. But Wayland kept church and state strictly separate, and he concluded that religion cannot be regulated by civil authorities because it is not part of the social compact that forms the civil authority (1963, 321); the compact applies only to regulating difficulties that arise from the state of nature. Instead of forcing a doctrinal unity, civil authority should guarantee a free formation of doctrines, providing that they do not threaten the continuity of civil society. Conversely, a forced religious orthodoxy would only undermine attempts to promote true virtue by adding to the possibility of revolt and civil war. If we think of Wayland's system against the background of Hawaiian chiefship, it becomes clear that Hawaiians could never be a virtuous people in this sense, as long as the distinction between the two classes remained unquestioned, and the commoners lived their lives through their chiefs.

I should repeat here that the correct path to political society was connected, as were human emotions and morally sound politics, with the developments in natural society, its level of virtue, and degree of revelation.[9] So when working in the field, the missionaries were able to put forth statements that, while recognizing the mutually enforcing relationship between moral truths, religion, and civil institutions, also inquired about the minimum conditions of salvation. That is, they had a deep interest in the changes that must be effected in natural society in order to bring out morally and intellectually rational human nature. "How much civilization and refinement the heathen must possess before they will be given to the Son of God for a possession, we know not, but we know that when any of the children of Adam shall have right views of the character of the Lord Jesus Christ, and exercise an evangelical faith in him, they will be entitled to mansions in heaven. This should be the grand object of all our endeavors" (Andrews and Richards to Evarts, Sept. 30, 1828, HP/HMCS).

The conception of the human mind inspired by empiricists gave rise to a straightforward scaling of cultural differences, or deviations from the standards of civilization. This is not to say that such a scale was constructed as any exact measure, but only to provide a common metaphor of thought, a tendency to think in terms of "a scale by which to mark all the grades between their state and that of Christian civilization" (Richards 1973, 33). Scaling was needed, of course, to assess the right dose of teaching and preaching, which were in every case worth the trouble since the system contained a logic that emphasized the universally shared capacities of the human mind for improvement. But because human improvement was a comprehensive whole, all this would have been in vain if separated from the proper moral foundation: "Education and civilization, without a firm belief in God's Word, will accomplish little or nothing for the heathen" (Bingham 1849, 240). Lorrin Andrews went even further. According to him, "the human mind needs to be expanded & exercised before it knows what use to make of moral or religious truths . . . Science & literature must expand the mind and religion must sanctify it" (Andrews to Wisner, Nov. 3, 1829, MSL). About the same time, Tocqueville saw the same in New England: "Religion is the road to knowledge, and the observance of the divine laws leads man to civil freedom" (1948, 41).

A person needed to conquer the heights of civilization on two fronts at the same time, one facing godliness, the other leaning toward empirical knowledge of God's creation. Where these fronts met, there would the human path reach the summit of its trajectory, and a civilized life with all its cultural products and institutions would emerge. Let us consider the reflections by Bingham when he evaluated the leading chief Kalanimōkū (c. 1770–1827): "A competent education would have made him an accomplished statesman" (1849, 308). When he died, Kalanimōkū had embraced only the Christian god, hence failing to fulfill the other requirement, which would have opened, at least in theory, the road to an enlightened system of politics. Jarves, the editor of the government newspaper *The Polynesian*, was not only a champion of liberal government, but he also engaged in developing a theory of civilization, which, in this instance, gave a very succinct yet abstracted expression to Bingham's concrete example. In Jarves' theory, natural society and political society were causally linked so that "in proportion as they [the Pacific Islanders] become influenced by the new religion, they discontinue their old customs, and the whole government must be revolutionized" (Editorial, *The Polynesian*, Jan. 2, 1841, 118). This, he argued, will happen by necessity. Therefore, in Kalanimōkū's time, the missionaries could not have represented the Hawaiian society in any way other than as a heathen nation dominated by a perversion of liberty, because, by the same necessity, the causal chain that would logically allow the collapse of despotism was not yet established to any satisfactory degree. Therefore, a defect or an unbalanced combination of faith and knowledge in the constitution of natural society resulted in an anomaly in the political constitution of society—despotism. This produced a state of affairs under which it was extremely difficult to set bounds for the artificial realm that would respect both the natural rights of the people and the rational limits for government. Without such balance, "confusion, discord and oppression were the natural results" (Dibble 1909, 382). In brief, traditional Hawaiian politics rested on an unnatural foundation, out of balance, and was thus arbitrary.

As a notable contrast to the evangelical theory of politics, society for Hawaiians existed only through their chiefs; without a chief society would be abolished. Thus there was no distinction between natural society and political society, a distinction which was the cornerstone in the covenant view. In the covenant mode, people would always be in a society of some sort, because social existence was part of nature's order, whereas in the Hawaiian conception society needed to be established in a kind of combination of its social and political sides. In the Hawaiian theory, everything was one, and in the absence of a chief would therefore collapse as one. It would be an error to dismiss the importance of the chiefs simply by making the abrogation of temple worship and chiefly tabus in 1819 an index of a similar change in the social system. A leading chief of the 1840s, most likely Miriama Kekāuluohi,[10] expressed this idea in a succinct, although Christianized form:

> O ke alii, o ke aupuni a me ka lahuikanaka, hookahi no ia mai ke Akua mai. O ke ola o ke alii, o ia ke ola o ke aupuni a me kona lahuikanaka: no laila, e malamaia ke ola o ke alii e ke Akua, no kona aupuni a me kona lahuikanaka apau.

> The chief, the government [*aupuni*], and the people have always been one from the time of God [i.e., from creation]. The chief's life is the life of the government and the life of his people: therefore, let the chief's life be preserved by God for his government and all his people (Kekāuluohi, attrib., 1848, my translation).

As a strong contrast, missionary culture was built on another kind of biblical foundation, which told that the original condition of humankind as a collection of free individuals was such that they could not organize themselves into hierarchic units without a deliberative consensus of some kind. This is why the moral condition of natural society was so important for the missionaries. As already indicated, this theory allowed for judgments of any human society regarding whether its morality stood firmly on God-given natural foundation (i.e., whether it was naturally founded) or whether it fell short, reaching the dimensions of either anarchy or tyranny.

In reality, these culturally bounded rational limits of government took years to accomplish. Paradoxically, the slow pace was due in part to the haste with which foreign reformers wanted to establish what they thought was a regular government. They were impatient in this work and would not wait for the Hawaiian "natural society" to mature. They chose to pursue changes in the "political society" first, and then wait until the Hawaiian natural society showed signs of maturation. This was a culturally malleable alternative as well. However, the institutions of the new Hawaiian political society (tax collectors, constables, and petty clerks of all kind) were often merely appended to the existing structures of ruling. On the local level in particular, the enforcement of law took on improvised forms to serve the customary interests of the *konohiki* class. It was not unusual for these middlemen to grab more than their fair share of the now sacred labor of the local population, occasionally reserving certain trees or fish completely for their own use. In 1846, Harvey Hitchcock reported from Moloka'i that although the law prescribed only one *kohohiki* for each *ahupua'a* land section, "these head men [*konohiki*] have enlarged the number to suit their convenience" (Wyllie 1848, 38). Judging by other similar reports, this practice was widespread, leaving the common people still very much subject to the patterns of ruling inherited from the sandalwood trade and intensified agriculture (Wyllie 1848, 41, 67–68, 92; Rowell to Richards, Nov. 16, 1846; Clark to Richards, Aug. 20, 1846, both in MSL; Bond in Damon 1927, 172–174; Kamehameha III and Kekāuluohi to Keaweamahi, Aug. 5, 1839; same to Capt. Mallet, Sept. 4, 1842, both in FOE.).[11]

Conceptually, these events were encapsulated in the reforms at the top of the chiefship. *Kālai'āina* as a practice of civilized and rich countries was effectively Hawaiianized to accommodate this form of political thinking and to root it meaningfully in Hawaiian history, and in its social tensions. The latter meant especially tensions between the chiefs and enterprising foreigners and displeased commoners, which generated difficulties in maintaining the material standards of chiefly living. The reform of chiefship was thus directed toward bringing Hawaii and the foreign lands within a single system of thought whose organizing concept was the Hawaiian *aupuni* and the laws attached to it. As far as we know, the reforms were received locally in the same terms as they were intended, as a relaxation of forced labor. "As proof that the present is a state of civil freedom in comparison to former times, I would mention that the common natives, in their religious exhortations and prayers, often speak of the change in this respect with wonder and gratitude. When praying for the enslaved in other lands, they always speak of slavery as having passed away here" (Wyllie 1848, 68).

Thus, despite the unsanctioned *konohiki* practice (or because of it), there seemed to have formed a general sentiment that freedom had been granted, which certainly was well-adapted for reproducing the sense of reciprocity and hierarchy customarily built into the notion of *aupuni*. Because of continuing and sometimes intensifying exploitation, however, there also developed favorable social conditions for the emergence of partisanship among the common Hawaiians, and this might have been interpreted by using political language of European origin. This was especially true because the constitution prescribed an elected house of people's representatives to be established in addition to the council of chiefs. However, such language did not surface until late in the century, and throughout the period of inventing the monarchy these structural features were interpreted by using already available conceptual tools, all derived from the notion of *aupuni* and its Western equivalent, government. As the final step toward the fully organized constitutional monarchy, we shall look at the interpretive patterns that evolved during this period of state-building, and ask why the political translation work remained within the narrow limits of "government."

However, we must first reconsider the notion of political economy as it lends itself to highlighting certain peculiarities of its reception by or, rather, its importation to the chiefly hierarchy. The historical meaning of political economy as a branch of governmental knowledge in Western Europe generally developed through a mutation in the motives of government, as "the issue of sovereignty shifted its focus from the legitimacy of leadership to its responsibility for managing the social configuration" (Shapiro 1993, 102). It was indeed this management function that was brought to bear on the process of straightening out the practices of Hawaiian *aupuni*. Yet the meaning of politics was, unlike in the West and in some of the mid-century Hawaiian dictionary entries, reserved for legitimizing chiefly rule, and not so much for describing what the chiefs did as chiefs. The result was a bastardized combination of virtuous politics, and a politicized view of economy.

This anomaly will be better understood if we allow for the fact that William Richards never translated "political economy" in its normal Western sense. The missionary theory of civilization depicted a graded historical trajectory for a heathen society, and so he first transposed the contemporary Western political economy to an earlier historical phase according to his own cultural memory. For Richards, this phase corresponded with European feudalism, the closest analogy through which Hawaiian land tenure was normally understood by foreigners. And just as European peasantry had been liberated from the feudal yoke and elevated to a position of freemen, ready to enter into political relations with one another, the future of Hawaiian society was set upon the same historical track. For the concept of political economy, this meant surrendering to the Hawaiian notion of *aupuni*. This was necessary in order to emphasize the change in chief-commoner relations. Although there was much discussion of managing the productive life of society, politics was retained in that which made proper management possible—virtuous relations between equals. We might take this as the theoretical reason for the prevalence of the notion of *aupuni* in the emerging discourse, for in it the theory of political virtue saw a vehicle of cross-cultural communication.[12]

The "Invention" of Monarchy

Richards' school survives mainly through the published lectures and little is known of its actual proceedings.[13] But in events immediately following the brief schooling of the chiefs there was a proliferation of the themes taught by Richards.

The missionaries and white accomplices worked their way into the chiefship by objectifying selected elements or spheres of Hawaiian society as capable of representing politics, in many ways evoking the themes found in Richards' lectures. In pursuing this course, they allowed, intentionally or not, a certain continuity for the Hawaiian conceptualizations, including the common Hawaiians, who evoked the traditional values of chiefly care as their *aupuni* assumed a foreign look. For the white reformers, the common people were by and large an ignorant mass. Yet the native rulers were thought of in more nuanced ways, as a class with a material interest in ruling. In rendering the chiefs' ruling interest in political language the stereotypes of royal politics came readily to hand for the *haole*. The outward Hawaiianness of the chiefship was transformed by applying various signs of monarchy and courtly decorum as defined in the diplomatic manuals of the time, thus establishing an easily accessible cultural link between the chiefs and the foreigners. However, the leaving of common Hawaiians outside the conceptual linkage inhibited rather than facilitated a profound change of *aupuni* and *kālai'āina* toward concepts expressing Western ideas of social contract and partisan politics, or even the political virtues advocated by the evangelical party. Even after colonization the Hawaiian society continued to be effected by the principles of chiefly hierarchy.

Among the prominent inventions of the period, besides the complex legal apparatus, was the diplomatic code, which the doctor and former missionary Gerrit Judd thought would enhance the civilized appearance of the young kingdom (Judd 1960, 131; Kuykendall 1989, 240). Earlier, in March 1844, Judd had employed an adventurous lawyer from New Jersey, John Ricord, to become the law adviser for the king, the attorney general in the new government. By June, after consulting with Kauikeaouli (or rather informing him), Ricord was ready to present the new diplomatic code (Ricord 1844), essentially modeled after the principles of the Vienna Conference of 1815. This code became "the basis of Court etiquette in the Hawaiian Islands" (Code of Etiquette, FOE, June 29, 1844). Besides prescribing rank orders, the mode of applying for royal audience, and the appropriate dress code, the new court etiquette set the Hawaiian standard for practically everything that constituted the royal symbolism. This was reminiscent of the European monarchies of the nineteenth century, from a national coat-of-arms to the opening ceremonies of the legislature. To better represent the progression of chiefship from arbitrary despotism to constitutional monarchy, several Hawaiian insignia were retained, particularly in the formal decoration of public occasions.

Something of this kind had already been in the works for a number of years. For instance, golden ribbons and the so-called Kamehameha buttons were in

1839 reserved for the exclusive use of Kauikeaouli, his chiefs, and the foreign consuls (KC/AH 22/5). Similarly, several new building projects had been initiated in Honolulu before 1845 (Greer 1977, 5–7), including road construction under the notorious leadership of Kekūanaō'a, governor of O'ahu.[14] However, the new ceremonial occasions, inaugurated in 1845, especially the opening of the legislature, exposed the novel insignia and royal symbolism to public view, thus evoking new but familiar images among the foreigners—although not always without ambivalence and irony—and a sense among the chiefs that the glory of *aupuni* was being restored.[15]

Although the royal pomp did not please but a few foreigners, it could not fail to awaken its audience to the existence of comparative equivalents—and of politics confined to the notion of government. Although the following description of the royal audience ridicules the ceremony in a manner typical of many of the visitors, it contains a rich collection of signs that were part of the semiotic landscape in which monarchy as a political entity was conceptualized. The story begins with Robert Wyllie, a wealthy businessman of Scottish origin, whom Judd had employed as the secretary of foreign affairs in March 1845, walking the guests to the new royal palace:

> At the gateway a guard of Kanaka [native] infantry presented arms, the royal standard was unfurled from the flag-staff and floated to the breeze. Passing up a broad, graveled alley, we ascended a flight of steps to the piazza, and were again saluted by a double line of officers, who were supposed to be the black rods in waiting. Entering the villa, we found ourselves in a wide hall traversing the center of the building, with saloons to the right and left. The King having not arrived, we had leisure to inspect the reception room. It was a spacious apartment, with windows on three sides, having green Venetian blinds opening to the piazzas, and two doors leading to the hall. It was handsomely carpeted, and the furniture consisted of a few plain mahogany chairs, with another of state, surmounted by a crown. A round table stood in the center, supporting alabaster ornaments, volumes of Wilkes' Exploring Expedition, and a richly bound Bible in the native dialect . . . The walls were hung with portraits of the Lonely One's [Kamehameha's] family—dingy chiefs and their ladies, smiling intensely, with round saucer eyes and thick lips—a painting of Blucher—two of the Kings of Prussia—and facing the throne, in a gorgeously gilt and carved frame, the King of the French . . . the approach of majesty was announced, and we hurried back to the hall.
>
> From the opposite side of the terrace appeared the regal sortege—brilliant in embroidery, gold lace, nodding plumes, and swords at their sides. On they came, two abreast—foremost, the King, with the Minister of Finance [Judd]; then a brace of Chamberlains, followed by the high chiefs and officers

of State, and the procession closed by the two young princes, Alexander and Lot.

In a few moments, his Excellency the Minister of Foreign Affairs [Wyllie] imparted the August intelligence of all being prepared for our reception. Forming in line—the Admiral leading, under pilotage of Mr. Wyllie—we entered the saloon, and approached the throne. The King was standing, and the courtiers ranged on either side. Our Admiral backed his topsails, and let go an anchor on the Lonely One's port beam. We were then telegraphed by name—shot ahead—hove-to abreast his Majesty—exchanged signals—filed away, and took position by order of sailing on the starboard bow!

His Excellency the Minister of Finance—who, by the way, was not an ill-looking nobleman—in full Court costume, and a field marshal's chapeau tucked under his arm, announced to the Admiral that his Majesty would deign to lend a willing ear to any observations upon religion, war, politics, or any other topics most agreeable . . . The King, Premier [Keoni Ana], and Judd, had broad red ribbons thrown baldric fashion over breast and shoulders, of such extreme breadth as to give the idea of the wearers having burst their jugular arteries (Wise 1849, 332–334).

A similar ritual order prevailed in the framing of the kingdom's legislature beginning in 1845, when Kauikeaouli gave the first of his annual keynote speeches and when the different ministers read their annual reports for the first time. In the legislative building, all the dignitaries were seated in designated places signaling the order of rank, Kauikeaouli's throne occupying the middle of the hall and the nobles, seated to his right in a semi-circle, faced the people's representatives, who took the left side of the throne. Also the foreign representatives and the missionaries had their places, respectively behind the nobles and the people's representatives and facing each other. Directly opposite to the throne were the judges and other government officers (*The Polynesian*, May 24, 1845).

The king was dressed in a costly and splendid uniform. He came attended by the queen, his cabinet, and military escort. As he entered the building, the new royal standard, containing the national coat of arms, designed at the herald's office in London, wholly from national emblems, was hoisted for the first time. The brass band, all native musicians, struck up the national anthem; guns from the fort thundered forth twenty-one times. The whole company arose, and the king walked with much dignity to his throne. A prayer was offered by Mr. Richards, chaplain of the court, after which, at the command of the king, all seated themselves. The king then covered his head with his chapeau in a graceful manner and read his speech . . . I must confess that gratifying reflections filled my mind upon viewing the well-ordered and appropriate ceremonies of the day . . . Still more gratifying is the reflection that this order has been brought out of disorder and savage barbarism in the short space of twenty years by my countrymen (anonymous traveler quoted in Judd 1960, 132).

The ceremonies such as the opening of the legislature were not in fact completely new to Hawaii, because the missionaries, foreign consuls, and naval officers had been conducting funeral processions and official receptions ever since Keōpūolani received a Christian funeral in 1823, and perhaps earlier. What was new was the historical context of the sudden and additional splendor, as Hawaii was seen by many as obtaining a place among nations in the world system defined by Western standards. This was ridiculed by many Western observers, but for Hawaiians this all had a fundamentally different meaning: Hawaii was being raised to the level of the culturally superior lands of Kahiki.

The so-called Paulet affair is a good example of this native sentiment. In the early 1840s, continuing difficulties with foreigners had led the chiefs and William Richards to proceed with a plan to gain diplomatic recognition for the Hawaiian government. In July 1842, Richards and Timothy Haʻalilio, the king's secretary, departed to pursue their mission. By April 1843, they had secured recognition of Hawaiian independence from the governments of England, France, Belgium, and the United States. At about the same time, in February, the Hawaiian Islands were seized by the commander of the English warship *Carysfort*, Lord George Paulet, who wanted to settle once and for all the long-standing disputes between the chiefs and the English residents. Paulet's occupation lasted until July, when Rear Admiral Richard Thomas, Paulet's superior, restored the islands to the native chiefship according to their newly recognized independence (for details, see Kuykendall 1989, 185–226). The restoration, and the diplomatic recognition of Hawaiian independence, were deeply felt by Hawaiians. Fusing together their own migrant origin and the biblical conception of history, they thought that they had finally suppressed so much of their heathen past that their *aupuni* could be recognized as an equal partner by other nations, whose histories were said not to have wandered so far from the God-given path. As a consequence, the evolving comparative political discourse was again focused on government, whose moral foundation, constitution, laws, and other principles were selected for critical evaluation.

These public invitations to practice cultural comparisons had been gaining momentum since James Jarves began his editorial career in the early 1840s. In one of his first calls through his weekly column, Jarves made an inquiry into the basis of cross-cultural comparisons: "We read of religious festivals, of orders of priesthood, the tyranny of the rulers, and other matters of this nature, and yet there are no connecting links to enable us to form any adequate idea of them, by which we could compare these institutions with those of other nations" (*The Polynesian*, Jan. 16, 1841).

Jarves' answer nearly duplicated the missionary theory of the origins of heathenism. For him, the comparisons should have been based on tracing the common origin of humans through innovations, in which "the gradual development of human mind, shown in its progress after truth, or its sinking deeper into error" was manifested. This line of reasoning, of which Jarves was an eloquent spokesman, established Hawaiian chiefship as a developmental stage in the common human history, together with such powers as England, France, or Germany. "Those who have watched the progress of Hawaiian polity must have been favorably impressed, with the rapid progress which they have of late made, toward a regular and settled form of government" (Jarves in *The Polynesian*, Mar. 13, 1841). On this progressivist theme the Hawaiian chiefs could not have been more in agreement, for their *aupuni*, still in the hands of native chiefs, was appropriating the desired properties of the foreign governments, whose power and presence was felt more strongly each day.

Readers should remember that the Hawaiian authors of this comparative discourse were primarily, if not solely, among the chiefs and the more prominent native converts, such as Malo and Hōpū. The great mass of common Hawaiians engaged in dealings that turned out to be quite hostile to both chiefly and missionary cosmopolitanism, as we shall see very shortly. Another relevant distinction must be made between the native converts and the chiefs: the evangelized natives effectively combined Hawaiian traditions of chiefly virtues and Christian morality, to the point where the two were virtually the same, while the chiefs never became converts in the sense preached by the missionaries. They rather held tightly by their traditional prerogatives to define cultural values. In this attempt, the chiefs, with the help of a few foreigners, mobilized ritualized Christianity and, equally, ritualized monarchy. The motive was of course to secure the chiefship by finding common elements between Hawaii and the lands of Kahiki, which, as I have said earlier, had materialized for Hawaiians in a quite radical and unprecedented manner. Thus, while the native converts, who recognized the rarity of evangelical Christianity, sought to find affinities between the chiefs' conduct and Christian ethics, the chiefs assumed a more worldly outlook and, consistent with the cultural theory supporting the chiefship, alienated their *aupuni* from its "original" Hawaiianness. This required a more "pragmatic" orientation toward religion, which was nothing new to the chiefs, but was a source of grave concern for the evangelicals. For instance, in the opening session of the legislature in 1845 Abenera Pākī, a member of the upper house who was not particularly noted for his Christian behavior, proposed a resolution that,

In the name of all the people of these islands, thanks be expressed by this body to the Governments of Great Britain, France, Belgium, and the United States, for the readiness with which they severally recognized the Independence of these Islands, thus receiving us into the fraternity of nations.

That these Resolutions be printed in the Hawaiian and English languages, and suspended in a frame in each of the Legislative Chambers (*The Polynesian*, May 24, 1845).

In Pākī's resolution we can see the core of an international order in which the national actors, or governments, have prescribed levels of competence. It is important that the national actors were indeed governments, not individuals, and that the rapprochement between the Hawaiian chiefship and the Western governments was filtered through the notion of *aupuni* (Pākī's phrase was "*na lahui Aupuni*," which means nations or people organized as in *aupuni*, people with government as opposed to people without it, as American Indians were often represented [*Ka Elele Hawaii*, May 29, 1845]).

The same reciprocity principle was repeated by the new attorney general, John Ricord, when he read his tedious report to the legislature the following day. Ricord made an explicit reference to comparative qualities of the several governments and stressed the duty of the Hawaiian government to render itself intelligible to foreign governments: "It is not enough that we should understand oar [sic] laws; they to [sic] must understand them and witness in them some civilized conformity to their own" (*The Polynesian*, June 14, 1845). The common root that Ricord was displaying before his Hawaiian audience was to be found in the Roman, Jewish, and English legal traditions, which were all applications of "the laws of Moses," a thoroughly familiar figure for Hawaiians. However, Ricord plainly denied that the Mosaic law would be directly applicable to the governance of modern societies. Yet merely by alluding to the person of Moses and by giving modern examples of the application of the Mosaic tradition, he had already taken the Hawaiian *aupuni* to the conceptual sphere of Western government. He had also produced a comparative equivalent for himself and for those foreigners who shared his conviction that a new monarchical government had just witnessed its political birth.

In a notable shift from the earlier practice, the laws were now published first in English, before Hawaiian, again indicating a break with the past and its somewhat perverse political principles. The political meaning of monarchy apparently caused some problems for Richards, whose duty it was to translate the statute laws of 1845 and 1846 into Hawaiian. In Ricord's preface to the statutes, he says that "the political principles of this code are not materially different from those sustained by the mildest forms of monarchy" (Statute Laws

1846, 6). Richards' Hawaiian version of this statement is as follows: "*O na kumu kalaimoku iloko o keia mookanawai, aole i ano e nui keia i ko na Aupuni oluolu nui e ae, na Aupuni alii hanau hoi*" (Kanawai 1846, 6). To my knowledge this is a rare or perhaps a unique occurrence of the word *kālaimoku* as a translation of the word "political." Yet it is immediately qualified by a compound expression *aupuni ali'i hānau*, or monarchy (lit. government of hereditary rulers). Again it seems that the political meaning of the new monarchy was mediated in Richards' translation through the Hawaiian concept of *aupuni*, and by the idea of its management, as the word *kālaimoku* implies.[16] Ironically, Ricord's analyses included an implicit message to the chiefs to use their power to render Hawaiian *aupuni* understandable across cultural boundaries. It was a call to bring wise men from Kahiki and declare the imported ideas culturally valuable.

To this we should add Kauikeaouli's speech (in fact drafted by Wyllie [FOE, May 1845]), in which it was made quite clear that the Hawaiian *aupuni* was kept through a god, as in the old times. As always, the god was conceived of in pragmatic terms far removed from the evangelical god who ruled in the hearts of people. As the god was the same as the god of the foreign governments, it gave certain advantage to assert its power, and it could be used as a prime example of making Hawaii more familiar to the outside world: ". . . the Word of God is the corner stone of our kingdom. Through its influence we have been introduced into the family of the independent nations of the earth" (*The Polynesian*, May 24, 1845).[17] Although, for Kauikeaouli, a proclamation such as this did not mean a personal commitment to the worship of Jehovah beyond mere ceremony, it once again elicited customary patterns of thought. As if to perfect the image of a newly born nation, the mission-led Hawaiian language paper *Ka Elele Hawaii* in one issue began publishing Richards' text on political economy (*Ka Elele Hawaii*, May 29, 1845), but it was never continued.[18] In the foreigners' eyes, Kauikeaouli assumed a domesticated position, the familiar figure of an enlightened and properly worldly monarch. When the premier Keoni Ana spoke of the advantages of the new system of government in early 1846, he commented on the king's new status as an equal of the common people, "inventing" history as Kekuaipi'ia had done for Kotzebue in 1824: "Now he is one of you. Then he was King and god" (*The Polynesian*, Feb. 14, 1846). That said, the cultural center of the reform remained the king himself, his lowering down and his granting a constitutional government. This Keoni Ana could not put aside, and hardly wanted to.

Indeed, it was not so much the promised commoner participation in government that prompted *haole* praise, but rather the bustle around the king and the imagined harmony that was being created. There was to be a system which was familiar, in contrast to the anomalous chiefship: "Politics are now rapidly becoming a system as in other lands," wrote Jarves (*The Polynesian*, Jan. 3, 1846). This body politic was not to give itself up to fractious partisanship; for it was rather a representation of holistic order, unwittingly in a manner of *aupuni*. It consisted, however, not of traditional—or traditionalized—care for the people, but rather of rules of conduct, king's speeches, road construction, and the like. All of these were used not only to prop up the tottering chiefly establishment, but also to provide foreigners with instances to witness the growing familiarity of the Hawaiian government. As this activity was conceptually tied to a centralized government, any independent initiative springing from amongst the local people met with suspicion if not outright rejection. This precluded any expansion of the developing political discourse toward forms of republicanism, so much desired in the meditations of the missionaries and many other Western observers.

CHAPTER 6

The Denouement
Untranslated Experiences

The growing number of contact studies suggests that culture contacts rarely, if ever, involve a simple imposition of the foreigners' culture. Even colonial situations are more complex than that. The weak surely have weapons, but the visibility of their resistance tactics is often low when observed through existing historiography. The Hawaiian experience is a case in point. The re-reading of Hawaiian historical material from culturalist perspectives has attracted scholarly attention to more subtle aspects of commoner life in the post-contact era (e.g., Ralston 1984; Sahlins 1992). This chapter continues this work by taking up some notable patterns of commoner resistance and examining the workings of the contact culture to see why resistance was ineffective, and what were its consequences for the emerging cross-cultural political discourse. As Thomas (1992) says, in contact cultures there is a certain selectivity in what becomes objectified, reflecting the structures of events that occur during the contact. This is nicely manifested in Hawaii, where the grafting of cross-cultural equivalents of politics took a turn toward cultural mediation centered on the notion of government. It is paradoxical that this allowed very few commoner feelings to be absorbed into the developing political language of the Hawaiian monarchy. This is not to say that the players, missionaries for example, were necessarily ignorant of the various meanings associated with the Hawaiian *aupuni*. They were, in fact, quite observant in recording these meanings, but the nature of the Hawaiian chiefship and the evolving circumstances did not favor constructing notions of participatory politics or anything resembling the full spectrum of the republican ideal. As previously, I will first explore the formal translation history before introducing more narrative. In the following I have selected meanings related to *aupuni* which carry beyond a mere appellation for "government" or "kingdom," and which reveal the cultural basis of the common people's efforts to resist changes in their *aupuni*.

Aupuni as Reciprocal Condition

The verb "to govern" was first recorded by Andrews in his 1836 vocabulary. According to Andrews, the Hawaiian equivalent was *hoʻomalu*, which he translated as "to bless, comfort, make comfortable, to rule over, govern as a chief, to keep in order the affairs of state" (Andrews 1836, 97), or *aliʻi*, meaning "to act the chief, to rule over, govern" and "a chief, a king, ruler" (10). Drawing on island sources, both Protestant and Catholic, Boniface Mosblech also used the two words to translate the French verb "gouverner," namely, *aliʻi* and *malu* (Mosblech 1843, 209). *Malu* lacks the causative prefix *hoʻo-*, but carries somewhat similar meanings as *hoʻomalu* (for *aliʻi*, see below). When Emerson and Bishop defined "government" in 1845, they wrote *"na kanawai hoomalu,"* referring to the body of laws and edicts that constitute the frame of governing, and *"ka hoomalu ana i ke aupuni,"* meaning the sum total of the activity of ordering a chiefly territory (Emerson and Bishop 1845, 65). They also applied *hoʻomalu* to translate the verb "to rule" *(e hoʻomalu aupuni)* and the noun "ruler" *(he luna hoʻomalu)* (137). Bishop's *Hawaiian Phrase Book* translated "civil officers" as *nā luna hoʻomalu*, and utilized the same phrase to translate "presiding officer" (Bishop 1854, 20–21).[1] Andrews in his dictionary sharpened his view on the word *hoʻomalu* and gave the following definition: "To rule over, especially in a peaceful way; to *govern* quietly; to make peace," and further as an adjective, "making or causing peace between differing parties" (Andrews 1865, 198, my italics). On the other hand, Hitchcock, in his *English-Hawaiian Dictionary*, was very straightforward in translating "to govern" as *"e hoomalu i kanaka"* (lit. to cause a shadow over people [in a positive sense], Hitchcock 1887, 97). He also gave *hoʻomalu* as a synonym for "to rule" (178). In revising Andrews' dictionary in the early 1920s, Parker added two aspects of *hoʻomalu*; first, "to bring under the care or protection," and second, "to seize and appropriate by process of law" (Andrews 1922, 180).

This translation seems to be close to the logic of Polynesian tabu, and approaches the sense of prohibition with which something was marked for the use of the chiefs only. In a complaint made sometime in the 1840s or 1850s to the Minister of the Interior, Keoni Ana, the *makaʻāinana* of Waiʻoli, Kauaʻi, felt rather indignant about the *konohiki* of the place, who had forbidden the use of a certain tree suitable for making shingles. The word that the people used for such a prohibition was *hoʻomalu*. The word was also used in government accounts to show, for example, how much cash was extracted by selling "prohibited" (*ho'omalu*) fish (IDM/AH, Box 1, Docs. 13 and 20, n.d.). In official use, king Kamehameha III spoke of his *malu*, which was translated as "government," for example, *"malalo o ko'u malu"* or "subject to my Government" (Proclamation by Kamehameha III, Apr. 13, 1846, LH/BM).

The present translation was confirmed in 1957 by Pukui and Elbert, who basically followed the revised version of Andrews' dictionary and added some new or previously unrecorded meanings. Of interest are "to keep quiet, still, as during taboo," "to restrict, confine, quarantine," "to suspend, as a license," "to precede, as at a meeting," "probation," "to judge," and "to call to order" (Pukui and Elbert 1957, 315; the last two appeared only in examples given).

As we have seen, the word *ho'omalu* implies a peaceful state of being, a protection enjoyed by people living under those in higher positions. It also implies the infamous submissive attitude on behalf of the governed. To enjoy the protection and peace provided by chiefs one had to be willing to accept the restrictions as part of the mutual harmony between chiefs and the common people. The falling figurative shadow *(malu)* of the chief is cool and comfortable, like the real shadow on a hot day. William Ellis relates a story of a conquered person who, to avoid being taken captive and sacrificed, could run to the conquering chief and ask for mercy by prostrating at the chief's feet. If the chief spoke to the person, he was to live under *malu* or protection of the chief, usually as a member of the chief's retinue (1979, 106). Later the native scholar Samuel Kamakau in his notes identified *malu* with words such as *kia'i* (to watch, guard, overlook; a guard, watchman, caretaker), *mālama'* (to take care of, attend, care for, preserve, care, preservation, support, etc.), *maluhia* (peace, quiet, security), *'olu'olu* (pleasant, happy, nice, etc.), *maha* (rest, repose, vacation, freedom from pain, at ease, comfort), and *haumalu* (quiet) (Kamakau, *Quotations*, n.d.). As *ho'omalu* became the standard translation of "to govern" it lost some of its quality as a word implying a state of blessedness and comfort.

Another equivalent of governing is *noho*, which was, strictly speaking, not codified until Pukui and Elbert's *English-Hawaiian Dictionary* (1964, 66). Besides *ho'omalu*, they gave three alternatives for the verb "to govern": *noho aupuni*, *noho ali'i*, and *noho*. *Noho aupuni* is given a tripartite translation: to rule, a reign, and a ruler (1957, 248; the last was added to the 1985 edition). *Noho ali'i* has more dimensions. It can mean a throne, reign, chieftainship, tenure as chief, a rule, to reign or act as a chief (1957, 248). Finally, *noho*, besides its common meanings of seat, chair, to live, to reside or to dwell, can be used to designate "to rule or to reign." Pukui and Elbert also noted that in this latter sense the verb *noho* usually takes a qualifier; for example, *noho moku*, to rule a district (1986, 268).

Going backwards in time, the verb "to govern" disappears in the dictionary renderings of *noho*, as well as of the phrase *noho aupuni*, although it was used, for instance, by Malo in his 1840 manuscript (Malo 1987, 39), and translated at the turn of the century as "to conduct government" (Malo 1991, 54). Instead, *noho ali'i* seems to have been the favorite of the past compilers (and *noho Mō'ī* after the introduction of the new title for the king). In his vocabulary, Andrews translated it as "king's seat or throne" (Andrews 1836, 109). From the late 1820s, *noho ali'i* began to appear in Bible translations to mean a throne or a king's seat, or, to be or to continue to act as a king, or to reign as a king. These meanings, together with their biblical references, were recorded in Andrews' dictionary (1865, 422) and they remained unaltered in the Andrews-Parker edition (Andrews 1922, 464). In 1887 Hitchcock made an exception to the use of *noho aupuni* and *noho ali'i* as equal alternatives in translating "to rule" (Hitchcock 1887, 178). As can be inferred from early translations, the word *ali'i*, the general epithet of a person in chiefly position, was sometimes used alone to signify governing and ruling (for later usages, see Andrews 1865, 50; Andrews 1922, 52; Pukui and Elbert 1957, 19). That *ali'i* surfaced as the first recorded equivalence of "to govern," together with the words *ho'omalu* and *malu*, is not at all surprising. The word *ali'i* must have been uppermost in the minds of the missionaries, at times suppressing Jehovah, given their desire to be allowed to land and stay in Hawaii.

Before moving on to more active expressions, we should pause at three words that, like *noho*, describe the more existential side of governance. Those words are *kū*, *ea*, and *ka'a maluna*. The latter was first given a meaning "to take the oversight or office" (Andrews 1836, 56), and was afterward intensified to include meanings of "exercising an office over others" (Andrews 1865, 229). It reached its peak when Pukui and Elbert translated it as "to rule others" (1957, 101). Literally, and emphasizing the existential imagery of the word, *ka'a maluna* means "to be situated above."

In the dictionaries there is no reference to the governing or ruling dimension of the words *kū* or *ea* until Pukui and Elbert's 1957 first edition (34, 155). In their first *English-Hawaiian Dictionary* they list *kū* and *ea* as two possible equivalents for the verb "to govern" (1964, 131). In the corresponding Hawaiian entries of 1957 *kū* is relatively unambiguous. In addition to the most widely used meanings—"to stand," "to rise," "to be upright or erect,"—Pukui and Elbert give the translation "to rule or reign, as a land" (155). While the earlier dictionaries are silent here, there is some indication in the native texts of related uses of *kū*. Kamakau uses the word similarly when he says *"ku i ke Aupuni"* (stand at the head of the government) or *"ku i ka moku"* (stand at the head of the district or island) (Kamakau 1867b).

Ea was first translated as "a spirit, vital breath, the breath, life" (Andrews 1836, 15). "Air," "breeze," and "wind" were added later (Andrews 1865, 64–65;

1922, 77–78). In 1957, two other groups of meanings were added: "sovereignty," "rule," "independence," and "to rise," "go up," "raise," "become erect" (Pukui and Elbert 1957, 34). At present, "sovereignty," "rule," and "independence" are the primary meanings (Pukui and Elbert 1986, 36). It seems that these latter translations of *ea* are based on a re-reading of the official correspondence concerning the short-lived cession of Hawaii by the British naval commander Lord George Paulet in the winter of 1843. At the time of ceding the islands, King Kamehameha III wrote a public declaration using the words *"ua haawi au i ke ea o ka aina o kakou,"* which was translated by the ex-missionary doctor Gerrit P. Judd as "I have given away the *life* of our land" (my italics). In the same declaration, Kamehameha III expressed the "hope that the *life* of the land will be restored when my conduct is justified" *(e hoihoi ia mai ana no nae ke ea o ka aina, ke hooponoia mai ka'u hana ana)* (Kamehameha III and Kekauluohi 1843, my italics). Similarly, when informing Kuakini, the head of the Hawai'i island, about the cession, his O'ahu counterpart Governor Kekūanaō'a used the word *ea*: *"Ua haawi iho nei ke Lii au i ke ea o ke aupuni ona ia Beritania Nui"* (My chief just gave the *ea* of his government to the Great Britain [FOE, Feb. 27, 1843]). On this occasion, the word *ea* was most likely used figuratively in the traditional spiritual sense, which saw a close link between the life of the chief and the fertility of the land. Moreover, the native choice of the word indicating life seems to have been closely tied to the seriousness of the situation and the presence of death on account of the British warship. Addressing another chief about the proceedings in Honolulu, Kekūanaō'a made death an explicit point of reference: *"Aloha oe e Timoteo Haalilio kuu hoa o na pililia a pau, a me na make hoi a pau a ka haole"* (Greetings to you Timoteo Ha'alilio my companion in all the troubles and also in all death from the foreigners [FOE, Mar. 6, 1843]).[3] When the cession was over on July 31, 1843, that day was made an annual day of celebration, *Lā Ho'iho'i Ea*, or, as it was called in English, Restoration Day. The element of anti-life was removed.

Later twentieth-century readings of *ea* as "independence" is particularly intriguing as the idea of independence had been expressed by using the word *kū'oko'a* (lit. to stand aloof) since at least the late 1830s (*Ke Kumu Hawaii*, July 4, 1838; Richards 1839, 64; *Ka Nonanona*, Oct. 3, 1843; *The Friend*, May 1, 1844; IDL/AH 1, Nov. 5, 1846; Kaimikuokoa 1854). This word was used throughout the nineteenth century (Kamakau 1869a; Baker, c. 1880).[4]

Let us now proceed to words that contain an active imagery of governing, which are *ho'oponopono*, *'ai*, and *ho'ohaku*. Ho'oponopono was rendered as an equivalent for "to govern" only by Emerson and Bishop in 1845. However, they also wanted to secure the meaning against possible misinterpretations by adding a Hawaiian definition *"e lilo i alii no kekahi poe"* (to become a chief for a people) (Emerson and Bishop 1845, 65). In other places *ho'oponopono* has been translated as "to put together," "to put in order or to rectify" (Andrews 1836, 50), "to rule over," "to be superintendent," "to put in order," "to regulate," "to correct what is erroneous" (Andrews 1865, 208; 1922, 197), "to put to rights," "to put in order or shape," "correct," "revise," "adjust," "amend," "regulate," "arrange," "rectify," "tidy up," "make orderly or neat," "administer," "superintend," "supervise," "manage," "edit," "work carefully or neatly," "to make ready, as canoemen preparing to catch a wave" (Pukui and Elbert 1986, 341). The foregoing list clearly suggests a wide range of specific meanings for *ho'oponopono*, but all seem to point to one central idea: setting things in order. As I indicated in discussing the meanings of *kālai'āina*, the Hawaiian lands were traditionally divided and redistributed after a conquest or the death of a chief. This business was often called *ho'oponopono* and it included, besides dividing the lands, appointing the right people as chiefs to the subdivisions, and overseers to smaller divisions (e.g., Ii 1983, 69–70; 1869d). This also involved more active participation of the chiefs than the idea of *ho'omalu* might imply.

A still more active connotation is carried by the verb *'ai*, the basic meaning of which is "food," especially vegetable food, and "to eat," "to destroy," "to consume." Early on, the translators added the meaning of enjoying the products of the land. From 1836 to 1957 this dimension was expressed in the language of Western economic discourse: *e 'ai i ka 'āina*, "to have the profits of the land" (Andrews 1836, 2; 1865, 23; 1922, 33). In Pukui and Elbert's rendition, the word "profit" was dropped and replaced by meanings that emphasized reciprocal relations between chiefs and their people. According to Pukui and Elbert, *'ai* can be translated as "to rule or enjoy the privileges and exercise the responsibilities of rule" (1957, 8). In combinations, the verb *'ai* has similar meanings, as for example, *'ai moku*, "to rule a district or island"; *ali'i 'ai moku*, "ruling chief of a district or island"; *'ai 'āina*, "to own, control and enjoy land" (for *ali'i 'ai moku*, see below). These translations are unquestionably closer to Hawaiian understandings of the position of their chiefs, and seem to correspond to the intentions of the early native writers (see Stokes 1932; Sahlins 1992, 110 fn. 23).

Unlike *'ai*, the verb *ho'ohaku* contains a connotation of illegitimate ruling or domination, a bossy type of lording over. The tone of the word is quite appropriate if we consider the half-illegitimate shadow economy that for years existed in the smaller land units between the people and their *haku'āina*. The latter would habitually extract a sizable portion of people's products and labor for their own use, despite the government's efforts to root out the practice.

The translation of the word "governor" makes a somewhat separate case, although it builds on the common imagery. The early translators used the composition *ali'i 'ai moku*. According to the vocabulary of the missionary Hiram Bingham, *ali'i 'ai moku* is "a governor, a chief who takes possession of, or divides a country, or enjoys its profits" (Bingham 1832, 23). Andrews, perhaps willingly in order to keep his vocabulary from expanding, avoided any wordy definitions and satisfied himself with the word "governor" (Andrews 1836, 10), a rendition he also used in his manuscript for the same vocabulary (Andrews, *Vocabulary*, n.d.). In the later 1830s, a young newspaperman, Stephen D. Macintosh, followed Bingham (or someone else with a similar translation) in his manuscript vocabulary (Macintosh, *Vocabulary*, n.d.). However, by 1845 *ali'i 'ai moku* had been replaced by *kia'āina* as the favored translation for "governor" (Mosblech 1843, 45, 209; Emerson and Bishop 1845, 65; Bishop 1854, 20), thus marking an official break with the traditional past of land-consuming chiefs.[5]

The induced break was of course not complete. The use of *ali'i 'ai moku* continued beyond 1845 and, correspondingly, the word *kia'āina* had been used synonymously at least from 1828 (Bishop 1828; Bingham 1832, 157; Andrews 1836, 68). In his vocabulary, Andrews opted for more words and defined the etymology of the word: "the support of the land, that is, a governor, governor of a state or island, a ruler." In comparison, the word *kia'āina* implies a more existential nature of governing, as if a condition of life (not to mention the sexual metaphor inherent in the word *kia*: pillar, prop, post, pole, etc.), than the words based on the root *'ai*. For example, in the 1865 dictionary, *'ai moku* is explained quite thoroughly as "a person who holds the rank of a chief over some district or island; one who enjoys the honors and profits of such a post without really owning the land," or "one who enjoys the fruits of the land but pays a part to the owner." To illustrate this managerial dimension, Andrews quotes the story of Lā'ieikawai, the cornerstone of Hawaiian language written fiction: "*e pau kona aimoku ana*" (his authority is ended). *Nā ali'i 'ai moku*, as "governors," is mentioned only in passing at the end of the same entry (Andrews 1865, 26). Under the entry *ali'i, ali'i 'ai moku* was translated as "the chief over a division, that is, the governor under the alii moi" (50). This translation was carried over to the revised version of Andrews' dictionary (1922, 51), and continued by Judd (1939, 89). In Pukui and Elbert's dictionary, the word "governor" was dropped altogether as a gloss for *ali'i 'ai moku* (1957, 19).[6]

Aupuni of the Worldly Rulers

The Hawaiian imagery of governing could have been used as a resource in various kinds of translation enterprises, but it will become clear that the cultural mediation was very much tilted in favor of Hawaii's officialdom. The embryonic fusion of evangelical republicanism and traditional chiefly virtues was played down by the chiefs and their *haole* ministers, including the missionaries hired by the government. Just as the traditional eating of the land was officially replaced as the epitome of chiefly existence, so too was the chiefly *malu* blocked from becoming the centerpiece in forging continuity or even identity between Hawaiian and Western "politics."

A turning point in advancing one-sided cultural translation was the decision of some of the missionaries to leave the mission and become attached, along with other foreigners, to the emerging monarchy, as advisors and ministers. William Richards was the first to leave the mission in 1838, followed by Judd in 1842, and Andrews in 1845. Very soon the other missionaries expressed their disapproval of the worldly look assumed by their co-workers in Christ, especially in Judd's case (Journal of Lowell Smith, June 2, 1842; Armstrong to an unknown recipient, June 8, 1844, M-7/AH; Baldwin to Greene, Nov. 8, 1845, HP/HMCS).[7] Even Richards, who had enjoyed the trust and high esteem of his colleagues, was suspected of questionable intents (Richards to Baldwin, June 9, 1845, MSL). The distance created in the mid-1840s between the mission and the chiefly powers, furthering the earlier post-Kaʻahumanu separation, was multi-dimensional. Richards was motivated by a bid to protect the chiefship to maintain some distance from the other missionaries, whom he considered too quick to advocate commoner rights: "It is a fact that there is a number of the Brethren whom I consider quite radicals in politics, & I therefore feel it necessary to act in my sphere somewhat independly [sic]" (Richards to Anderson, Jan. 1, 1842, HP/HMCS). Ironically, this reasoning precluded rather than aided missionary influence in the Hawaiian government.

Those left in the field began to more openly advocate republican values than they had previously dared. This change was largely due to the new circumstances in which the missionaries saw first hand how the government regulations were out of touch with local conditions. The monarchy was becoming more organized, culminating in the establishment of government ministries and privatization of lands beginning in 1845. Consequently, the number of laws and regulations multiplied, and all of this eventually rested on the shoulders of perplexed commoners.[8] The missionaries in the field generally felt that the laws were multiplying too fast, and that too little attention was being paid to lessening the burden of the taxes being collected to run the new bureaucratic machine, and to pay off the foreign debt the chiefs had accumulated in their business transactions (Kekāuluohi to Kekūanaōʻa, May 4, 1842, FOE).[9] The majority of missionaries were thus taking the side of the common people, and it was clear that such criticisms were alienating the missionaries in the field from those in the government. In addition to Richard Armstrong (who later changed his mind and joined the government as minister of public instruction), concerns were expressed over the foreigners in government by Baldwin and Smith, and also Levi Chamberlain, John Emerson, and Cochran Forbes. It appears that their critical stance was largely shared by the missionaries in the field (Kuykendall 1989, 256; Baldwin to Greene, Nov. 8, 1845, HP/HMCS).

This split in the mission was further intensified by the so-called petition movement among common Hawaiians. While the king and his new *haole* ministers were getting ready for the great opening of the 1845 legislature, people all around the islands were holding protracted prayer meetings that much resembled those during the revival in the late 1830s. The sole purpose of these meetings was to pray "that the Lord wd give them [Hawaiians] black rulers" (Baldwin to Greene, Nov. 8, 1845, HP/HMCS). The new legislature might have been a good thing, but staring back at the natives across the aisle of the legislative building, would be sun tanned yet recognizably white faces, missionaries, and adventurers cum government ministers and advisers for the king. Beginning in approximately April of that year, these meetings eventually led to drafting petitions to the king and the legislature. Some of the petitions were published in *Ka Elele Hawaii* and translated in *The Friend*, which for a time entertained a critical posture toward the new government. The petitions were opposed mainly to three related issues: the appointment of foreigners to government posts, the allowing of Hawaiian citizenship to foreigners, and the selling of land to foreigners. There were a few other causes of grievance as well, such as heavy taxation, the plethora of laws, and the poverty of the king (e.g., IDM/AH, Apr., Nov., 1845; FOE, June 12, Aug., 1845; LFP/AH, June 25, July 2, 1845; NDOC/162). All of these issues were, however, expressions of the fear of the common people that foreigners were on the move to take over the Hawaiian *aupuni* and turn Hawaiians into a landless class of wanderers. Some of the petitions were long and elaborate letters signed by hundreds, or sometimes thousands of common Hawaiians. Apparently some were written by mission-educated intellectuals such as Malo, although it is uncertain if he was involved in the actual writing. He nevertheless was active in "promoting the movement," as Kuykendall says (1989, 259).

One of the prominent figures in the movement was Z. Kaumaea of Maui. Besides spearheading some of the collective petitions, he himself drew up at least one of them, which advised Kauikeaouli in organizing the five government ministries. Kaumaea's advice consisted of an interesting combination of Christian jargon and references to traditional Hawaiian virtues of harmonious living. He fluently introduced the five newly created government ministries, but in defining their duties he gave them a coloring of the same ideals we have encountered in the writings of Malo and Hōpū. In fact, Kaumaea created an historical continuity between his understandings of the traditional chiefship and of the government reform, only this time he introduced a commoner's point of view. As was the pattern in the other petitions, Kaumaea also put his trust in Kauikeaouli. Kaumaea proposed that, in order to invigorate the *ali'i*-ship, Kauikeaouli should be placed above the laws, for he was the parent (*makua*) from which the ministries and hence everything else emanated. In the same manner, Kaumaea also referred *kālai'āina* back to its origin in the genealogical knowledge of the chiefs' pedigrees, and only after that would he deal with the issues of governing (IDM/AH, Box 2, Nov. 1845). All in all, such resistance, although familiar in content, was unusual in form, and it was taken quite seriously in government chambers. Kauikeaouli assigned a three-man secret committee, consisting of Ioane 'Ī'ī, Aarona Keli'iahonui, and John Ricord, to investigate the origin of petitions, as it was suspected that either the missionaries or some other foreign residents, notably the U.S. Commissioner Brown, had stirred up the movement.

In the letter of assignment, probably written by Judd, the petition movement itself did not receive nearly as much attention as did the possibility of foreign instigation, so that the movement was labeled "insidious" and "insurrectionary," while the foreigners were said to be motivated by a desire to effect a "political change in our domestic policy." The Hawaiian version of the same letter treated the movement as unlawful and forbidden: "*kekahi mau hana malu ana*" (lit. forbidden doings). The word "political" was left untranslated, as the Hawaiian text said, "*me ka manao e hoohuli i ko'u aupuni ma ke ano o ka hooponopono ana i ka aina*" (while thinking to change my *aupuni* in the manner of adjusting the affairs of the land) (FOE, June 12, 1845). But because the possibility of an independent commoner protest was practically ruled out, and the word "political" was attached to the foreigners' motives of altering the form of government, it seems that the chiefs and their *haole* ministers excluded common Hawaiians altogether from government-centered political discourse. The secret committee heard several witnesses, including Hawaiian church members and the missionaries Alexander and Baldwin, but all they could find out was that the petitions emerged from a religious context, for they were usually written after church services. Baldwin had announced a prayer meeting for the good of the government, but had not been present when the petitions were made (Baldwin to Richards, June 9, 1845; Baldwin to Greene, Nov. 8, 1845, both in HP/HMCS; native testimonies are filed in FOE, June 14, 1845).

Baldwin had himself identified the petition meetings as being "political" (Baldwin to Richards, June 9, 1845, HP/HMCS), and had made that known to the people (what expressions he used is unknown), but all this had little or no effect on the conceptual map of Hawaiian society. For the commoners the goal was to preserve the old social order, with the honors of the chiefs, and the commoners virtuously living under chiefs and thus contributing to chiefly honors. In Baldwin's parish, some sixteen hundred natives signed their names in support of the traditional hierarchy: "*Aole i pau ko makou minamina i ka nani o na 'lii, a me ko makou noho ana malalo ou e ka Moi a me na 'lii malalo ou. O ko haawi e aku no ka ia i kou noho alii ana malalo o na haole*" (FOE, Aug. 1845). The sentence could be translated as follows: "We still value the glory of the chiefs and our living under you the king and the chiefs under you. And for this you placed your chiefship under the foreigners." The people of Kona, Hawai'i, expressed the same desire in more poetic language: "Here is this reason of our petitioning you [king and legislature]. You should take good care of the ruling chiefs and the blood called chiefly blood, the *pi'o* and the *wohi* ranks for the *aupuni* and the true Hawaiians, whose task it is to take good care of the land, and the axes, and the spades, and the bitter yam,[10] and the dwellings, and the *kapa* and *malo* cloth, and the vegetable and meat foods, and the tax money, and all things. Death and life are not for us [to decide], this matter is for the king only" (my translation, original in LFP/ AH, June 25, 1845).

These ideas, combined with Malo's and Hōpū's criticism of the chiefly establishment, provide us with a more elaborate picture of Hawaiian commoners as notoriously subservient "*kanaks.*" Still, in the 1840s, hierarchy was a prized social value, according to which all respectable life stemmed from inequality. To be more precise, all sources indicate that this valued inequality is not to be confused with the arbitrary use of power, or a total suppression of all commoner interests. These were unacceptable, and excesses in the chiefs' use of power finally generated a crisis of legitimacy. This was expressed in petitioning on a massive scale, and a turning away from the official Protestantism after Catholicism made its way permanently into the islands in 1839.

These were clearly two very different forms of resistance. The Protestants choose petitions, although it seems that their motives were the same as those of the Catholics: to stop the traditional, reciprocal hierarchy from disappearing. But those who had turned to Catholicism seemed to think that it had already vanished, that the chiefs' *aloha* had run out, replaced by ceaseless exploitation. The school laws of the early 1840s are particularly revealing on this point. In the old days, people had flocked to mission schools to gain prestige, but by the 1840s the schools had become a burden. Children were required by law to attend, and parents were ordered to support the teachers (mainly by working land given to the teachers). The Catholic schools soon became popular if for no other reason than that their teaching was gratuitous. The government responded by agreeing to pay the teachers' salaries, but it failed to raise enough cash to do so, and again the parents were made liable for the deficit. Occasionally, the teachers, too, "made high demands upon" the families (MH 40, 191), thus becoming another link in the hierarchy, where every person of some notice tried to eat from the land and improvise on the established work rule of the islands. Persons in lower positions would do work as a tribute or a recognition of the status of the person stationed above.[11]

For many Hawaiians, the status system itself was still legitimate, and they worried that the system would be replaced by a rule of the *haole*. *Haole* could not by definition be the objects of native homage, or cornerstones in any complex arrangement of obligation, status, and honor. The *haole* had already taken the reins of *aupuni*, and the laws they made were seen as oppressive. In more remote areas common people enlisted in the cause of the Catholic Church, and hoped to thereby escape from what they considered oppressive school laws and to protest more generally the state of affairs in the Hawaiian *aupuni*.

The missionary Richard Armstrong relates some dramatic events on the southern tip of Hawai'i island, Ka'ū: "On his late tour around Hawaii, the king went ashore at a Romish village in Kau; as his custom was, he called the villagers together to give them some advice, hear their grievances, &c; but not a word could he get out of them. Governor Young, of Maui, made an attempt to address them, and get them to answer some simple and civil inquiries; but he also failed; so with others. The king told them it was plain that they did not love him nor regard him as their king, and with this took his anchor and left them, having been ashore only a few hours. He speaks of it as a decided proof of the evil tendency of Romanism" (Armstrong to ABCFM, Nov. 7, 1843 in MH 40, 192).

The petitions were even more alarming than the presence of Catholic congregations, because they came from the ranks of the established church and implicated what had been the strongest ally of the chiefs, the Protestant mission. This was surprising in a way that the troubles with Catholics were not. The latter were also culturally malleable, being a familiar melding of open hostility with and a form of worship different from that of the ruling chiefs, a situation reminiscent of the uprising of the supporters of the old native religion in 1819. To quote one missionary: "Many of them [Catholics] are insolent and ripe for rebellion, and all that is wanting is the presence of a foreign power to lead them on. Of this our rulers are aware, and it is a source of great perplexity to their minds" (Bishop to ABCFM, Sept. 15, 1843 in MH 40, 190). Following the secret committee report on petitionings, there developed among the foreigners in the government a need to put their political identity in writing, or rather to assume a political identity and make it a permanent and binding principle of all the king's ministers in the new government. The document, whose Hawaiian translation is apparently lost, was entitled "Political Creed and Principles as Professed Individually by the Members of the Present Administration of His Majesty Kamehameha III" and dated June 20, 1845. It was drafted by the new foreign minister, Robert Wyllie, together with Judd and Ricord. (Richards is known to have approved these principles; cf. Richards to Baldwin, June 9, 1845, MSL, in which Richards claims to be "root body and branch a monarchist.") The declaration stated that the foreigners in government service would support monarchy and serve faithfully until native Hawaiians gained sufficient training to take over their place in the government. More specifically, they outlined once more the progressivist theory of civilization, which did not grant political citizenship for common Hawaiians. Although Hawaii was widely thought to be a political entity with diplomatic ties and a legitimate government, its people were regarded as semi-barbarous and immature. In the foreigners' minds, they had barely secured even the potential for being capable of political activity, in the more or less distant future, and only if the defective chiefly government could be altered to bring forth habits of industry in the people, and to support "a nation of consistent Christians" (Richards to Anderson, Aug. 1, 1838, HP/HMCS). The fourth and fifth articles of the declaration expressed this old idea quite well:

> I admit that chiefly owing to the American missionaries, the Natives have made great progress in letters and religion, and that they are capable of being so trained as to be able to conduct the affairs of Government efficiently, but I consider that they are as yet very far from having arrived at that pitch of civilization.
>
> I consider that they [Hawaiians] can only be brought to that pitch, by promoting education, the careful study of proper Books, and the practical training which they may receive by ascending through the different gradations of offices under Foreign Ministers (FOE, June 20, 1845).

As an interpretation of commoner resistance, the declaration and its pledges were perfect examples of translating grass-roots activity into an abstract language of government. It did so by way of constructing a cross-culturally sustainable view of a society moving toward becoming a mature and permanent political system. This was done mainly by focusing on foreigners as the potentially disruptive factor, and placing common Hawaiians within a stereotypical image of the passive peasant who is only too easily led astray (cf. Ralston 1984). Again, generalizing their mediated experience of Hawaiians as incapable of sustaining an ordered political society, this small band of foreigners were blind to the much-valued autonomy being displayed by petitioning commoners. Instead of initiative and autonomy, they saw impulsiveness, impropriety, and subversiveness. It would have been easy to put a republican cloak on the shoulders of Hawaiians who, after church services, gathered together to present their thoughts publicly and to vote on whether to petition the king (FOE, June 14, 1845). When, in the eighth article, the *haole* trio pledged to "discourage all Republican tendencies," they specifically promised to guard against any attempt to place the islands under the "dominion of Whites" (FOE, June 20, 1845). There was no mention of any threat of a republican kind originating from within the ranks of common Hawaiians.

Although the authors of the petitions never suggested that Hawaiians wanted a republic, there remained in the minds of government ministers a lingering thought that perhaps common Hawaiians could be induced to support a republican movement as they were known to be both easily led and increasingly dissatisfied with their condition. The natives could defend what they considered proper values, but as these values contradicted the republican theory of the creation of a civil society capable of producing political action, so the petition movement was also received more as a pathology than as a sign of progress.[12] The petitioners opposed the government reform, which was intended to spearhead a new political birth of the Hawaiian nation. They thus took sides with age-old custom and refused the personal independence now being prescribed. Their views were close to what the missionaries understood to be avoidance of responsibility: "There is a strong disposition in this people to throw off upon another those burdens and labors which they ought, for their own and their families' best interest, to assume themselves" (MH 42, 157). This was, of course, just another way to describe life in a hierarchic system in which status was attributed to a person who had other people to do his or her work. The missionaries shared the common view that the Hawaiian chiefship had been "a system of oppression" that "had for ages crushed and well nigh annihilated every vestige of manly independence" (MH 42, 420). A nation refused personal independence must be immature, hence naive, ignorant, and easily manipulated by foreign agents, hence politically incompetent.

While the commoner sentiment was barred from government circles, it was also deemed necessary to likewise prevent any missionary involvement "in the purely political concerns of the King's Government" (FOE, June 20, 1845). As the missionaries in the field were suspected of having helped natives prepare petitions, the *haole* ministers took action to prevent a partisan idea of politics from becoming a standard interpretation of Hawaiian commoners. This was a significant step because the missionaries in the field were able to create a conceptual bridge between traditional chiefly virtues and evangelical republicanism.[13] Thus there formed a great divide between the local affairs of the land and the state builders in Honolulu. This effectively split the mission, and the gate-

keepers—Judd, Wyllie, and Ricord, and also Richards—checked further dissemination of interpretive patterns that might give the commoner resistance
access to a comparative discourse of politics.

The government mouthpiece, *The Polynesian*, joined in by condemning attempts to interpret politically the commoner prayer meetings which had been
held prior to petitionings. The paper strongly opposed "giving a political turn to
private and public prayers" (*The Polynesian*, July 26, 1845). *The Polynesian* had in
fact excluded such possibility even before petitions began to flood the government offices. In January 1845, Jarves' column identified the opposition party as
consisting of individual foreigners without a unified platform of action. There
was to be no "formidable party of subjects [meaning common Hawaiians]" (*The
Polynesian*, Jan. 18, 1845).

In conclusion, the building of monarchy and the development of the comparative political discourse occurred simultaneously, forming an almost symbi-
otic relationship, for as the reform progressed, certain conceptual and culturally
standardized entities became more usable as interpretive patterns. Not that it
all would have been *haole* doings. The missionary disintegration was in fact mediated by a more significant Hawaiian disintegration. In the 1830s, the dynamics of Hawaiian society produced the royal rebellion and Christian revivalism,
exposing and releasing unexpected difficulties for chiefly rule, as well as for the
civilizing goals of the mission. The 1840s, in turn, saw the mission itself split in
response to these difficulties.

This split effectively aided the conceptual continuity of the political translation work rooted in the chiefly hierarchy, with the qualification that the
meanings of blessedness and comfort were blocked from entering the official
understanding of Hawaiian royal *aupuni* as a standard in comparative discourse.
In the short run, the attempt to create a Western type of political society from
above failed, because the same means that were used in achieving this goal were
simultaneously working against it. The system of *kālai'āina* was applied from top
to bottom without any attempt to heal deficiencies in the reciprocal relations
between the chiefs and the common people. Regulated working days, uncommon restrictions, and taxation in real money were all attempts to create new
connections between the chiefs and the commoners, the "regularity" necessary
for instituting political society. These attempts fell short of their objective,
while disregarding the traditional meaning of Hawaiian *aupuni* as the embodiment of *malu*. In time, this inability to reconcile the balance of give and take between chiefs and commoners, and the failure by the economizing white *ali'i* to
even appreciate such conceptions, were taken into the Hawaiian view of life as
resentments of things lost. Whether real or imagined matters little. Years later,

malu appeared again, but this time transformed to carry meanings closer to republican government than to Hawaiian ideals of chiefly "protection." In the Hawaiian language geography book compiled by Harvey Hitchcock Jr. in 1873, *aupuni* was defined as a democratic and benevolent order: *"Ua kohoia kekahi poe kanaka na lakou i ka oihana o ka hoomalu ana i ka lehulehu, a e imi aku i na alanui o ka naauao a me ka waiwai, kahi e holo ai ka lahui, a i oluolu hoi ko lakou noho ana"* (Some people are chosen by us for the task of governing [ho'omalu ana] the masses and to search for the road of wisdom and wealth along which the nation may go and to make their living comfortable) (p. 54).

Hitchcock's republican rendition of *malu* is hardly recognizable as Hawaiian *aupuni*, whose genius was never grounded in principles of personal autonomy and popular election. Rather, the security and comfort provided by the chief's *malu* was intimately tied to a person's duty to seek a chief and to "hold himself at the call of his chief" (unidentified missionary to Anderson, Oct. 13, 1835, MSL). The natives entertained this notion for some time. In the 1860s, Samuel Kamakau, disillusioned with Protestant ways, turned to Catholicism, which had already assumed an air of original Hawaiianness the Protestants in Honolulu could never match. Kamakau began to write articles on Hawaiian history for the major Hawaiian language newspapers. Occasionally he engaged in criticism which brought to light commoner sentiments so deeply buried beneath the practices and terminology of the monarchy. In May 1869, he was at his gloomiest and, although idealizing the past, was able to present a view of Hawaiian life that had been anticipated in the petitions a quarter of a century earlier:

> . . . in the old days people who lived in out-of-the-way places were heavily burdened by labor performed for the chiefs, landlords [haku 'āina], and land agents [konohiki]. But although the work was hard, that today is even more so when families are broken up and one must even leave his bones among foreigners. In the old days, the people did not work steadily at hard labor but at several years' interval, because it was easier then to get food from the fishponds, coconut groves, and taro patches. Hogs grew so fat that the eyelids drooped, bananas dropped off at a touch, sugarcane grew so tall that it leaned over, sweet potatoes crowded each hill, dogs fattened, fish cooked with hot stones in the early morning filled the food gourd, and a man could eat until he set the dish aside. This was the generous way of living under a chief who made a good lord; the people were fed and every wish of the chief was gratified. Labor done in the patch of the chief was a rental paid for the use of the land and everyone was benefited thereby. Today the working man labors like a cart-hauling ox that gets a kick in the buttocks. He shivers in the cold and dew-laden wind, or broils in the sun with no rest from his toil. Whether he lives or dies it is all alike. He gets a bit of money for his toil; in the house where

he labors there are no blood kin, no parents, no relatives-in-law, just a little corner for himself . . . (Kamakau 1992a, 372).

The laws that were drafted from 1838 to 1846 and beyond were intended to encourage common people to industry and self-reliance, and to realize the social conditions necessary for creating the political society of free equals. Instead, they produced a sentiment of reflective criticism of the workings of *aupuni*. But this sentiment, paradoxically, was interpreted as a disturbance of the order assumed by the chiefs to prevail in the state of *aupuni*, and by the *haole* ministers to prevail in an ordered body politic. It took decades for such disturbances to become integrated into the political conceptions of the Hawaiian monarchy as a pattern of explicit political activity, formally and cross-culturally comparable to those of the West. In the meantime, commoner demonstrations were seen as improper acts of resentment and loss of love for the chiefs. They were felt to originate in misunderstandings, or in foreign agitation, and were seen as unfit to be interpreted as organized politics. Or they were categorized as falling within *"ka oihana o na luna"* the business of the [government] officials, as politics was defined at the time (Emerson and Bishop 1845, 117). This prevented the concept of *kālai'āina* from becoming the formalized and general equivalent of perceiving politics as a universal phenomenon, which would have made itself visible in Hawaii as well as in foreign lands. We may end this discourse by quoting an anonymous poet, whose piece of lyric, missionary as he might have been, presents a negative image of the sentiment that went untranslated.

E imi i ka waiwai,	Seek wealth,
E pono ai oukou;	That you may be prosperous;
Ke dala me ka aina,	Money and land,
A me ka hale hou.	And a new house.
O ko ke kino keia,	These are material things,
E huli a loaa,	Seek until you find,
E malama no hoi,	Take care indeed,
E aua a hoopaa.	Hold back and secure them.
Ka makamaka ole,	The friendless one,
Oia ka pomaikai;	Is the prosperous one;
O lilo wale kona,	Lest his be lost completely,
Ke noi mai o hai.	When others request.
Heaha la ka hewa,	What indeed is the wrong,
Ke kapa mai lakou;	When they say;
He paakiki, he ino,	Hard, evil,
He pi, he aua no?	Miserly, stingy indeed?

Kokoke lakou ike,	They will soon know,
Ka make loa ka!	It is death!
Ka mai, ka hemahema:	Illness, infirmity:
Popilikia la!	True distress!
O ko Hawaii make,	Hawaii's demise,
Mamua o ko hai;	More than anything else;
Ka nele i ka waiwai,	Is the lack of wealth,
Ke hiki mai ka mai.	When illness appears.
E nana i ka hana,	Observe the actions,
(A hana like pu:)	(And work together too:)
O na haole imi waiwai,	The wealth-seeking foreigners,
Na kumu o kakou.	Are our teachers.
Noloko o ka nui,	From within the plenty,
Manawalea ai,	You will find beneficence,
I koe ko ke kino,	The material needs will remain,
Ke nui mai ka mai.	When illness is thriving.

(Ka Elele Hawaii, Dec. 22, 1848, my translation with Puakea Nogelmayer)

Conclusion

This study has been more than just an anthropology of Western political ideas as they were played out in the Kingdom of Hawaii. I have tried to go beyond a simple analysis of Western projections upon Hawaiian culture to explore how these projections were made part of the scene of culture contact, and what real impacts they had. In a study like this, our own conceptions of politics will eventually become a burden, and unwittingly blur the boundaries between us and Western observers of the nineteenth century. For this reason I have proposed a way to transcend the dichotomy between, on the one hand, abstract and universal conceptions of politics (or structural functionalism), and on the other, particularistic substantialism (or radical cultural relativism), which we often find in studies of politics at cultural encounters. My thesis has been that in culture contacts between Western and non-Western people, there can develop localized comparative discourses which reflect genuine cultural inventiveness of the parties involved. I have also suggested that the substance of culture, that is, the specific meanings available in contact situations, is embedded in the interacting notions through which cross-cultural conceptual innovation is channeled. Therefore, the degree of cross-cultural appropriation of concepts in the everyday has a direct bearing on the degree to which cultural boundaries are crossed.

Refusing to define politics a priori is a meaningful way to look at the history of the concept's formalization, as it takes place "in the field." With such an approach, we can avoid endlessly redefining our working concepts (e.g., politics, government), before we even begin looking for their particular appearances. If I take the spirit of his argument correctly, Nicholas Thomas (1994) has suggested a similar approach to the concept of "colonialism." Concepts such as this usually possess a folklore of their own, which tends to be overridden and ignored by abstract definitions from outside of the field. It is primarily for this reason that I chose to study the formation of a cross-cultural political discourse in the Kingdom of Hawaii during the missionization period. With the assistance of anthropological theories, I was able to detect and interpret the specific historical contexts relevant to the structuration process of political comparisons. We saw how these contexts became entangled in the process, and how resulting interpretative patterns gave new coherence to these same contexts. The result was what was known as "politics" and "government," and also, to a limited extent, mediation between the cultures.

In more concrete terms, the unique status that the Hawaiian chiefs afforded the Protestant mission between 1825 and 1839 colluded with interests and cultural notions of the white trading community, and through some key concepts—namely church and state—elevated the concept of politics to the center of foreigners' intercourse with the mission. While the chiefship was objectified in political terms, as a result of intense missionizing, and while everything was at the same time effectively controlled by the chiefs, the emerging political discourse became an essential part of the foreigners' perspectives. However, this discourse did not directly involve Hawaiians, who participated mostly using indigenous concepts. These were mediated through the same group of people who gave the decisive impulse to this same controversial political discourse—the missionaries. In the second phase of our chronology, the mission began to lose its influence, which had been considerable to that point. This was most evident in the collapse of the mission school system, which had previously covered nearly every inhabited corner of the islands, and had made the word of God the daily bread of thousands of Hawaiians. The collapse had a deeply disillusioning effect on the missionaries, whose attentions were redirected to what they identified, using their own cultural notions and social theories, as the Hawaiian political system.

The missionaries were able to make sense of the defects of the Hawaiian polity by resorting to a familiar although rapidly weakening political theory that was based on the idea of covenant—a morally binding relationship between the members of a polity. As bearers of this theory, the missionaries represented Hawaiian chiefship—identified by them as political society—as disfigured and perverted. The perversion itself was engendered by an unhealthy condition in the Hawaiian version of natural society, which was seen to be morally defective, and discouraging of individual enterprise and autonomy. It was a shock to the representatives of the religion of the "strange white men" that the Hawaiians so effortlessly captured the word of God, while scarcely recognizing its "democratic spirit."

Because the Hawaiian system was judged defective, and was accused of causing the major civilizing apparatus to break down, it was felt that a change of a political kind had to be induced. But, more importantly, the missionaries felt that their own identity as religious messengers was being threatened by chiefly "politics." The chiefs effectively appropriated the new religion and received it through their own cultural idioms, and after becoming fully aware of this the missionaries launched a new plan to reformulate the heathen system of governance so as to avoid being again swallowed by it. Thus, in theoretical as well as cultural terms, the beginning of Hawaiian politics can be properly located in the conflicting positions of the main groups of actors, and their reciprocal cultural appropriations of each others' ideas and actions. All this resulted in the missionaries acquiring a growing knowledge of the cultural logic of the Hawaiian society, including its "politics," and their concomitant need to recontextualize Hawaiian reality. They did so in ways that involved fundamental questions concerning the nature of human character as an autonomous, yet social being.

In the final stage of our narrative, the universalizing frame of the international community of nations and governments was made to embrace also the Hawaiian chiefdom, which was itself speedily absorbing the signs of a European-inspired monarchy. After this recontextualization, there developed some formalized comparative knowledge between Hawaiians and foreigners. Yet, the organizing term was "government" rather than "politics." This was mainly because the involvement of some of the missionaries in the Hawaiian state-building project resulted in the alienation of the very people—the missionaries in the field—who were best placed to translate the prevailing popular Hawaiian sentiment into a political language that would have some cross-cultural significance and standardizing power.

As a result, by 1845 the cross-cultural comparative discourse had been codified by fusing together the notions of *aupuni* and government, and the various practices belonging to each. In fact, the sphere of equivalents was restricted to the highest echelons of society. An all-important feature in this process was the readjustment of the Hawaiian historical consciousness regarding the necessity of change, and the discard—or rather reformulation—of the old ways. By combining biblical ideas and Hawaiian traditions, several key Hawaiians, together with the missionaries, constructed a discontinuity in the Hawaiian history. Simultaneously, they evoked a return to the common origin of nations, a new continuity with the histories of foreign lands. Sadly, this also opened the gates for *haole* co-rulers and made the accumulation of government revenue a project larger than life itself. A common universe of *aupuni* was thus created, a hybrid notion which even today lives on as a tension between "the way of the land" and "the way of the chiefs." This tension has been quite literally carved into the land. Ka'ū, the southern tip of the island of Hawai'i, and Wai'anae, the south-west coast of O'ahu, are examples of places that share a long history of Hawaiian nativism and resistance against the foreigners in Honolulu, places where Catholi-cism found refuge already in the 1820s and 1830s as a major source for inverting authority. Similar places of cultural refuge can still be found there today. The vi-tality of this tradition today is signaled by the fact that most native Hawaiians cling to the Catholic Church, and today the Catholic Church is ten times the size of the original church brought by the ABCFM missionaries.

These observations about the present have theoretical relevance, because they tell us about structural constraints that prevented fuller use of the poten-tialities of cultural translation in the field of politics, something that would have resulted in a comparative discourse that extended beyond government bureau-cracy. Whatever the common Hawaiians did, the gatekeepers in the Hawaiian government would not treat them as a political entity.

On several occasions I have examined the concrete experiences and sense-making patterns of the people involved in this history of political discourse and its translation. I have tried to present post-contact Hawaiian society as a context that was ever-present, but determinant only to a point of facilitating the selective use of some already existing interpretative patterns, such as the Hawaiian con-ception of *aupuni*. In other words, the argument is contextual in that contextual circumstances directed the use of available cultural tools, all of which were "there," but only some of which were applied. A good example is the missionar-ies' rising awareness of having been used by the traditional Hawaiian rulers. The use of certain cultural tools, mainly the notion of the autonomous citizen, con-tributed to the development of a new context—the monarchy—that then pro-ceeded to modify the use of the same tools, and even to prevent their more extensive use. We have seen this in the ways common Hawaiians were repre-sented politically (i.e., monarchy vs. republicanism). From this emerges a theo-retical formula: Context is not external to social action.

This was visible when the concept of politics first appeared on the multicul-tural scene of Honolulu and Lahaina between 1825 and 1827. The concept was mediated by conflicting Hawaiian structures: first prostitution and Christian tabus, and second the authoritative position of the missionaries and the presence of sex-starved sailors. Prostitution was first transformed into an issue of the inde-pendence of chiefly authority, then into one of regulating relations between church and state, and finally into a typical political language of the liberal state. The discourse that formed was not all-determining. It was relatively confined to the intercourse between missionaries, sea captains, and traders. The chiefs inter-preted these events as they were used to doing: "It is for us to decide."

We can now better appreciate the need to understand the cultural logic on both sides of this contact, notwithstanding the centrality of events in concrete situations. For it is through events that the systems may begin to penetrate each other. In this respect, the foregoing history of politics as an experienced concept may have been too uniform. As Dening, Sahlins, and Thomas have proposed, the foreign presence in Hawaii and elsewhere in Polynesia was localized and outside of its own normal context. This naturally demands that more attention be paid to the indigenous cultural systems and how they encompass the foreign elements as events. Nevertheless, one has to understand both sides, each as whole cultural systems, in order to see how the scattered foreign elements interacted with the more fully present native ones, and in order to evaluate the structures of fused notions.

Thus the mediated events constitute the terrain for transcending the question: "Did Hawaiians have politics?" And yet, it may be untimely to jettison this question as altogether futile and misleading. Let us consider the alternatives. There are two basic directions we can take. We could take the question at its face value and try to clear our investigative path of all misrepresentations and ideological debris, and reach the immaculate bottom of the issue à la Clastres (1977). Alternatively, we can study the question itself, in all its historicity. The first alternative always presumes at least an implicit idea of politics, toward which the research process is constantly leading. Otherwise we would have very little to discover; the research process would never undertake to find anything but its own ontological or, if you will, cultural roots. The second alternative, the one I have been pursuing, consists of a conscious effort to reconstruct the historical path that leads to the contextually specific question of the existence of politics. It leads to a cultural motive to claim that politics is part of the observed reality. In this latter sense we can answer the question, "Did Hawaiians have politics?" with a "yes," while avoiding the hermeneutical dilemma of unconsciously imposing an idea of what politics is. Hawaiians did have politics, but the fact of their having it is itself a construction that became reality, indeed an invention, but genuine and meaningful, and hence effective.

In writing this book I have many times thought about this effectiveness and its manifestations today. For example, in 1996 a group of Hawaiian activists reestablished Hui Kālai'āina, the Hawaiian party that was originally founded in 1888. On the party's homepage was written that the Hawaiian name Hui Kālai'āina "literally" means political party (http://members.xoom.com/HUIKALAIAINA, Sept. 3, 2001). This is another indication of the strength with which Hawaiians have symbolically taken over foreigners' meanings and now use them creatively. It is true that kālai'āina had different meanings when the Hawaiian kingdom was being molded to suit the mid-nineteenth-century international order. But, as then, today's activists will find ways to Hawaiianize politics, or to politicize Hawaiianness.

Indeed, it is not just that Hawaiian concepts are used in recontextualizing foreign notions. An interesting anecdote is found in the revised edition of Samuel M. Kamakau's *Ruling Chiefs of Hawaii* (1992a). In the book, the Hawaiian god Kū, who is usually associated with conquest and human presence in general, is described also as the god of politics. The caption below a photograph of a wooden (*'ōhi'a*) image of Kū says "god of war and politics." Compared to the first edition (1961), Kū has now acquired new political dimension besides the old function of the war god. A more recent on-line publication by the Hawaiian artist and writer Herb Kāne says of the *luakini* temple that it was "dedicated to Ku as patron of politics and warfare" (Kāne 1997, chapter on religion). We could easily dismiss this new epithet of Kū as being an insignificant and accidental choice, were it not at the same time a link to a more distant cultural practice. Remember what the missionary Hiram Bingham said about the nature of traditional Hawaiian politics: "the change of government, the war, as they call it" (Bingham to Worcester, May 13, 1820, HP/HMCS). In spite of himself, Bingham was our contemporary, a relativist who understood that politics was present in conjunctions not readily available to the natives of his own country. Not that he would have approved these anomalies of hiding politics under the cloak of religion, "the policy of the chiefs." The point is, rather, that he was able to perceive the difference, and yet give it an intelligible twist in his own terminology, exactly what an anthropologist or a political scientist would do now, almost two hundred years later.

If Bingham could do this, then native Hawaiians were surely able to seize a notion from *his* cultural stock and invest it with local meanings, and a century and half later expand the scope of the idea of politics to include a god. Of course, the West has provided little help; throughout the Christian world, God has been called upon to bless arms and protect against the enemy. In Hawaii, this was relived as early as 1824 when a nativist rebellion of Kaua'i was crushed by troops blessed by Jehovah. Or, consider another recent event relating to the re-publication of Kamakau's historical writings in the original Hawaiian, their first appearance since their being printed in two Hawaiian language newspapers in the 1860s. The editors entitled the book *Ke Kumu Aupuni* (Kamakau 1996), and on the occasion of its publication it was given an English translation "The Foundation of Nationhood" (*Honolulu Star-Bulletin*, June 10, 1997). This was an intimation that *aupuni* can acquire meanings not directly linked to "government," but inspired by a combination of the needs of the present and sentiments that were repressed in the 1840s, but have been revived from time to time ever since.

Equally familiar, yet more elaborate continuities can be found in our own contemporary scholarship. If some of the American missionaries saw political activism in the native petition movement in 1845, so did Sahlins in his analysis of the secularization of the commoner resistance (1992, 127). It is as if Sahlins would have taken the side of the missionary Dwight Baldwin, whose sermons in Lahaina inspired common Hawaiians to openly express their resentments to their chiefs. And if we could bring James Jarves or John Ricord back to life, they would certainly engage in debate with Sahlins, and warn against him and all those who were too eager to see politics in religious meetings. Baldwin, not unlike Sahlins, was a cultural relativist who might have agreed with Sahlins that, "if the movements sometimes took idiomatic forms unfamiliar to Western conceptions of politics, as in the Great Awakening of 1837–39, this too was testimony to the indigenous character of the revendications" (1992, 126). It seems that whatever was the appearance of resistance, politics it was after all. Paradoxically, it leads to the same conclusion as R. H. Barnes' idea that politics, as well as economics and kinship, among other things, belong to the group of anthropological topics that, due to their *commonsensical* nature, are less exposed to difficulties of comparison than metaphysical categories, like experience of time (1987, 129). Whether we take Sahlins' or Barnes' argument as our foundation, the outcomes will strangely resemble each other. We have a diverse series of political structures and meanings, which would nevertheless be all part of the more abstract and universal category of politics, either by its commonsensical nature or by means of discovering politics beneath less familiar (not part of "common sense") modes of behavior

True, for the West a fair amount of disenchantment is a far more reliable sign of politics than, say, religious revivals. In the West political leaders were, and still are, expected to possess a somewhat secularized identity if they wished to be treated as rational creatures at all (a status which the post-Ka'ahumanu chiefs in particular were acquiring under missionary "tutelage"). This means that a person acting politically is supposed to have an interest, and if it were shown to all the world it would appear naked and defenseless, and so should be hidden. In a completely rational world, which Jarves and Ricord among others imagined for the new era in Hawaii, politics would be an independent field, without need of support from any other field of human activity, most especially religion. But even Jarves and Ricord knew that sometimes a rational political persuasion must be couched in legitimating language, mythical, religious, or what have you.

To return to Bingham, his apparently relativistic views on Hawaiian politics were accompanied by a typically modern Western idea of ideological deception, an assumption that power manifests itself in pure forms beneath mystification. If Bingham was prone to describe the native Hawaiian religion "as an engine of government" (Bingham to Worcester, May 13, 1820, HP/ HMCS), and equally reluctant to say the same thing about his Protestant faith, so we find among modern commentators those who think that traditional chiefly rule was in need of an ideological justification, an engine of government, so to speak. Valeri, for example, sees the real business of politics in the Hawaiian chiefship as having been legitimated culturally by invocation of a ritual senti- ment, which was then relived in everyday life. According to Valeri "ritual pro- duces social order by producing conceptual order—sense" (1985b, xi). But Valeri also argues that this conceptual reproduction of society entails a "sup- pression of aspects of reality" (xi), something expressed as a problem of legiti- mizing "the nobility's rule" (xii).

This is not a new tendency in Hawaiian cultural studies. For example, Martha Beckwith, in her well-informed introduction to Kumulipo chant, points out "the social and political importance" of genealogical chants, which they owe to their "conventional acceptance" among the Hawaiians (Beckwith 1990 [1951], 30). Similarly, twenty years later, Katharine Luomala, in the preface to Beckwith's translation of Kumulipo, maintains that the chiefs in their "political bid for power" were "*using* ancient cosmogonic beliefs" (Luomala 1990, vxiii, my emphasis). More recently Linnekin seems to argue that the cosmological meaning of genealogies could always be used "as a pretext for politically moti- vated action" (Linnekin 1990b, 102). True, but we could ask why should the motive be split into politics and culture, because the cultural motive for the chiefs to be "the life here on earth" was certainly enough to explain the motive. This explanation tends toward essentializing the cultural motive as a more gen- uine practice of status, and the political motive as somewhat more self-conscious and corrupt, and hence allowing the idea of spurious culture creep in.

Some other authors were anxious to seek evidence of the crumbling ritual order and its manipulation by self-conscious chiefs, the "engineers" of govern- ment. Handy's popularized "Government and Society" (1933) ends with a celebration of Kamehameha's extraordinary personality and skill as an inde- pendent chief, the irony of which is that few pages earlier he had explained in plain language the divine nature of Hawaiian chiefship. As the first historically recorded chief who ruled over all the islands Kamehameha provides, of course, a more than adequate object for Western political thinking, which emphasizes individual action independent of all ritual constraints (see Valeri 1985b, 144– 145), with earlier chiefs having been mediated through oral traditions and em- bedded in myth. Thus the ritual process is that of mystifying power, not far from the "average Western common sense" (Sahlins 1999, 407).

In Valeri's analysis there is a recognized yet unsatisfied need to bring politics and culture more closely together so that culture will not appear so easily as a legitimizing asset (which it can occasionally become). The mystifying aspect of ritual cannot be understood without considering the sense through which power is comprehended by the rulers and the ruled. Valeri calls this "dialectics of sense and mystification" (1985b, xii). His emphasis on the analysis of conceptual conditioning of experience (see 1985b, 347) is thus undermined by "mystification," or what could be called a functionalist obsession with the latent function of value integration, which is logically but not ideologically close to the concept of false consciousness. The analysis is necessarily functionalist because it cannot assure the modern reader that cultural notions were used intentionally by Hawaiians as pretext for real politics. But if Hawaiians acted culturally, why is there this need to use culture as an explanation of political action that is conditioned by the very same culture? I think this uneasy proposition is made possible only by introducing the concept of politics initially into analysis, and then adding "the sense" (after realizing that the otherwise lonely and raw concept of politics is resistant to the all-encompassing hold of culture, and therefore needs an explanation). The problem with the theory is that the sense does not eliminate the disturbing concept of politics, which will not cease to demand explanation unless we add a mystifying function to sense.[1]

These and many other modern commentators who conceptualize Hawaiian chiefship in terms of politics and culture tend to identify the political, in the hierarchical continuum of chiefs and commoners, with self-interested action, as the political constant of human societies, and make self-interest a corollary of the material organization of society. The particular problem with this idea is not so much its occasional emphasis on self-interest, which undoubtedly exists in unlimited forms. Rather it lies in depicting self-interest analytically as separate from cultural categories, which are supposed to be used to giving self-interest generally acceptable sense. For example, Johnson and Earle write that if research cannot reveal adequate material reasons for war, it must have been a result of "political competition" (1987, 232; see also Earle 1991), the political being a label for the will to power which only needs a cultural mantle to hide its utilitarian drive. In this approach, the material remains the sphere of real relations of power, thus politics, and the cultural is reduced to the role of masking the materiality of power. At best, material and cultural elements are seen as mutually related, but only to the effect that the fundamental conceptual division of labor between them remains intact.

These remarks are not intended to ridicule some of our finest historical anthropology, but instead to remind the reader of the highly problematical nature of the concept of politics, and its heavy load of Western folklore which, as Sahlins himself has pointed out, deserves an anthropology all its own (Sahlins 1996). This study has been an attempt to provide something of that kind. Keeping this motive in mind, I think my suspicious attitude toward any casual use of the concept of politics in cultural encounters, and these musings over the continuities of rather old political thought, will be perhaps tolerated.

Appendix

List of Consulted Hawaiian Language Dictionaries and Vocabularies

The several Hawaiian language dictionaries and vocabularies that have survived either as published volumes or archival items were an indispensable source in my search for the translations of Western political concepts into Hawaiian. The method used in this search was a simple one. I worked backwards from later dictionaries and vocabularies until no trace of the word under inspection was found. The reporting is done in a reversed order. In all cases, the word was first looked up in the European language section, and after that the corresponding entry in the Hawaiian section was checked. The order of the word check was thus: European language → Hawaiian → European language, wherever this was applicable (some dictionaries and vocabularies have only Hawaiian entries).

In this appendix is presented as complete a listing as I have been able to draw of the different vocabularies and dictionaries of the Hawaiian language. I have also included manuscripts that are known to have existed but are now apparently lost. The directions of entries in the published works containing more than 4,000 words, and which can be properly called dictionaries, are footnoted.

I assume that the following list is nearly complete in terms of the information we have at our disposal today, but this does not exclude the possibility that some works have been unknowingly omitted. I have modified a similar but shorter listing by Elbert (1954). Like his, mine does not include Catholic sources. The Catholic missionaries prepared several short grammars, language studies, and vocabularies in manuscript, and in 1834 they printed a grammar that also contained a vocabulary of some two thousand words. These works were probably shipped to Rome when the Catholic mission became a diocese in 1941 (Yzendoorn 1927; Catholic Church, n.d.).

Date of Publication	Probable Date of Compilation	Author	Nationality
1784	1778	Anderson (with Cook)	British
1955	1778	Samwell	British
1789	1787	Dixon	British
1822	1791	Quimper	Spanish and American
1812, 1814	1804	Lisiansky	British
Not published, lost	before 1818	'Ōpūkaha'ia	Hawaiian
1822	1819	Arago	French
Unpublished, lost	1824	Loomis	American
Unpublished	1825	Bloxam	British
1825	1822–1824	Bishop and Ellis	American and British
Unpublished	before 1826	Whitney	American
1841	1828	Botta	Italian
Unpublished	1828	Bishop	American
1834	1828–1831	Bachelot	French
Unpublished	1832	Bingham	American
1834	1834	Dumont d'Urville	French
Unpublished	before 1836	Macintosh	American
Unpublished	1834	Andrews	American
1836	1834–1836	Andrews	American[a]
1843	1843	Mosblech	French[b]
1845	1845	Emerson and Bishop	American[c]
Unpublished, lost	before 1847	Richards	American
1854	1854	Bishop	American
Unpublished	1852–1855	Remy	French
Unpublished, lost	before 1865	Baldwin	American
Unpublished, lost	before 1865	Bishop	American
Unpublished, lost	before 1865	Judd	American
Unpublished	1843–1846	Kamakau	Hawaiian
1865	1836–1865	Andrews	American[d]
1887	1882–1887	Hitchcock	American[c]
1890	1890	Fukuoka and Taki	Japanese
1922	1915–1922	Andrews and Parker	American[a]
1936	1936	Hawaiian Language League	Hawaiian and American
1938	1938	Shaw	American
1939	1939	Judd	American
1945	1945	Judd, Pukui, and Stokes	Hawaiian and American[e]
1957	1949–1957[f]	Pukui and Elbert	Hawaiian and American[a]
1964	1957–1964	Pukui and Eblert	Hawaiian and American[c]
1965	1957–1965	Pukui and Elbert	Hawaiian and American[a]
1971	1965–1970	Pukui and Elbert	Hawaiian and American[e]
1985	1972–1984	Pukui and Elbert	Hawaiian and American[e]

[a] Hawaiian-English.

[b] Marquesan-Hawaiian-French and French-Marquesan-Hawaiian.

[c] English-Hawaiian.

[d] Hawaiian-English with an English finding list.

[e] Hawaiian-English and English-Hawaiian.

[f] The following years are only suggestive, reflecting the ongoing work of Elbert and Pukui.

Notes

Introduction

1. I have deliberately avoided making a distinction between culture and tradition. Both are historical, yet tradition can be used in a more narrow sense of an explicitly formulated connection with the past and objectification of aspects of culture, whereas culture as a theoretical concept involves also all subconscious and routine relations with the past. However, such distinctions are not relevant to the present argument.

2. Recently three valuable projects have made much of this material more accessible: the publication of a good selection of Kamakau's newspaper series from the 1860s by the 'Ahahui 'Ōlelo Hawai'i (Kamakau 1996), and the on-line projects at the Bishop Museum (The Hawaiian Language Newspaper Index Project) and the University of Hawai'i Libraries (digitalization of Hawaiian newspapers on microfilm).

Chapter 1: Natives and Foreigners

1. A good summary description of the situation in 1818 can be found in the text of the Russian circumnavigator Vasilii M. Golovnin. Besides giving a brief sketch of Hawaii as a stopover and wintering place for northwest coast traders, he also relates some details on the early residents:

> Such frequent and lengthy visits of foreign ships soon acquainted the Sandwich Islanders with the use of many European objects and even with the customs of civilized nations. This process was accelerated greatly by the strong desire of the present ruler [Kamehameha] to enlighten his people. By his honest and fair dealings with the Europeans [Golovnin specifically notes that by Europeans he means mostly Americans] and by his kindness to them he attracted many sailors from the trading ships and even some artisans who settled among the Sandwich Islanders and married native island girls. At the time of Vancouver's visit here (1791–1794)

the King [Kamehameha] already had about eleven Europeans in his service, while now there are about 150 of them in the Islands, among whom are ship builders, locksmiths, boiler makers, joiners and many carpenters and blacksmiths (Golovnin 1974, 28, see also 61; for a description of the wandering type, see e.g., Golovnin 1974, 55; Campbell 1967, 119; Cox 1957, 33; Ross 1849, 46–47).

2. An early historical example is Ka'iana, the nephew of Kalani'ōpu'u and a warrior who in 1787 sailed with Captain John Meares to China and the northwest coast of America, and returned home several months later bearing muskets. Two years later, Captains John Kendrick and Robert Gray took onboard a chief's son "Atto" (his name was probably Kū), and another Hawaiian named Kalehua, both of whom then visited America in 1790 (Ingraham 1918, 2, 8, 12). Kalehua returned to Hawaii in May 1791, and acted as an interpreter for Vancouver because Ka'iana, for some reason appeared to have lost his knowledge of English (Manby 1929, 15–16; Vancouver 1984, 447, 449–451, 476). In February 1793, Vancouver's crew met yet another Hawaiian, Kualelo, who had visited England and returned home the previous year. This man had used his experience of foreign lands as an effective means to enhance his commoner status. He had been given land by Kamehameha, and by marrying a high-ranking woman had gotten still more (Menzies in Vancouver 1984, 810).

To give even a close approximation of the number of the early post-contact Hawaiian sailors and adventurers is impossible, but evidently dozens, perhaps hundreds of young Hawaiians, both male and female, took a passage to Kahiki during the thirty-six years between 1787 and 1823. During this period some two hundred Hawaiians were recorded as absentees, mainly recruited by whalers (Schmitt 1968, 175, 182). Some Hawaiians became minor sensations, like a certain Kānehoa who, before returning to Hawaii in 1817, spent eight years in Russia receiving basic Western education and a Russian Orthodox baptism (Barratt 1988, 344–345). No systematic effort to teach Hawaiians was attempted, however, before the organization of the Foreign Mission School in Cornwall, Connecticut, in 1816. Between 1816 and 1832 the Sandwich Islands Mission educated and brought back to Hawaii eleven native men (compiled from The Missionary Album, 1969). The most triumphant of these early voyages took place in 1823, when high chief Liholiho with some other chiefs and attendants sailed to England hoping to materialize the symbolic alliance between the British crown and Hawaii.

3. In the translation I have followed Fornander (1916–1920, vol. 4, 374), with minor alterations. A shorter passage of the same part of the Kūali'i chant is also reproduced by Kamakau (1991b, 115–116). In the Kamakau version the original Hawaiian is slightly different at times, as is the translation, but I think it unnecessary to mix the two versions or to offer alternative wordings. I have followed Kamakau in one respect, namely by spelling Fornander's Tahiti with the initial K to emphasize the difference between the island of Tahiti and the mythical homeland of Kahiki. I have also added modern diacritical markers to the original Hawaiian.

4. The dawn in the chant of Kūaliʻi designates social order, besides being a metaphor for human ascendancy. Thus, night represents the pre-human era but also the state of society without order. Kamehameha's advancing conquest, for example, was compared to the passing of night and the dawning of day:

ʻO ʻoe ia e Kalani nui Mehameha,	You, O heavenly chief, Ka-mehameha,
E hea aku ana i ka ʻiwa kīlou moku la,	great warrior, hero who hooked the islands together,
E ko-mo! ʻAʻole i wehewehena, ʻaʻole i waihona kona pō,	you we greet in welcome: "Come in!" Dawn has not begun to break, night has not departed,
O ka hōʻā keia e—.	torches still burn.

(Pukui and Korn 1988, 10–11)

5. This is also reflected in forms of worship, the common name of which is *hoʻomana*, that is, "to cause one to have *mana*, to empower" (Valeri 1985a, 89). Thus gods' ability to empower people was made dependent upon people worshiping gods. It is telling that when the abolition of the Hawaiian tabu system was at hand in the fall of 1819, the decisive step was first taken by one of the few truly high-ranking chiefs, Keōpūolani, mother of the high chief Liholiho who then ruled all the islands. Referring to the high chief Kamehameha, who had died the previous May, Keōpūolani said: "He who guarded the god is dead and it is right that we should eat together freely." [The eating tabu which separated men and women at meals, and forbade women some foods, was made to symbolize the entire system of tabus.] (Kamakau 1992a, 224).

Relating to this, the English missionary William Ellis, who traveled around Hawaiʻi island in 1823, tells an interesting story. According to the natives of Kona, Hawaiʻi, Kamehameha's war god Kāʻili (short for Kūkāʻilimoku) used to be seen flying about near his temple in the form of a fireball. Ellis was keen to explain the natural cause of such a phenomenon and, after giving the explanation, he asked the natives if they saw the same fireballs even though the worship had been discontinued and the image destroyed. Their answer was firmly negative (Ellis 1979, 75).

6. The alliances between chiefs and commoners and high chiefs and lesser chiefs were all part of this logic of genealogically mediated *mana*. The system gave Hawaiian society a certain fluidity, and led to constant evaluations of the usefulness of current commitments, because of the potential of enhancing one's *mana* either through usurpation or re-alliance. The practice of *ʻimihaku*, or the search for the lord, was the manifest essence of alliance formation, and generated instability in chiefly dynasties. The *mana* was in perpetual flux, due in part to the pattern of *ʻimihaku* itself.

7. For a description of this rite I have consulted ʻĪʻī's and Samuel Kamakau's

accounts (Ii 1983, 37–38, 43–44; Kamakau 1992b, 142–144). The best available analysis is undoubtedly that of Valeri (1985b, 326–327), who cites other primary sources that describe *hono*.

8. Traditionally, Lono's possession of the land was only temporary. The myth describes Lono as a late-coming god, who after a stormy marriage in Hawaii returned to Kahiki, from which he promised to come back again. The story was incorporated—perhaps a post-Cook event—into the *makahiki*, at the end of which the fertility god was ritually defeated by the high chief and sent back to Kahiki. Lono's departure marked also the opening of the temples of Kū (Ii 1983, 72; Malo 1991, 150–152; Beckwith 1989, 31–41; Sahlins 1981, 17–28; 1985, 209–214; 1989; Valeri 1985b, 214–215).

9. There is some evidence also from the later contact period that the chief's person remained sacred and subject to great care. Sometime between 1838 and 1842, King Kamehameha III's secretary Timoteo Ha'alilio wrote a troubled letter to the governor of O'ahu, Mataio Kekūanaō'a. He asked the governor to send soldiers to guard the king's residence on O'ahu, and issued a list of persons who were allowed to come and go freely without being stopped by the soldiers. Just a few moments earlier a foreigner had come into the house while the king and his closest men were eating. The unobstructed entrée of the foreigner caused much alarm and agitation among the Hawaiian nobility. According to Ha'alilio, "ua kokoke mai ka make, death was near." The "fencing" of the house had failed, which was the reason for Ha'alilio's troubles, since he and Kekūanaō'a were the hosts for the occasion (NDOC/164; see Greer 1991, 97).

10. In 'Ī'ī's account there were four fronds, while Kamakau notes only two. It seems likely that the former is correct, four being a sacred number. Unlike Kamakau's account, 'Ī'ī's is based on personal experience.

11. It is said that a form of Kū, Kūho'one'enu'u, was represented by a tree brought from Kahiki by Haumea, to whom this tree was given by 'Olopana's daughter Mulei'ula as a reward for her help in delivering Mulei'ula's child (Kamakau 1991b, 6–8).

12. The word *ulele* is rendered '*alele* in the Kamakau version, meaning "messenger" (another version of '*elele*). Apparently the two versions have been mixed, because the Fornander version gives the translation "messenger" for *ulele*, which literally means "to leap at, get into action, do quickly, do at once; one moving swiftly" (Pukui and Elbert 1986, 368).

13. It may be added that at the end of the *makahiki* ritual Lono was addressed as Lononuiākea (K. Kamakau in Fornander 1916–1920, vol. 6, 44–45).

14. The terms *haole* and Kahiki were sometimes interchangeable, as the Hawaiian words for Irish potato (*uala kahiki*) and tomato ('*ōhi'a haole*) indicate.

15. When the intercourse with foreigners and Hawaiians became a matter of everyday life, and Hawaii was firmly connected to the outside world, Kahiki as an expression and category gradually shifted to the background and acquired meanings that were at once more narrow (Tahiti or any of the southern groups) and clearly legendary (great migrations). In official correspondence, the phrase '*āina 'ē* (other lands,

i.e., lands elsewhere) had largely replaced Kahiki by the 1840s. For instance, when King Kamehameha III appointed ex-missionary Gerrit Judd the minister of foreign affairs, this expression was used (FOE., Nov. 2, 1843). Kahiki was replaced also in more quotidian talk. When the widow of the King Kamehameha IV, Queen Emma, set out for her trip to Europe in the 1860s, she was said to go to *'āina 'ē*, not to Kahiki (*Ke Au Okoa*, May 8, 1865). Kahiki did not disappear completely, however: *"He nui na keiki kane i makemake e holo i kahiki,"* many young boys wanted to go abroad, reported a newspaper (*Ke Alaula*, Nov. 1866). In poetic contexts, Kahiki was also widely used: *"Make i Tahiti* [Kahiki], *i ka aina polikua a Kane,"* he died in Kahiki, the invisible land of Kāne [one of the major gods who came from Kahiki], was said in a lament for Timothy Ha'alilio, the Hawaiian ambassador who died at sea on his way home from Europe and America (*Ka Elele Hawaii*, Oct. 21, 1845).

16. As we shall see, there was a significant, crafted continuity between the old indigenous tabu observances and the nineteenth-century biblical tradition, the old tabus being a sign of godliness and regard for gods, which was seen as a virtue much in line with the virtues of Christian worship. Kamakau, for example, compares those who were careless in observing tabus to unbelievers in the Old Testament. In their own specific ways, each was supposed to have been foolish (Kamakau 1992b, 64).

17. In reverence to the ancient wisdom, Kamehameha left the *aupuni* to his son Liholiho, but his war god, Kūkā'ilimoku, to his nephew, Kekuaokalani. The cycle of ruling and usurping was thus built into the inheritance as a structural condition, which Kamehameha's other relatives well knew. To eliminate the possibility of history repeating itself, the ruling chiefs stripped their gods of divine potency—with well-known consequences. In the ensuing war in December 1819, Kekuaokalani and his followers were defeated (Gast and Conrad 1973, 235–236) and the *aupuni* was left standing without its traditional rival, the younger sibling armed with the government-snatching god.

18. Besides these explicit orders, there were rumors, like one circulating in March 1793. According to Vancouver, the Maui paramount Kahekili was rumored to have threatened to kill all white men in his territory (Vancouver 1984, 875). Similarly, Liholiho's cousin and main rival after Kamehameha's death, Kekuaokalani, was alleged to have said he would kill all whites settled in the islands once he had defeated Liholiho (Freycinet 1978, 20; for similar incidents in 1813 and 1818, see Hunnewell 1909, 15, and Reynolds 1938, 146, respectively). These rumors followed a pattern, which reflected, beyond simple fear or inherent jealousy, different chiefs' strategies for appropriating foreign manufactures and know-how; death threats were habitually issued by chiefs who had failed to establish a close mercantile and military alliance with the foreigners.

19. Although known by the scholars for decades, the essential part played by the native helpers and Tahitians associated with Hawaiian chiefs still waits for an in-depth study (Kuykendall 1989 [1938], 103; Barrère and Sahlins 1979, 23; Barrère 1969, 77; Kame'eleihiwa 1992, 143–144; Sahlins 1992, 89, fn. 16, 91). Tahitians

were particularly instrumental in explaining to the Hawaiian chiefs what radical changes had taken place in the Christianized Society Islands (Tyerman and Bennet 1831, 399, 401–403, 407, 418–419, 470, 481–486). Likewise, one should not underestimate the influence of the spiritual father (*ora matua*) of the Tahitian converts, the English missionary William Ellis. He was the first Western priest to conduct a Christian sermon for the Hawaiian chiefs in a comprehensible manner, as he was fluent in Tahitian, which was quite well understood by Hawaiians. This historical event took place on April 17, 1822 (Tyerman and Bennet 1831, 416–417).

20. To give an idea of the method of combining elements of Christian doctrine and ritual with technical know-how in literacy, let me quote the missionaries' joint description of a public examination held in Honolulu on January 9, 1823. Note also the presence of the Hawaiian and Tahitian helpers and the organization of schools. All this is shrouded in the naive innocence so typical of the missionary writings in the early 1820s:

> On the 9inst. [ninth moment of the day] we had examinations of our schools at this place which now comprize [sic] more than 200 pupils, most of whom appeared in decent order at the chapel, with a good number of spectators— Br. T[hurston]. conducted the examination—which was in our view more flattering than any former one which we had.—Not less than 12 Chiefs & Chiefses [sic] including the favorite queen Kamamalu, & her sister Kinau— the king's [Liholiho's] brother Kauikioule [Kauikeaouli] & his sister Nahie- naena & Opiia [Pi'ia] one of the wives of the late king [Kamehameha]—with her present husband Laanui, bore an interesting part of the examination; nor was the king's copy-book with its fair, neat pages, & his communication before alluded to, which was read to the assembly, less interesting.—The assistant teachers, Honorii [Honoli'i], Auna the Tahitien, James Kahuhu, Kanae & Taumi [Kaomi] appeared at the head of their respective schools and assisted in the examination—The two latter, with *Abner Morse* read original compo- sitions—The queen recited about half of Watt's catechism, Kahuhu read with fluency a passage from the Bible, Kapiolani the wife of Naihu [Nāihe] & Tuhio their friends presented their first essays in composition, & Naihu with simplicity handed in a declaration written by his own hand, containing four words—'Aroha au ia Tehova'—*I love the Lord*.—Opiia exhibited fair hand writing with many others—Honorii gave an address to the pupils, & Br. T. closed the exercises with prayer (Bingham, Thurston, Chamberlain, and Loomis to Evarts, Jan. 11, 1823, HP/HMCS).

21. Ka'ahumanu, one of Kamehameha's wives, was Liholiho's *makuahine*, or a female relative of the parental generation. Her ties to Liholiho were strengthened when she was made his foster mother (*makua hānai*). There was no real blood tie between the two, but Ka'ahumanu, who was of a prestigious Maui island lineage, provided Kamehameha a means to enhance the alliance between Maui and Hawai'i families. After Kamehameha's death, Ka'ahumanu dexterously used her position to

promote Maui interests, pushing out Liholiho, who, through her biological mother Keōpūolani, represented conciliation between the lineages of Hawai'i and Maui.

22. There is an apparent connection between this sudden interest in the *palapala* and the arrival, in the spring of 1822, of the Reverend William Ellis and his Tahitian helpers, who soon found their ways in the households of Hawaiian chiefs (see Journal of Sybil Bingham, Aug. 9, 1822).

23. As the system of *palapala* became more organized, the status of native teachers grew as well: "The general influence of *the teachers* is very great; often greater than is desirable: for it sometimes makes them feel that they are nearly on a level with the chiefs; and they have not sufficient stability of character to bear so sudden promotion" (Richards to Evarts, Apr. 14, 1828, HP/HMCS).

24. For a more detailed account of this transformation of the traditional role of the paramount chief, see Sahlins 1981, esp. 64–66. Sahlins' argument is basically as follows: As the lower-ranking chiefs took over the appropriation of foreign goods and the control of lands, the high chief's traditional foreign connection (Kahiki) was transformed into a defense of what was considered native, that is, the opposite of Western customs and paraphernalia. The encroachment of the Hawaiian nobility upon Liholiho's sovereignty was seen immediately after his succession to the paramountcy in 1819 (Freycinet 1978, 20–21).

25. Kalanimōkū and Hoapili were both Keōpūolani's husbands, although several months before her death Keōpūolani decided to have but one husband according to Christian custom, and chose Hoapili.

26. According to the journalist-historian James Jarves, a similar edict was declared in February 1823, and a fine of one dollar—a considerable sum of money in a situation where the chiefs had monopolized the circulation of specie—was imposed for anyone working on the Sabbath (Jarves 1843, 234). It is difficult to say whether Jarves got the date wrong and actually meant the edict given just prior to Liholiho's departure, since the other standard sources are equally vague on dates. Nevertheless, the logic of events is clear if not their sequence: The Maui chiefs claimed a share in the area traditionally reserved for the sovereign, who then decided to convert his symbolic link to Great Britain into material support of his reign.

27. I think one cannot overestimate the immanent influence of the chiefs, for it was certainly not the whole mass of the people that attended to Christian order. As in all times of crisis, the normal course of Hawaiian life was subject to ritual upheavals, and the relatively small party of Jehovah could not enforce the new tabus without being present. Charles Stewart, a little less celebratory in his accounts, says that on Maui, "the news of the war at Taui [Kaua'i], and the absence of the most powerful rulers, have excited in the farmers and common people throughout the district [Lahaina], a more general spirit of drunkenness than at any time since our arrival among them. For the last few days, by far the greater portion of the whole population have been in a state of intoxication; and given up night and day to gambling, riot, and fighting, and every species of revelry" (Stewart 1970, 314–315).

28. The chiefs' habitual practice of participating in these proselytizing activities was a source of irritation for the missionaries, who felt that their own cause was being usurped and compromised. One particular instance was the chiefly monopoly over distributing writing utensils and later, to a lesser extent, books (Bingham to Evarts, Oct. 27, 1823, HP/HMCS).

29. If this concept reflected the missionary thinking, it was not part of the terminology that the mission invented for conveying their ideas to Hawaiian audiences. It seems that it was of native origin and was then adopted by the missionaries. Remember that the Hawaiian term *pō* refers not only to night but also to the times before the arrival of human beings and human order—all that stands for the divine, uncontrollable, and dangerous. Human culture, knowledge, and skills are the opposite of *pō*, which was easily turned into the opposite of the enlightenment, or the new human order through the worship—and control—of Jehovah. The concept was Hawaiian but so was the manner in which it reflected missionary thinking: god + worship = human order = enlightenment.

30. They were even addressed as "brethren who live together with the chiefs" *(nā hoahānau e noho pū ana me nā aliʻi)* (Letter of Boas Mahune, Aug. 6, 1838, IDM/AH).

31. At the time this was really a matter for the highest chiefs, but in the long run Christianity became an important engine for a more widely spread cultural objectification. In the Christian schools and meetinghouses, great but constantly diminishing masses of common Hawaiians were made to abandon their traditional past and adapt to the new forms of life, such as Christian marriages and codes of decency. Christianity also facilitated the rise of a new class of native intellectuals, pious and successful in their studies. These prominent scholars of the mission schools, quite in line with missionary theories, regarded the traditional past as the time of losing sight of the true God, Jehovah, whom their distant ancestors had once known, and they thus at least partially denounced this idolatrous period in their history (Barrère 1969; Dibble 1839, 18–19; 1909, 11–13; Kahananui 1984, 194–195; Kamakau 1991a, 49, 63; 1991b, 118; 1992a, 210; Malo 1991, 62, 73, 237; Pogue 1858, 25–26). It became their Dark Ages, which was first put at a distance but later revived in the form of an ethnographic interest in folklore. Here again the Christian intellectuals were prominent in collecting traditional material and reconstructing pre-contact Hawaiian society, first around 1836, then in the early 1840s, and continuously from the 1860s (HEN: Thrum, 35a, 254, 258; Piianaia 1987; Emerson 1991; Thrum 1918).

32. Kekuaipiʻia made it very clear that the chiefs were absolutely conscious of their choice and otherwise in perfect control of the situation, for she said that "if we see that the faith in question does not suit our people, we shall exchange it for another" (Kotzebue in Barratt 1988, 252). Barratt's notes (p. 253) give more sources for similar chiefly responses.

33. Note the paradigmatic use of the word stranger, a categorical synonym for enemy.

34. It is also of interest that some of the Hawaiian priests were most ready to accept the new worship, and a few engaged in the service of *palapala* (Journal of Levi Chamberlain, Aug. 12, 1827; Journal of Seth Andrews, July 4, 1837). The high priest of Kamehameha, Hewahewa, who was in favor of the missionaries and their god, had advised Liholiho to stop the traditional worship in 1819 (Ellis 1979, 80). His behavior can be understood as being typical of a Hawaiian expert in the tradition of his kind, for he himself was a descendant of the foreigner priest Pā'ao, who had inaugurated a cult of foreign gods in Hawaii. It would be interesting to know more about the part the priests played in the dissemination of *palapala*, especially in view of any systematic variation in the orientations of the different types of priests. Might there have been a pattern among the priests of Kū, to which Hewahewa belonged, to ally with the forces of Jehovah, and did the Lono priests see it as more attractive to join the defenders of the Hawaiian gods (cf. Sahlins 1981, 64–66)? Also deserving study is the connection between the nativist party and the Catholic missionaries who arrived in 1827, particularly since the Catholics were commonly called rebels *(he kipi)* and disturbers of the people *(he haunāele)* by the chiefs in power (FOE, Nov. 27, 1842).

35. When Kalanimōkū decided to build a temporary church in Honolulu late in the summer of 1825, he, according to Bingham's account, "employed about 3,000 men" to perform the work. Bingham, who never tired of measuring buildings, said the church covered "an area of 19,440 square feet" (Bingham to Burder, Sept. 13, 1825, HP/HMCS).

36. For a more detailed study of the conditions of the common Hawaiians and their patterns of resistance, see Ralston 1984, and Sahlins 1992, 25–35, 57, 87, 90, 149–163. An interesting contemporary document that gives a summary description of the variety of commoner tactics is Newbury 1835.

Chapter 2: The Politics of Virtue

1. Yet Union College, relatively popular among the missionary candidates, had a more liberal aura (Rudolph 1962, 73; Schmidt 1957, 59).

2. According to the missionary way of thinking, the heathen were in a brute condition primarily due to their lack of enlightenment. A non-Christian was described as "having reason without exercising it" (Tyerman and Bennet 1831, 432).

3. Dibble said clearly that this was already a proverb during the early period of missionizing. Interestingly, it is missing from Pukui's extensive collection of Hawaiian sayings (1983).

4. The Hawaiian custom of attaching oneself to the household of one's superior, the practice of becoming someone's *'ohua*, also inhibited the missionaries' attempts to remain an independent group. As it happened, they also became landholders under their respective chiefs, established households, and engaged in a number of *'ohua* relations (Levi Chamberlain to Baldwin, Aug. 29, 1848, KC/AH 35/28).

Chapter 3: Culture in the Making

1. Regarding the expression *ka lā kapu*, it may be noted that *kapu* soon became a measurement of time equaling one week, or the passing of one Sabbath. Before the abolition of the tabu system in 1819, four tabu days was also a rule in the Hawaiian lunar month. The mission was naturally hesitant to adopt the Hawaiian word *kapu* and instead introduced the Hebrew-based *ka lā Sabati* (Ke Kanawai o Iehova 1825), and the Greek word *hebedoma* for "week." Apparently *kapu* retained much of its old currency (use of *hebedoma* was largely restricted to the few mission-educated convert-intellectuals). Even some of the missionaries used *kapu* to measure time when dealing with Hawaiians (Richards to Kuakini, IDM/AH, Box 1, Feb. 18, 1840). Besides, the frequent prayer meetings were generally called "*kapu* meetings" (e.g., Lahaina Station Report, 1834, HMCS).

2. Attempts to discipline the women apparently failed, at least in Lahaina, where the missionary Lorrin Andrews counted approximately 500 Hawaiian prostitutes in 1845 (*Ka Elele Hawaii*, Sept. 9, 1845).

3. For similar incidents, see Daws 1968, 75–81.

4. The perceived threat had deep roots beyond prostitution. Long before the arrival of the missionaries, foreign residents and visitors had developed, to safeguard their own importance to the chiefs, a certain reluctance to teach new skills to Hawaiians or in any way to alter the conditions that would have affected their transactions in the islands. Archibald Campbell, who was employed in making sail canvas for Kamehameha's ships, witnessed the practice sometime in 1810:

> Having informed him [Isaac Davis, Kamehameha's trusted foreigner] that a loom was necessary, he ordered Boyd, his principal carpenter, to make one. This, however, Boyd declined, from an illiberal notion held by many of the white people, that the natives should be taught nothing that would render them independent of strangers. He told the king he did not know how to make looms; upon which I undertook to make one myself; although, by so doing, I incurred the displeasure of many of my countrymen. Davis had a native servant called Jack, who worked as a Tailor, and was a very handy fellow. This man showed much anxiety to observe how I proceeded; but his master told me by no means to allow him, as he was so quick he would soon learn to make a loom himself. When I said I had no wish to make it a secret, he replied, that if the natives could weave cloth, and supply themselves, ships would have no encouragement to call at the islands. Another instance of this narrow way of thinking occurred, when a brother of the queen's, whose name I do not remember, but who was usually called by the white people, John Adams [this was Kuakini], wished me to teach him to read, Davis would not permit me, observing, "they will soon know more than ourselves" (Campbell 1967, 99–100).

Given that the Hawaiian way to succeed in life was very much tied to one's ability to attract the attention of a chief and to become one of the chief's people, it is no wonder that Hawaiians were anxious to learn foreign skills, which so much fascinated the chiefs. The reluctance to teach the natives these skills was very likely of foreign origin. This was, however, structured by patterns of Hawaiian chiefship. Customarily, Hawaiian chiefs did no physical work; the chief only gave orders to bring whatever was needed. If foreign merchandise was the desired object, those who could supply the demand naturally had the advantage. The mission came to Hawaii to teach natives and thus was a natural adversary to foreigners who thrived by protecting their skills.

5. At a relatively early stage of regular culture contact, there developed, especially in Honolulu, a specialized sailor jargon. This had elements from European languages (Botta 1984, 31), but remained Hawaiian-based until the latter half of the nineteenth century (Roberts 1992).

6. For more details of Poki and his opposition to Ka'ahumanu, see Jarves 1843, 282–283; Bingham 1849, 340–343; Dibble 1909, 204–206; Kamakau 1992a, 284–291; Kuykendall 1989, 123–130; Bradley 1968, 183–184; Kame'eleihiwa 1992, 85–93; Sahlins 1992, 74–76.

7. I found it extremely difficult to translate Malo's use of the word *ae*. In the published English version it was translated as "country," which I think is awkward. In another context *ae* was translated as "blight," but that is not appropriate in this context.

8. For Whitney and Richards, the rise of Catholicism was always a sign of corruption, whereas Protestant ascendance and expansion of commoner rights carried hopeful signs. In the case of France, sins of revolution and Napoleon were both recognized and denounced, the former for forsaking the word of God, the latter for autocracy, both leading to excessive bloodshed. The demand for good order represented by Napoleon was, however, treated with some understanding. This general work was preceded in 1830 by a four-page Hawaiian translation of William IV's address to the English parliament declaring an official revival of the word of God (*O ke kauoha maikai* 1830). The missionary habit of recounting histories, especially English history, as oscillation of good and bad morals and rulers was continued for quite some time. For example, Sereno E. Bishop, son of the missionary Artemas Bishop, taught English history at the Lahainaluna Seminary in the late 1860s in exactly the same mold: the objects of evaluation were once again the prevalence of Christian worship, especially Protestant forms, and the status of the common people, and also the existence of a written constitution (Sereno Bishop c. 1868).

9. A similar, although much later, case is that of Kepelino Keauokalani, another Hawaiian chronicler, who associated Wākea, the chief who according to tradition first instituted "image-worship," with Henry VIII. Because Wākea was considered in the Christianized Hawaiian tradition to be the chief responsible for the loss of the true god, he became "Hawaii's evil chief." He and Henry VIII "were alike" (Kepelino 1932, 66).

10. We should, however, guard against placing too much emphasis on the ad

hoc nature of these constructs. The chiefs, living at an international stopover for commercial shipping, were relatively well-informed about the nature of the foreign lands. For example, William Ellis wrote the following vignette of Liholiho just prior to his voyage to England: "His general knowledge of the world was much greater than could have been expected. I have heard him entertain a party of chiefs for hours together, with accounts of different parts of the earth, describing the extensive lakes, the mountains, and mines of North and South America; the elephants and inhabitants of India; the houses, manufactures, &c. of England, with no small accuracy, considering he had never seen them" (Ellis 1979, 324–325).

Chapter 4: Political Economy

1. It was most likely forgotten due to Ka'ahumanu's illness and death, and the tumultuous succession of Kauikeaouli and Kīna'u.

2. According to Kuykendall, "Beginning with Captain Finch in 1829, there was scarcely one of the foreign naval commanders who visited Hawaii down to 1838 who did not offer the king and chiefs advice on some subject" (Kuykendall 1989, 158–159). Introduction of private ownership, abrogation of labor dues, and standardization of taxation all figured in nearly every foreign suggestion. But all of them—perhaps excluding Miller's proposal, which was aided by Bingham—were wanting in one essential respect: they provided no culturally intelligible theory of divinity and history, but were practical pieces of advice couched in a taken-for-granted Western liberalism.

3. The subject of restricting the enjoyments of the mercantile community was less ambiguous. Bingham, at least, was rather sarcastic to the foreign residents and sea captains, who signed a petition against the new measures (Bingham to Evarts, Nov. 25, 1831, MSL).

4. Compare this to the situation in 1826, when the mission counted at least four hundred native teachers throughout the islands and about one hundred more, who were spreading the word directly employed by local chiefs (SIM 1826a).

5. For particulars of Kauikeaouli's rebellion, see Sahlins 1992, 121–125, which is by far the fullest account. See also Kame'eleihiwa 1992, 157–167; and Kamakau 1992a, 334–340.

6. Baldwin also recognized the significance of language: "Where we attempted to portray the sinner's guilt, we doubtless failed to give it all that point, which we shd in our own vernacular tongue" (Baldwin to ABCFM, Nov. 3, 1834, MSL).

7. The Hawaiian organization of trade had of course attracted missionary attention much earlier. In a letter to the mission board, Artemas Bishop predicted that "should personal property be guaranteed to the common people as their inviolable right such a spur would be given to industry as has hitherto been unknown" (Bishop to Evarts, June 1, 1825, MSL). But, again, the 1830s differed from previous years in that the commercial life of Hawaiians became an essential part of missionary concerns.

8. Traveling in central Oʻahu in May 1822, a two-man deputation from the London Missionary Society heard the following story: "Our guide said that once he came hither, being very weary and fainting with thirst, he had offered a native, who was with him, a dollar to fetch him a drought of water from the stream below. The man refused, saying, "What good would a dollar do to *me*, for it would soon be known that I had it, and then I must give it up to the chief?" (Tyerman and Bennet 1831, I, 455).

9. In the instructions the mission (or more properly Bingham) drafted for Richards, the idea of the close correlation of godliness and political system was confirmed once more: "It being the general conviction of the mission that Christian philanthropy requires a great increase of attention in the agriculture, manufactures, commerce, government &c of the Sandwich Islands, & that philanthropists may now . . . very properly be invited to engage personally, in the business of cultivating the arts, & improving the political economy of the Islands on the principles of benevolence . . ." (SIM 1836b).

10. In August, he wrote his missionary colleagues in Hawaii that he had found many people interested in "the subject of Political Economy at the Sandwich Islands," but that the threshold of leaving was still too high for the moment (Richards to the Members of the Sandwich Islands Mission, Aug. 1, 1837, MSL).

11. This wording also reflects the serious reservations the missionaries had concerning Richards' new role in the service of the chiefs.

12. Malo had, in fact, been the first Hawaiian commoner to complain in public about the chiefs' excesses. In 1837, he wrote a public letter for the native paper *Ke Kumu Hawaii*, one that, unlike his essay of 1839, went untranslated and was thus explicitly directed to the native audience. As a Christianized Hawaiian, Malo's frame was derived from the Bible, and although his subject was the arrival of Christianity at Hawaii, the letter contained strong criticisms of the chiefs' practices. For example, "Here is another thing; do not exclusively burden the Hawaiian people with [your] wrongdoings while easing the load of foreigners; and do not burden the common people while easing the living of the chiefs; and do not burden the poor while saving the favorites. Instead, this is the right way, equal burdens and reliefs to the common people as well as the chiefs, to the long-term residents as well as the newcomers" (Malo 1837, 52, my translation).

13. To my knowledge the first person to have alluded to the essential link between the revival and the plans to reform the chiefship was Sereno E. Bishop, in 1902. Although his motives to connect the two events were far from being based on any analysis of the relations that prevailed between the chiefs and common Hawaiians, he was on the right track in giving Christianity a central place. According to him, "This great awakening was the predisposing cause of the extraordinary change which soon followed in the willing elevation by the king and chiefs of their serfs to the status of independent freeholders, and of voters for representatives in the legislature" (Bishop 1902, 43).

14. The word "political" appeared first in Andrews' vocabulary of 1836. The

entry for the Hawaiian word *aiāhulu* contains the following explanation: "To pray or poison to death, to procure the death of another by any fraudulent means, or for any *political* or selfish purposes" (Andrews 1836, 3, my emphasis). The appearance of the word political in this entry does not, however, indicate that the word would have been taken, in itself, as an explicit object of translation. In the modern Hawaiian dictionary the word *aiāhulu* has also lost the meaning Andrews was able to decipher. The meaning is now "ungodly" or "wicked," probably based on the more specific meaning, "someone who is careless in observing tabus" (Pukui and Elbert 1986, 9).

15. Andrews had learned Hawaiian so well that he took much pride in it and felt the inadequacy of any English translation. The typical missionary despair in facing a "savage" and "imperfect" language had been replaced for him by paternalistic admiration. In the introduction to his dictionary, Andrews remarked that, "The Hawaiians possessed a language not only adopted to their former necessities, but capable of being used in introducing the arts of civilized society, and especially of pure morals, of law, and the religion of the Bible" (Andrews 1865, vi; see also Andrews 1864). This attitude was not uncommon among missionary families. For instance, Rev. Henry H. Parker, a son of a missionary and the principal reviser of Andrews' dictionary, was famed for his outright refusal to preach in English (Elbert 1954, 13). The paternalistic side of this admiration was reflected in the very outspoken manner in which Andrews, for example, tried to establish what he called "the best and purest Hawaiian" he could obtain from his informants (Andrews 1865, iv). In practice this strategy involved concentration on the language of the *ali'i* and a few outstanding converts (language which apparently differed from that of most Hawaiians), and avoidance of terms that would indicate aspects of sexual intercourse and other elements of Hawaiian life that were too much for the agents of civilization.

16. This vocabulary has usually been attributed to Andrews and only recently has its identity been seriously questioned. According to Marguerite Ashford (1987), the vocabulary is most likely Kamakau's list of synonyms, which he was appointed to prepare in 1843 by the faculty members of Lahainaluna Seminary (Lahainaluna, *Faculty Records*, Sept. 27, 1843). According to the records of the faculty meetings, Kamakau's vocabulary was intended to be used as a basis for a new Hawaiian-English dictionary (*Records*, Feb. 11, 1846; this source also indicates that the vocabulary was completed or nearly completed by that date). When the Hawaiian Legislature in 1860 decided to finance Andrews' Hawaiian language dictionary, Kamakau's vocabulary had already become an important part of the work.

17. The Hawaiian word *akeakamai* means literally "to desire wisdom," and perhaps is, despite its perfect Hawaiian appearance and construction, a direct translation from the Greek *philosophos*. At least the word was used by the missionaries to translate natural philosophy and, later, science.

18. Kauakahikahaola and Kālaikuahulu were respected orators and genealogists, and close advisors to the high chief Kamehameha.

19. There are two other words that build on *kālai'āina*, but which have appeared

in a dictionary only very recently. *Kalakalaiaupuni* as a translation for "political" was recorded in Pukui and Elbert's dictionary in the 1985 edition (Pukui and Elbert 1986, 501). The word has a similar connotation as *kālai'āina*, but its object is not land in general but *aupuni* or government. In the Hawaiian-English section, *kalakalaiaupuni* was translated as "political activity; to do such" (p. 121). The expression *loea kālai'āina* as a translation for politician and *loea kālai aupuni* for statesman also debuted in the 1985 edition (pp. 209, 501, 533). *Loea* is a word meaning skillful person or expert. *Loea Kalaiaina* was the name of a Hawaiian language weekly, which ran for about two and a half years from 1897 to 1900 as a mouthpiece for the Hawaiian nationalist Home Rule Party. Political party as *'ao'ao kālai'āina* is also a relatively recent codification, appearing first in Pukui and Elbert's first edition in 1957 (p. 25). At the turn of the century the organizers of the Home Rule Party used the phrase to designate themselves as a political party (*Home Rula Repubalika*, Nov. 2, 1901).

"Political expert," *kilo aupuni*, is another 1957 codification (p. 140). In the precontact and early post-contact period, the word *kilo* was used to name the class of people that studied the signs in different parts of nature to tell future events. It seems that *kilo* were classified according to the parts of nature in which they were specializing. Kamakau lists experts in sky, stars, clouds, and earth, who were all called *kilo* (1991a, 8; see also Kepelino 1932, 130). *Kilo aupuni* does not conform to this logic, since it was not from *aupuni* that *kilo* read the signs of the future, but rather from the natural phenomena for the preservation or establishing of *aupuni*. However, it is possible that because of their function in the high chief's household they were also called *kilo aupuni*.

Finally, there are the Hawaiianized loan words for political, namely, *polikika*, *polokika*, and *polotika* (Pukui and Elbert 1957, 312–313), which have been in use at least from the early years of the twentieth century. A writer in *Ka Nupepa Kuokoa* in 1927 used the phrase "hana politika" in the sense of "political affairs" or "politics" (Kalei 1927).

Chapter 5: Natural Rights, Virtuous Wealth

1. It is impossible to present the contents of Richards' lectures in full detail. Here I concentrate merely on the major theoretical points since they will help us understand the cultural context of these ideas and their connection to Hawaiian structures of meaning.

2. Puakea Nogelmeier graciously helped me to clarify the most difficult parts of the text.

3. In his 1841 report to Charles Wilkes, the commander of the United States Exploring Expedition, Richards was more direct, and perhaps disappointed because the reforms were taking root very slowly. According to him, ". . . even to the present day, it is next to impossible to convince the elder chiefs that authority and subordinations can be maintained by any other means. An old chief said to me, 'If we can not take away their [the common people's] lands, what will they care for us? They will be as

rich as we.' . . . no landholder considered himself safe in his possessions, and therefore even ridiculed the idea of making extensive improvements" (Richards 1973, 23). More than anything else, this evaluation seems to reflect an altered condition in chief-commoner relations, as the intensified competition between the chiefs led to intensified relations of production, thus undermining the traditional values of reciprocity and care. These issues were on the table already in 1838 when Richards was conducting his school of political economy (or Kauikeaouli's, to be more precise). Thus, "In this land [Hawaii], the governing people (*po'e ho'omalu*) have become wealthy, a wealth-grabbing people. The [common] people are not diligent at work, and there is not much wealth in the land . . . Some chiefs think that if the present practices are ended, the riches of the chiefs will also be gone and their ruling will be a thing of the past. These thoughts belong to ignorance" (Richards 1839, 140, my translation).

To assure the chiefs of the benefits of reform, Richards revisited the feudal history of England, to which he likened the traditional land system in Hawaii. In this line of thought, the Magna Charta and the abrogation of feudal relations were enough to prove that the source of English wealth was in the land reform, which was itself based on a religious reform. In the final analysis, the word of God was again the guarantor of wealth and longevity of government: "*Ina aole hoohiki ke alii pela, aole paha loaa ia ia ke aupuni.*" (If the king did not allow [the observance of the word of God], perhaps he would not get the government [*aupuni*]) (Richards 1839, 141, my translation).

4. Richards' missionary colleague Lorrin Andrews made a telling remark in his translation of David Malo's essay on native depopulation in 1839: "The reader will notice that David Malo recognizes a certain ingredient here, as necessary to the prosperity of a nation, that many writers on political economy leave out or forget, viz: *The fear of God, and obedience to his laws*" (Andrews in Malo 1839).

5. When elections became an established part of the structure of the transformed chiefship, in the early 1850s, the word of God and its different interpretations gathered momentum at the polls (e.g., IDM/AH, Box 1, nos. 71, 75).

6. When Richards translated this law in 1842, these attributes simply disappeared, presenting the foreigners with a collection of laws without the keynote that dominated the native discussions.

7. The publication of these laws was postponed due to the death of Kīna'u on April 4, 1839. The date of publication, June 7, was also the date of proclaiming Kekāuluohi the successor of Kīna'u as the effective co-ruler and paramount advocate of Christianity. Her speech, or rather her "word," on that day was short but highly saturated in the symbolism of *aupuni*:

> Ua lohe mai la no oukou. Eia ia'u ka aina, ua hele aku la hoi kela makuahine. Eia hoi ia'u. Eia hoi, ko'u wahi manao, e like me ka olelo a ka mea i make aku la, mai hoowalewale oukou i ka'u keiki, a e malama oukou i ka pono a ke Akua.

You have heard. The land is in my possession [from Kauikeaouli], that mother [Kīnaʻu, Kauikeaouli's adoptive mother] has gone. It is indeed with me. Here is also my thought, according to the word of the deceased, do not tempt my son [Kauikeaouli], and observe the right way of God (FOE, June 7, 1839, my translation).

As could be expected, on that occasion Kauikeaouli made no reference to God. However, the third speaker, Christian veteran Hoapili, had only God in his mind, when he recommended God's way "until the end arrives" (FOE, June 7, 1839).

8. The standard edition of 1837 sold at least 75,000 copies in the United States and was widely taught in schools. It was also translated into several languages and generally used by American missionaries wherever they operated (Blau 1963, xlii, xlx). The date of the book's arrival at Hawaii is not known. First published in May 1835, it might have arrived with the eighth company of missionaries sent by the ABCFM in December 1836, or the mission board might have sent it by any vessel bound to the islands. It is also unclear which edition became the basis of the Hawaiian version. The eighth company could have brought only the first edition, to which an unsatisfied Wayland made considerable changes in 1837. This was the year when the second edition was published, and Richards was in the United States. Because the Hawaiian version was published in 1839, I think it more likely that the second edition was used. The reasons Wayland was chosen to convey a moral point of view in Hawaii, despite his Baptist faith, are most probably his exceptionally good reception at American schools, and his ability to provide "enlightenment to the faithful" (Cremin 1980, 28).

9. An often repeated theme in the missionary writings is the Hawaiian way of expressing affection, joy, and sorrow: disfiguring bodily movements, loud wailing and crying, and, at the death of a chief, inflicting of wounds, knocking out teeth, and cutting hair—acts explicitly forbidden in Deuteronomy. In the eyes of the missionaries, this manner of expression, in its unrestrained flow of emotions, was one of the surest signs of barbarism. Of course in the right context, such as a revivalist Christian prayer meeting, unrestrained emotions were allowed to some extent, and even welcomed by some (see Daws 1961). Moreover, weeping in general was not considered a vice if the person could only combine the tears with the least possible bodily movements (Samuel and Nancy Ruggles, Journal, May 3, 29, 1820; cf. Richards in Stewart 1970, 338–340). Choosing an example at random, the following quote describes a step toward a rational society as assisted by Christian principles: "Her [Kaʻahumanu, "the Queen Regent"] reception here [Kailua, Hawaiʻi] by the people was as usual cordial and affectionate, tho unattended with any of those extravagant excesses which formerly ever followed the arrival of any distinguished ruler. On the contrary we assembled by her request and offered to the throne of Grace our thanksgivings and praises for her safe arrival. Formerly, guns would have been fired, wailings of Joy would have rent the air, dances and revelry would have succeeded. Tho not less than ten thousand people assembled here soon after her

arrival there was the utmost order and stillness prevalent during the whole time of their stay" (Bishop to Evarts, Nov. 30, 1826, HP/HMCS). The early missionary letters and diaries are dotted with similar remarks in which properly contained human emotions are given a constitutive status in laying the foundations of a correct social and political order.

10. The text was attributed to her by Bishop Museum archivists.

11. The constitution of 1840 "succeeded rather in complicating the organization and probably increasing the burdens," because its clear-cut pyramidic logic failed to effectively account for and do away with the more complex local relations of subordination. According to Sahlins, the constitution created an added layer of officials (tax collectors—*luna 'auhau*) on top of the existing *konohiki* system (1992, 111).

12. The manner of viewing social relations as objects of government was indeed built into the foreign-made statute laws of 1845 and 1846, which were intended to establish government ministries and the judiciary. For example, the work of the minister of public instruction consisted, among other things, of supervising what were called "parental duties" and "filial duties," which meant seeing to the proper execution of the Christian moral code in Hawaiian homes (*Statute Laws* 1846, 198–203). After these "duties" left the think-tank legislature they remained largely a dead letter, but they did indicate a shift in how government approached individuals and their lives. The most distinct instances of these new governmental dimensions, such as the "duties," were nevertheless framed as means to promote Christianity among the common people, not as tools of a Western-type political economy. There was also a clear emphasis on enlightening the people and thus rendering them better equipped to enter the political society. This theory was, however, much transformed by the common Hawaiians, to whom "the great mass of laws" *(na kanawai lehulehu)* represented "a real source of oppression and trouble" *(he kumu nui keia o ke kaumaha a me ka pilikia)* (NDOC/162), and, perhaps, a perversion of Christianity. The worship of the Christian god and the tenets of Christianized *kālai'āina* were understood in a traditionalized sense as benefiting *aupuni* and the honor of the high chiefs, not as means to accumulate personal wealth without regard of the collective. Thus the fifty-two petitioners from Kona, Hawai'i, criticized the chiefs for letting greedy foreigners settle in the islands: "It is the foreigners who acquire wealth whom we refuse—those people are not true Hawaiians" (LFP/AH, June 25, 1845).

13. Apparently only two documents remain of Hawaiian origin, both concerning Richards' yearly salary of $600. It appears that Kīna'u was responsible for providing the money from her lands on O'ahu, and that there was some reluctance on her part because she thought Richards was engaged only on a part-time basis (Kamehameha III to Kīna'u, June 27, 1838, FOE; Kana'ina to Kīna'u, 1838, IDM/AH).

14. As an indication of the continuity of the corvée mode of production, road construction was considered "government work" *(hana aupuni)* and its execution was not an excuse to disregard other work, as Kekūanaō'a explained: "Those who

carry food for horses are required to do it early—before light, so also those who carry milk, they are to bring it before light and leave it with their customers: then go immediately to the work of the government" (FOE, Feb. 15, 1841). No wonder Malo included Kekūanaō'a in his list of chiefs who continued to abuse their power long after the new laws had been adopted (Malo to Richards, June 2, 1846, FOE).

15. The air of change was thick in the chiefly circles, as the following quote from the journal of the House of Nobles shows:

> Discussion was held and the opinion stated that a seal be made for the Kingdom.
>
> Passed: that the Kingdom have a seal.
>
> Passed: that Mr. Richards write out a description of the Kingdom's seal and present it to the legislature.
>
> Passed: that T. Haalilio's [the mission-trained secretary for Kauikeaouli] seal be given to G. P. Judd.
>
> Passed: that Mr. Richards be in charge of writing a description of the Hawaiian flag.
>
> It is a major task for the legislature to arrange for seals for the main officials of the Kingdom and the seal(s) of the governors.
>
> Passed: a statement that a seal be made for the major finance officials and the governors with the King's new crown made in a badge and then his office inscribed around it. The same to be done for judges.
>
> Passed: New badges for legislators and major government officials shall be the Kamehameha III badge for all connected with the military and other officials, and the King's servants (kanaka, men).
>
> Passed: Dress for the legislature shall be tails and the new badge (Journal of the House of Nobles, May 8, 1845, LFJ/AH).

Judd's report to the legislature for the year 1845, his first year as the minister of finance, indicates that one-fifth of all government expenditures were directed toward various construction schemes of monarchical buildings in Honolulu, including the new royal palace and the king's summer retreat. Among other construction projects were new rooms for the treasury, a new main road, bridges, and prisons, but it is unclear whether they were included in said fifth (MIR 1845, 4–5, 9–10).

16. This appears to have been before the Hawaiian expression for monarchy was established as aupuni mō'ī, according to the new title for the king, mō'ī. In Stokes' (1932) opinion the word was invented by the foreign advisors to King Kamehameha III—perhaps Gerrit P. Judd—during the reorganization of the Hawaiian government in the early 1840s, and gradually replaced the word ali'i nui as the title for "king." Sahlins (1992, 21) criticizes Stokes' view based on two rather independent arguments: First, the word mō'ī would fit perfectly within the divine king theory, because according to Malo the central image in the royal luakini temple was called mō'ī (Malo 1991, 165; 1987, 110; Cook and King 1784, 160). This would

indicate that during *luakini* rituals the king and the god were interchangeable. Second, in George Dixon's Hawaiian vocabulary from 1786–1787, the word for king was *"myre"* (Dixon 1789, 268), an anomaly that no one has been able to explain.

Sahlins' first point relies heavily on a structuralist premise, according to which we can derive the meaning of a variety of things from one paradigmatic scheme (i.e., the king's divinity). In the case of Hawaiian chiefship this is quite strongly supported. Dixon's strange spelling might well have been a product of his bad ear. To start with, English sailors used the letter "y" to indicate the sound *[ai]*, and, excluding the initial "m," Dixon's word for "king" would be pronounced *[airi]* or *[aire]*, which resembles the Hawaiian word *ari'i*, or *ali'i* as it is spelled today. This would conform with other journalists' translations for "king." However, Dixon recorded the word *aree* (the modern *ali'i*) and rendered it as "a chief," making a clear distinction between chief and king. If we again include the initial "m," the pronunciation would be *[mairi]* or perhaps *[maire]*. This latter case would still be a mystery, for *maile* is a vine used for garlands on important occasions, and is associated with Laka, the goddess of *hula*.

It nevertheless appears strange that Dixon would have used an idiosyncratic spelling for the clear and distinctive sounding *mō'ī*. He was able to record a rather similar word *moe* (to sleep) without resorting to anglicized spelling (Dixon 1789, 269). Furthermore, *mō'ī* does not contain the alternate consonants "l" and "r," or "k" and "t"; neither does the vowel structure have any difficulties, perhaps excepting the "i" which was often spelled with "e" by English speakers. But in Dixon's case, his success in spelling *moe* with "e" would add to the possibility of his spelling *mō'ī* with "i," and also of his constructing syllables resembling *mō'ī* more than his *"myre"* does. Besides, the Anglophone James King of the Cook expedition spelled the word *mō'ī* as *"Maee,"* meaning the central temple image (Cook and King 1784, 160). The bad ear hypothesis cannot be ruled out, but this speaks against it.

17. While in the United States, Ha'alilio was asked to write something to "a lady's album." Richards apparently took a great deal of interest in Ha'alilio's reflection, for he copied it and translated it for the official journal of the Hawaiian government:

> It is with admiration and great joy that I have seen this country, its people, and all they have accomplished for themselves, both for the body and the soul, through energy and intelligence. All these valuable things have really been obtained by piety and a sincere faith in the true God.
>
> Thus it has appeared to me in my various journeyings, for in all places which I have visited or in which I have dwelt in this country, both among the highest and the lowest classes, I have seen that they worship God. It is on this account, viz., the sincerity with which they worship God, that success attends every work to which they put their hands (*The Polynesian*, June 14, 1845).

18. Political economy, or *kālai'āina*, became a minor fad in the missionary circles. *Ka Elele Hawaii*, for instance, featured a pseudonym Kalaiaina, who most emphati-

cally repeated the lesson of hard work as the groundwork of all wealth. He also took up the usual comparison, the American Indian who remained idle (*Ka Elele Hawaii*, Oct. 21, 1845).

Chapter 6: The Denouement

1. A similar translation was carried over to the small English-Hawaiian vocabulary, which was published by the Hawaiian Language League in 1936. In this work, however, "ruler" was translated as *mana hoʻomalu* (Hawaiian Language League 1936, 31). Here *mana* implies an authority.

2. An Italian visitor of the late 1820s translated the word "governor" (*governatore*) as *"malama"* (Botta 1841, 362). This is certainly a confusion of the title and function of the Hawaiian "governor," but because *malama* has the meaning of "caretaking," the confusion carries a valuable indication of the traditional ideal of a reciprocal relationship of caring and loyalty between chiefs and their people.

3. By linking death and foreigners with the so-called *"a"* possessive, Kekūanaōʻa made a distinction between troubles that, when given an *"o"* possessive, come and go as nature dictates, and troubles caused by malicious acts. Death in this case is intentional and relative to illegitimate killing, and is clearly at odds with the established order of things.

4. Richards used the word *kūʻokoʻa* in his translation of Wayland's textbook of political economy. The specific context is the American Revolutionary War. A literal translation of his wordings would be "and America stood aloof and became a separate government" (*a ku okoa o Amerika, a lilo i aupuni kaawale*). In this text, *kūʻokoʻa* was not yet canonized as what it became at the international recognition of Hawaii's independence in 1843. Rather it was used in its more common sense to indicate difference and separation, just like the word *kaʻawale*. We do not see the expression *aupuni kuʻokoʻa*, "independent government or kingdom," until 1843. Before that date, *kaʻawale* was the usual word to denote independence. For instance, in the translation of Woodbridge's geography seven years before the translation of Wayland, Richards and his colleague Samuel Whitney indicated the independent nature of the American states by using the clause, *"ua noho kaawale,"* "they were ruled independently." The status of the rulers of one state in relation to those of other states was described as *"okoa"* (*He Hoikehonua* 1832, 120). This, apparently, was the old native usage in reference to coexisting chiefdoms and land allotments between the chiefs.

5. When the Hawaiian chiefship was restructured to better correspond with the European monarchies, in the early 1840s, the use of *aliʻi ʻai moku* appears to have declined, at least in official discourse. The head chief of Maui island, Ulumaheihei Hoapili, was among the last to have left a trace of this expression, when he signed the Lahaina harbor regulations in 1838 (*Ke Kumu Hawaii*, Dec. 19, 1838).

6. The only surviving work listing Hawaiian synonyms, Kamakau's *Quotations*, was probably compiled during the 1840s, and in it *aliʻi ʻai moku* and *aliʻi kiaʻāina* were given as synonyms (Kamakau, *Quotations*, n.d.).

7. Judd attempted to put the chiefs' economy on a sound and businesslike basis. In the new office his outward conduct was somewhat changed from his days as a missionary. "He [Judd] excuses himself for having attended balls & . . . parties, because he is a politician, & must sustain that character among the men of the world" (Journal of Lowell Smith, Apr. 6, 1844). According to Baldwin, "he smokes tobacco through the streets, gives licenses to sell rum, can set up a billiard table for the king, & either does or allows other things which they [the missionaries] cannot reconcile with a Christian profession" (Baldwin to Greene, Nov. 8, 1845, HP/HMCS).

8. According to Henry Wise, the "masses of subtle laws" were "equal in magnitude to the huge proportions of a Chinese dictionary" (1849, 330).

9. Chester Smith Lyman recorded a summary of these troubles in May 1846, which was an exceptionally dry spring on Oʻahu: "The distress among the natives is of course great. To render the matter worse the Govn't Taxes are required to be paid in gold or silver but these metals on that Island [Oʻahu] are exceedingly scarce. Mr. Richards told me that the whole amt. of money collected fr. that Island was not sufficient to pay the Governor's [Kekūanaōʻa's] salary. To procure money the people are obliged to go to some of the larger towns, Hilo or Honolulu, for employment that will yield it their lands at home are neglected & when once away they seldom return . . ." (Journal of Chester Smith Lyman, May 15, 1846).

10. Used in times of famine.

11. Another way to manipulate the school system, especially among older boys, was to attend school "merely for the sake of getting rid of the *koele*" [i.e., the labor tax] (Ives to Richards, Nov. 3, 1846, MSL).

12. Sahlins makes an interesting point when he says that Hawaiians became politicized en masse in 1845, because the traditional avenue of religious protest had disappeared. The chiefs having forsaken the church and become supporters of Protestantism only nominally, there was no use in resorting to the strategy of the late 1830s, namely denying the chiefs any role in mediating between this world and the divine. The Hawaiian Great Awakening worked to this effect, but the chiefs had their ways of getting even; they dropped their earlier godliness (Sahlins 1992, 127–129, 156). However, by labeling the petition movement political, Sahlins is in danger of prematurely taking sides in the debate of 1845, when the contemporary actors had not yet settled the political nature of the petitions.

13. Perhaps this was not true directly, but rather through their proselytizing, which was well understood by the missionaries in government service. They wished to see even more Christian influence among the people. Their views, however, were closer to a general policing than any form of liberation theology. In June 1846, the missionary-turned-judge Lorrin Andrews spoke at the Kawaiahao church in Honolulu and stressed the "need of a stronger Gospel influence in respect to the political condition of the nation." He reminded his audience of Christianity's role in character-building, and lectured to them that "the nation needs a

conscience, or the new laws will be but a dead letter" (Journal of Chester Smith Lyman, June 1, 1846).

Conclusion

1. To be fair, Valeri only points in that direction, and his analysis is basically concerned with "sense" rather than "the efficacy of Hawaiian religious representations" (Valeri 1985b, xii). Throughout his study he remains loyal to that emphasis.

Bibliography

Abbreviations

ABCFM	American Board of Commissioners for Foreign Missions, Boston
AH	Archives of Hawaii, Honolulu
BM	Bishop Museum Archives, Honolulu
HL	Hamilton Library, Honolulu
HMCS	Hawaiian Mission Children's Society Library, Honolulu
LMS	The London Missionary Society
MH	*Missionary Herald* (see Newspapers and Periodicals)
MR	*Missionary Register* (see Newspapers and Periodicals)
SIM	Sandwich Islands Mission

Newspapers and Periodicals

Home Rula Repubalika, semi-weekly newspaper, Honolulu
Ka Elele Hawaii, semi-monthly paper, Honolulu
Ka Nupepa Kuokoa, weekly newspaper, Honolulu
Ka Nonanona, semi-monthly paper, Honolulu
Ke Alaula, monthly paper, Honolulu
Ke Au Okoa, weekly newspaper, Honolulu
Ke Kumu Hawaii, semi-monthly paper, Honolulu
Missionary Herald, monthly paper, American Board of Commissioners for Foreign Missions, Boston
Missionary Register, monthly paper, Church Missionary Society, London
Sandwich Island Mirror and Commercial Gazette, monthly paper, Honolulu
The Friend, semi-monthly paper, Honolulu
The Hawaiian Spectator, quarterly paper, Honolulu
The Polynesian, weekly newspaper, Honolulu

Ministerial Reports of the Hawaiian Kingdom

MIR	Report of the Minister of the Interior

Archival Collections and Their Acronyms

ABCFM-HEA   American Board of Commissioners for Foreign Missions–Hawaiian Evangelical Association, correspondence, 1820–1920, HMCS

AG/AH   Attorney General, Kingdom of Hawaii, AH

FOE   Foreign Office and Executive files, Kingdom of Hawaii, AH

HEN   Hawaiian Ethnographic Notes, BM

HP/HMCS   ABCFM-Hawaii Papers, 1820–1900, HMCS, originals at the Houghton Library, Harvard University

IDL/AH   Interior Department, Letter Books, Kingdom of Hawaii, AH

IDM/AH   Interior Department, miscellaneous items, Kingdom of Hawaii, AH

JPL   Journals and Papers of Elisha Loomis, microfilms, HL

J/HMCS   The Journal Collection, 1819–1900, HMCS

KC/AH   The Kahn Collection, AH (numbered items)

LFJ/AH   Legislative Files, Journals, Kingdom of Hawaii, AH

LFP/AH   Legislative Files, Petitions, Kingdom of Hawaii, AH

LH/BM   Letters in Hawaiian, Kapiʻolani-Kalanianaʻole Collection, BM

LP/BM   Lahainaluna Papers, BM

M/BM   Hawaiian Chants Collection, BM

MSL   Missionary Letters, 1816–1900, HMCS

M-7/AH   Papers of Richard Armstrong, AH

M-59/AH   Hawaiian Chiefs, Letters, AH

M-125/AH   Papers of Jules Remy, AH

NDOC   Numbered Documents, Foreign Office and Executive files, Kingdom of Hawaii, AH (no dates)

TW/HMCS   Translation Workbooks Collection, HMCS

Works Cited

Ahahui Kalaiaina. c. 1899. *Olelo Hoalohaloha no ka Mea Kiekie ke Kama Alii Wahine Victoria Kaiulani Kalaninuiahilapalapa.* Ke Komite Hooko o ka Ahahui Kalaiaina. LH/BM.

Alexander, Arthur C. 1937. *Koloa Plantation 1835–1935: A History of the Oldest Hawaiian Sugar Plantation.* Honolulu: Star-Bulletin.

Alexander, Mary C. 1953. *Dr. Baldwin of Lahaina.* Berkeley: Privately printed.

Amasa. 1834. A letter to Hiram Bingham, dated Nov. 24, 1834. *Ke Kumu Hawaii,* Dec. 10, 1834:22.

Andrew, John, III. 1976. *Rebuilding the Christian Commonwealth.* Lexington: The University Press of Kentucky.

Andrews, Lorrin. 1836. *A Vocabulary of Words in the Hawaiian Language.* Lahaina-luna, Maui: Press of the High School.

———. 1864. "Value of the Hawaiian and English Languages in the Instruction of Hawaiians." *Hawaiian Evangelical Association Proceedings.*

———. 1865. *A Dictionary of the Hawaiian Language, to which Is Appended an*

English-Hawaiian Vocabulary and a Chronological Table of Remarkable Events. Honolulu: Henry M. Whitney.

———. 1922. *A Dictionary of the Hawaiian Language.* Henry H. Parker, ed. and revisions. Honolulu: The Board of Commissioners of Public Archives of the Territory of Hawaii.

———. (attributed). N.d. *A Vocabulary of Hawaiian Words with English Definitions, Illustrated by Short Sentences in the Hawaiian Language.* Microfilm copy of original ms., HL.

Andrews, Seth L. *Journal.* BM.

D'Anglade, Marie G. B. [1893] 1987. *A Tree in Bud: The Hawaiian Kingdom, 1889–1893.* Alfons L. Korn, trans. Honolulu: University of Hawai'i Press.

Asad, Talal. 1973. "Two European Images of Non-European Rule." In Talal Asad, ed., *Anthropology and the Colonial Encounter.* London: Ithaca Press and Atlantic Highlands, N.J.: Humanities Press.

Ashford, Marguerite K. 1987. "The Evolution of the Hawaiian Dictionary and Notes on the Early Compilers, with Particular Attention to Manuscript Resources of the Bishop Museum Library." *Bishop Museum Occasional Papers 27.* Honolulu: Bishop Museum Press.

Ashworth, John. 1987. *'Agrarians' and 'Aristocrats': Party Political Ideology in the United States, 1837–1846.* Cambridge: Cambridge University Press.

Baker, Robert Hoapili. ca. 1880. *I ka Lehulehu. To the Public.* Broadside. Kalakaua's Scrapbook, 1872–1887. Kapi'olani-Kalaniana'ole Collection. BM.

Barnes, R. H. 1987. "Anthropological Comparisons." In Ladislav Holy, ed., *Comparative Anthropology.* Oxford and New York: Basil Blackwell.

Barratt, Glynn. 1988. *The Russian View of Honolulu, 1809–26.* Ottawa: Carleton University Press.

Barrère, Dorothy B. 1969. "The Kumuhonua Legends: A Study of Late 19th Century Hawaiian Stories of Creation and Origins." *Pacific Anthropological Records* 3. Honolulu: Department of Anthropology, Bernice P. Bishop Museum.

Barrère, Dorothy, and Marshall Sahlins. 1979. "Tahitians in the Early History of Hawaiian Christianity: The Journal of Toketa." *The Hawaiian Journal of History* 13:19–35.

Barth, Fredrik. 1987. *Cosmologies in the Making: A Generative Approach to Cultural Variation in Inner New Guinea.* Cambridge: Cambridge University Press.

Beaglehole, J. C. 1967. *The Journals of Captain James Cook: The Voyage of the Resolution and Discovery, 1776–1780,* parts 1 and 2. Hakluyt Society Extra Series 36. Cambridge: Cambridge University Press.

Beckwith, Martha W. [1940] 1989. *Hawaiian Mythology.* Honolulu: University of Hawai'i Press.

———, ed. and trans. [1951] 1990. *The Kumulipo: A Hawaiian Creation Chant.* Honolulu: University of Hawai'i Press.

Belcher, Edward. 1970. *Narrative of a Voyage Round the World, Performed in Her*

Majesty's Ship Sulphur, during the Years 1836–1842. 2 vols. Folkestone and London: Dawsons of Pall Mall.

Benjamin, Walter. 1992. *Illuminations.* Harry Zohn, trans., and Hannah Arendt, ed. London: Fontana.

Bhabba, Homi K. 1994. *The Location of Culture.* London: Routledge.

Bingham, Hiram. 1832. *A Lexicon of the Hawaiian Tongue Taken from the Apograph of H. Bingham by W. P. Alexander.* TW/HMCS.

———. 1849. *A Residence of Twenty-One Years in the Sandwich Islands; or the Civil, Religious, and Political History of Those Islands: Comprising a Particular View of the Missionary Operations Connected with the Introduction and Progress of Christianity and Civilization among the Hawaiian People.* 3d ed. Hartford, Conn.: Hezekiah Huntington.

Bingham, Sybil M. "Journal on Board the *Thaddeus* and First Years in the Islands, 1819–1823." Typescript, J/HMCS.

Bishop, Artemas. 1828. *Vocabulary of the Hawaiian Language, with Notes on the Structure of the Language.* Microfilm of the original ms, HL.

———. 1835. "He olelo no ka pule malama hou." *Ke Kumu Hawaii,* July 22, 1835:113–114.

———. 1838. "An Inquiry into the Causes of Decrease in the Population of the Sandwich Islands." *The Hawaiian Spectator* 1:52–66.

———. 1854. *Na Huaolelo a me na Olelo Kikeke ma ka Beritania, a me ka Olelo Hawaii, no na Haumana e Ao ana i kela a me keia* [Hawaiian-English phrase book]. Honolulu: Henry M. Whitney.

Bishop, Sereno E. ca. 1868. *Moolelo Beritania.* BM.

———. 1902. "The Native Protestant Churches of Hawaii." *The Pacific Commercial Advertiser,* Jan. 1, 1902:41–43.

Blau, Joseph L. 1963. "Introduction." In Francis Wayland, *The Elements of Moral Science.* Joseph L. Blau, ed. Cambridge, Mass.: The Belknap Press of Harvard University Press.

Bloch, Ruth H. 1985. *Visionary Republic: Millennial Themes in American Thought, 1756–1800.* Cambridge: Cambridge University Press.

Bloxam, Andrew. 1825. *Dictionary of Hawaiian Words.* BM.

Botta, Carlo. 1841. *Viaggio intorno al globo principalmente alla California ed alle Isole Sandwich regli anni 1826, 1827, 1828 e 1829.* Vol. 2. Torino: Fontana.

Botta, Paul-Émile. [1831] 1984. Paul-Émile Botta, Visitor to Hawai'i in 1828. Edgar C. Knowlton Jr., trans. *The Hawaiian Journal of History* 18:13–38.

Bradley, Harold W. [1942] 1968. *The American Frontier in Hawaii: The Pioneers 1789–1843.* Gloucester, Mass.: Peter Smith.

Brumann, Christoph. 1999. "Writing for Culture: Why a Successful Concept Should Not be Discarded." *Current Anthropology* 40 (special issue):S1–S27.

Calder, Alex, Jonathan Lamb, and Bridget Orr. 1999. "Introduction: Postcoloniality and the Pacific." In Alex Calder, Jonathan Lamb, and Bridget Orr, eds.,

Voyages and Beaches: Pacific Encounters, 1769–1840. Honolulu: University of Hawai'i Press.

Campbell, Archibald. 1967. *A Voyage Round the World, from 1806 to 1812 . . . with an Account of the Present State of the Sandwich Islands, and a Vocabulary of Their Language.* Facsimile Reproduction of the Third American Edition of 1822. Honolulu: University of Hawai'i Press.

Catholic Church. N.d. *Index of the Chancery Archives.* Diocese of Honolulu.

Cayton, Mary Kupiec. 1977. "Who Were the Evangelicals? Conservative and Liberal Identity in the Unitarian Controversy in Boston, 1804–1833." *Journal of Social History* 31(1):85–107.

Chamberlain, Daniel. "Copy of a Journal Kept by Capt. Daniel Chamberlain on a Mission to the Sandwich Islands, 1819–1820." Typescript of the original at the Houghton Library, Harvard University, J/HMCS.

Chamberlain, Levi. "Journal, 1822–1849." Typescript, J/HMCS.

Charlot, John. 1985. *The Hawaiian Poetry of Religion and Politics: Some Religio-Political Concepts in Postcontact Literature.* The Institute for Polynesian Studies Monograph Series 5. Lā'ie, O'ahu: Brigham Young University, Hawaii Campus.

Clastres, Pierre. 1977. *Society Against the State: The Leader as Servant and the Humane Uses of Power among the Indians of the Americas.* Robert Hurley, trans., in collaboration with Abe Stein. New York: Urizen.

Cohn, Bernard S. 1983. "Representing Authority in Victorian India." In Eric Hobsbawn and Terence Ranger, eds., *The Invention of Tradition.* Cambridge: Cambridge University Press.

Colnett, James. 1940. *The Journal of James Colnett.* Toronto: The Champlain Society.

Comaroff, Jean, and John Comaroff. 1991. *Of Revelation and Revolution. Christianity, Colonialism, and Consciousness in South Africa, Vol. 1.* Chicago: The University of Chicago Press.

Conkin, Paul K. 1968. *Puritans and Pragmatists: Eight Eminent American Thinkers.* Bloomington: Indiana University Press.

Conkin, Paul K. 1995. *The Uneasy Center: Reformed Christianity in Antebellum America.* Chapel Hill: The University of North Carolina Press.

Constitution and Laws of the Hawaiian Islands, Established in the Reign of Kamehameha III. 1842. Lahainaluna.

Cook, James, and James King. 1784. *A Voyage to the Pacific Ocean . . . in His Majesty's Ships Resolution and Discovery.* 3 vols. London: W. and A. Strahan for G. Nicol and T. Cadell.

Cowing, Cedrik B. 1995. *The Saving Remnant: Religion and the Settling of New England.* Champaign: University of Illinois Press.

Cox, Ross. [1832] 1957. *The Columbia River.* Edgar I. Stewart and Jane R. Stewart, eds. Norman: University of Oklahoma Press.

Cremin, Lawrence A. 1980. *American Education: The National Experience 1783–1876.* New York: Harper & Row.

Damon, Ethel M., ed. 1925. "The First Mission Settlement on Kauai Being Extracts from the Manuscript Journals of Rev. Samuel Whitney and Mrs. Mercy Partridge Whitney, 1819–1824." *The Friend* 95(9):204–210; 95(10):224–235.

———, ed. 1927. *Father Bond of Kohala: A Chronicle of Pioneer Life in Hawaii.* Honolulu: The Friend.

Daws, A. Gavan. 1961. "Evangelism in Hawaii: Titus Coan and the Great Revival of 1837." *The Sixty-Ninth Annual Report of the Hawaiian Historical Society for the year 1960.* Honolulu: Hawaiian Historical Society.

Daws, Gavan. 1968. *Shoal of Time: A History of the Hawaiian Islands.* Honolulu: University of Hawai'i Press.

Dening, Greg. 1980. *Islands and Beaches: Discourse on a Silent Land Marquesas, 1774–1880.* Chicago: The Dorsey Press.

———. 1982. "Sharks That Walk on the Land: The Death of Captain Cook." *Meanjin* 41(4):427–437.

Dibble, Sheldon. 1839. *History and General Views of the Sandwich Islands' Mission.* New York: Taylor and Dodd.

———. [1843] 1909. *A History of the Sandwich Islands.* Honolulu: Thos. G. Thrum.

Dixon, George. 1789. *A Voyage Round the World; but more particularly to the North-West Coast of America: Performed in 1785, 1786, 1787, and 1788, in the King George and Queen Charlotte, Captains Portlock and Dixon.* London: Geo. Goulding.

Dodge, Ernest S. 1965. *New England and the South Seas.* Cambridge, Mass.: Harvard University Press.

Douglas, Bronwen. 1993. "Pre-European Societies in the Pacific Islands." In Max Quanchi and Ron Adams, eds., *Culture Contact in the Pacific.* Cambridge: Cambridge University Press.

Duhaut-Cilly, August B. 1983. "Shadows of Destiny: A French Navigator's View of the Hawaiian Kingdom and Its Government in 1828." Alfons L. Korn, trans. *The Hawaiian Journal of History* 17:1–39.

Earle, Timothy, ed. 1991. *Chiefdoms: Power, Economy, and Ideology.* Cambridge: Cambridge University Press.

Elbert, Samuel H. 1954. "The Hawaiian Dictionaries, Past and Future." *The Sixty-second Annual Report of the Hawaiian Historical Society for the Year 1953.* Honolulu: Hawaiian Historical Society.

———, ed. [1959] 1982. *Selections from Fornander's Hawaiian Antiquities and Folklore.* Honolulu: University of Hawai'i Press.

Ellis, William. 1825. *Journal of a Tour around Hawaii, the Largest of the Sandwich Islands.* Boston: Crocker & Brewster, and New York: John P. Haven.

———. [1827] 1979. *Journal of William Ellis: Narrative of a Tour of Hawaii, or Owhyhee; with Remarks on the History, Traditions, Manners, Customs, and Language of the Inhabitants of the Sandwich Islands.* Rutland and Tokyo: Charles E. Tuttle.

Emerson, John S., and Artemas Bishop. 1845. *He hoakakaolelo no na huaolelo Beritania, i mea kokua i na kanaka Hawaii e ao ana ia olelo* [English-Hawaiian vocabulary]. Lahainaluna: The Press of the High School.

Emerson, Nathaniel B. [1903] 1991. "Biographical Sketch of David Malo." In David Malo, *Hawaiian Antiquities (Moolelo Hawaii)*. 2d ed. Nathaniel B. Emerson, trans. Bernice P. Bishop Museum Special Publication 2. Honolulu: Bishop Museum Press.

Emerson, Oliver P. 1928. *Pioneer Days in Hawaii*. Garden City, N.Y.: Doubleday, Doran & Co.

Evans-Pritchard, E. E. 1940. *The Nuer: A Description of the Modes of Livelihood and Political Institutions of a Nilotic People*. Oxford: Clarendon Press.

Fornander, Abraham. 1916–1920. *The Fornander Collection of Hawaiian Antiquities and Folk-Lore*. Thos. G. Thrum, ed. Memoirs of the Bernice P. Bishop Museum, vols. 4–6. Honolulu: Bishop Museum Press.

Friedman, Jonathan. 1997. "Global Crisis, The Struggle for Cultural Identity and Intellectual Porkbarreling: Cosmopolitans versus Locals, Ethnics and Nationals in an Era of De-hegemonisation." In Pnina Werbner and Tariq Modood, eds., *Debating Cultural Hybridity: Multi-cultural Identities and the Politics of Anti-racism*. London: Zed Books.

Freycinet, Louis Claude de Saulses de. [1829] 1978. *Hawai'i in 1819: A Narrative Account by Louis Claude de Saulses de Freycinet*. Ella L. Wiswell, trans., and Marion Kelly, ed. Pacific Anthropological Records 26. Honolulu: Department of Anthropology, Bernice P. Bishop Museum.

Fuchs, Lawrence H. 1961. *Hawaii Pono: A Social History*. New York: Harcourt, Brace & World.

Gast, Ross, and Agnes C. Conrad. 1973. *Don Francisco de Paula Marin*. Honolulu: The University Press of Hawai'i for the Hawaiian Historical Society.

Golovnin, Vasilii M. 1974. *Chapters on Hawaii and the Marianas in V. M. Golovnin's Voyage around the World on the Sloop of War Kamchatka Performed by Order of His Majesty the Emperor in the Years 1817, 1818, and 1819*. Ella Wiswell, trans. Miscellaneous Working Papers 2. Pacific Islands Program, University of Hawaii.

Greenleaf, W. H. 1964. *Order, Empiricism and Politics: Two Traditions of English Political Thought, 1500–1700*. London: Oxford University Press.

Greer, Richard A. 1977. "Honolulu in 1838." *The Hawaiian Journal of History* 11:3–38.

———, ed. 1991. "Riot, Mutiny, Killing, and Cannibalism: George Brown's Maui Tour." *The Hawaiian Journal of History* 25:93–102.

Grimshaw, Patricia. 1989. *Paths of Duty: American Missionary Wives in Nineteenth-century Hawaii*. Honolulu: University of Hawai'i Press.

Gunson, Niel. 1978. *Messengers of Grace: Evangelical Missionaries in the South Seas, 1797–1860*. Oxford: Oxford University Press.

Hale, Horatio. [1846] 1968. *Ethnography and Philology: United States Exploring Expe-*

dition during the Years 1838, 1839, 1840, 1841, 1842. Ridgewood, N.J.: The Gregg Press.

Handy, E. S. Craighill. 1933. "Government and Society." In Helen Pratt, ed., Ancient Hawaiian Civilization. Honolulu: The Kamehameha Schools.

Handy, E. S. Craighill, and Mary K. Pukui. 1972. Native Planters in Old Hawaii: Their Life, Lore, and Environment. Bernice P. Bishop Museum Bulletin 233. Honolulu: Bishop Museum Press.

Hanson, Alan. 1989. "The Making of the Maori: Culture Invention and Its Logic." American Anthropologist 91(4):890–902.

Harrison, Lawrence E., and Samuel P. Huntington, eds. 2000. Culture Matters: How Values Shape Human Progress. New York: Basic Books.

Hartman, Geoffrey H. 1997. The Fateful Question of Culture. New York: Columbia University Press.

Hawaiian chiefs. 1836. Letter to "friends in America." HP/HMCS.

Hawaiian Language League. 1936. Vocabulary of Common and Every-Day Words. Compiled by a Professor of Columbia University. Translated into the Hawaiian Language by The Hawaiian Language League. Honolulu: Royal Printing Press.

He hoikehonua. 1832. He hoikehonua, he mea ia e hoakaka'i i ke ano o ka honua nei, a me na mea maluna iho. Prepared by Samuel Whitney and William Richards. Oahu: Mission Press.

He kumukanawai a me ke kanawai hooponopono waiwai, no ko Hawaii nei pae aina. Na Kamehameha III. i kau. 1839. Honolulu.

Heimert, Alan. 1966. Religion and the American Mind from the Great Awakening to the Revolution. Cambridge, Mass.: Harvard University Press.

Heyrman, Christine L. 1984. Commerce and Culture: The Maritime Communities of Colonial Massachusetts, 1690–1750. New York and London: W. W. Norton.

Hinds, Richard B. 1968. "The Sandwich Islands: From Richard Brinsley Hinds' Journal of the Voyage of the 'Sulphur' (1836–1842)." E. Alison Kay, ed. The Hawaiian Journal of History 2:102–135.

Hitchcock, Harvey R. Journal, 1834–1853. J/HMCS.

———. 1873. Ka Honua Nei; Ka Buke Mua o ka Hoike Honua, nona Kamalii o na Kula Maoli o ke Aupuni. Hooponoponoia e ke Kuhakula Nui, mamuli o ke kauoha a ka Papa Hoonaauao. Honolulu.

———. 1887. An English-Hawaiian Dictionary; with Various Useful Tables. San Francisco: The Bancroft Company.

Hobbs, Jean. 1935. Hawaii: A Pegeant of the Soil. Stanford: Stanford University Press.

Hobsbawn, Eric. 1983. "Mass-Producing Traditions: Europe, 1870–1914." In Eric Hobsbawn and Terence Ranger, eds., The Invention of Tradition. Cambridge: Cambridge University Press.

Hobsbawn, Eric, and Terence Ranger, eds. 1983. The Invention of Tradition. Cambridge: Cambridge University Press.

Holman, Lucia R. 1986. *Journal of Lucia Ruggles Holman*. Brookfield Center, Conn.: The Congregational Church of Brookfield.

Howard, Alan. 1985. "History, Myth and Polynesian Chieftainship: The Case of Rotuman Kings." In Anthony Hooper and Judith Huntsman, eds., *Transformations of Polynesian Culture*. Auckland: The Polynesian Society.

Howe, K. R. [1984] 1988. *Where the Waves Fall: A New South Sea Islands History from First Settlement to Colonial Rule*. Honolulu: University of Hawai'i Press.

Hunnewell, James. 1909. "Honolulu in 1817 and 1818." *Papers of Hawaiian Historical Society* 8. Honolulu: Hawaiian Historical Society.

Ii, John Papa. 1869a. "Na hunahuna no ka moolelo Hawaii. *Ka Nupepa Kuokoa*, March 13, 1869.

———. 1869b. "Na hunahuna no ka moolelo Hawaii." *Ka Nupepa Kuokoa*, March 20, 1869.

———. 1869c. "Na hunahuna no ka moolelo Hawaii." *Ka Nupepa Kuokoa*, May 8, 1869.

———. 1869d. "Na hunahuna no ka moolelo Hawaii." *Ka Nupepa Kuokoa*, Dec. 18, 1869.

———. [1959] 1983. *Fragments of Hawaiian History*. Mary Kawena Pukui, trans., and Dorothy B. Barrère, ed. Bernice P. Bishop Museum Special Publication 70. Honolulu: Bishop Museum Press.

Ingraham, Joseph. 1918. "The Log of the Brig Hope: The Hope's Track among the Sandwich Islands, May 20–Oct. 12, 1791." *Hawaiian Historical Society Reprints* 3. Honolulu: Hawaiian Historical Society.

Jarves, James Jackson. 1838. "Sketches of Kauai." *The Hawaiian Spectator* 1:66–86.

———. 1843. *History of the Hawaiian or Sandwich Islands, Their Antiquities, Mythology, Legends, Discovery by Europeans in the Sixteenth Century, Re-Discovery by Cook, with Their Civil, Religious and Political History, from the Earliest Traditionary Period to the Present Time*. Boston: Tappan and Dennet.

Johnson, Allen W., and Timothy Earle. 1987. *The Evolution of Human Societies: From Foraging Group to Agrarian State*. Stanford: Stanford University Press.

Judd, Bernice, Janet E. Bell, and Clare G. Murdoch. 1978. *Hawaiian Language Imprints, 1822–1899: A Bibliography*. Honolulu: The Hawaiian Mission Children's Society and The University Press of Hawai'i.

Judd, Gerrit P., IV. 1960. *Dr. Judd, Hawaii's Friend: A Biography of Gerrit Parmele Judd (1803–1873)*. Honolulu: University of Hawai'i Press.

Judd, Henry P. 1939. *The Hawaiian Language and Hawaiian-English Dictionary*. Honolulu: Hawaiian Service.

Judd, Henry P., Mary Kawena Pukui, and John F. G. Stokes. 1945. *Introduction to the Hawaiian Language (An English-Hawaiian Vocabulary) Comprising Five Thousand of the Commonest and Most Useful English Words and Their Equivalents, in Modern Hawaiian Speech, Correctly Pronounced, with a Complementary Hawaiian-English Vocabulary*. Honolulu: Tongg.

"Ka 'Ainoa . . . [and] Liholiho's Kingdom." *Lahainaluna Paper* 4, Jan. 30, 1842. LP/ BM.

Kahananui, Dorothy M., ed. and trans. [1838] 1984. *Ka Mooolelo Hawaii: Hawaiian Language Reader Based on Sheldon Dibble's Ka Mooolelo Hawaii.* Honolulu: Committee for the Preservation and Study of Hawaiian Language, Art and Culture.

Kaimikuokoa. 1854. *He vahi palapala o Kaimikuokoa i kona mau makamaka e manoa nui ana i ke kuokoa ana o ke aupuni Havaii.* Honolulu: Catholic Press.

Kalei. 1927. "Ka Puuhonua." *Ka Nupepa Kuokoa,* Jan. 27, 1927.

Kamakau, Samuel M. 1865a. Makee Alii. *Ka Nupepa Kuokoa,* Oct. 14, 1865.

———. 1865b. Kumumanao. *Ka Nupepa Kuokoa,* Oct. 28, 1865.

———. 1867a. Ka Moolelo o Kamehameha I. Helu 16. *Ka Nupepa Kuokoa,* Feb. 23, 1867.

———. 1867b. Ka Moolelo o Kamehameha I. Helu 17. *Ka Nupepa Kuokoa,* March 2, 1867.

———. 1867c. Ka Moolelo o Kamehameha I. Helu 42. *Ka Nupepa Kuokoa,* Sept. 21, 1867.

———. 1867d. Ka Moolelo o Kamehameha I. Helu 46. *Ka Nupepa Kuokoa,* Nov. 9, 1867.

———. 1867e. Ka Moolelo o Kamehameha I. Helu 47. *Ka Nupepa Kuokoa,* Nov. 16, 1867.

———. 1868. Ka Moolelo o Kamehameha I. Helu 84. *Ka Nupepa Kuokoa,* Aug. 1, 1868.

———. 1869a. Ka Moolelo Hawaii. Helu 100. *Ke Au Okoa,* Jan. 21, 1869.

———. 1869b. Ka Moolelo Hawaii. Helu 123. *Ke Au Okoa,* July 22, 1869.

———. 1870. Ka Moolelo Hawaii. Helu 54. *Ke Au Okoa,* Dec. 22, 1870.

———. 1961. *Ruling Chiefs of Hawaii.* Mary K. Pukui, Thomas G. Thrum, Lahilahi Webb, Emma Davidson Taylor, and John Wise, trans. Honolulu: Kamehameha Schools Press.

———. 1988. *I ka Wa o Kamehameha. In the Time of Kamehameha: Selected Essays by Samuel M. Kamakau.* Malcolm Naea Chun, ed. and trans. Honolulu: The Folk Press.

———. [1964] 1991a. *Ka Po'e Kahiko: The People of Old.* Mary K. Pukui, trans., and Dorothy B. Barrère, ed. Bernice P. Bishop Museum Special Publication 51. Honolulu: Bishop Museum Press.

———. 1991b. *Na Mo'olelo a ka Po'e Kahiko: Tales and Traditions of the People of Old.* Mary K. Pukui, trans., and Dorothy B. Barrère, ed. Honolulu: Bishop Museum Press.

———. [1961] 1992a. *Ruling Chiefs of Hawaii.* Revised ed. Mary K. Pukui, Thomas G. Thrum, Lahilahi Webb, Emma Davidson Taylor, and John Wise, trans. Honolulu: Kamehameha Schools Press.

———. [1976] 1992b. *The Works of the People of Old: Na Hana a ka Po'e Kahiko.*

Mary K. Pukui, trans, and Dorothy B. Barrère, ed. Bernice P. Bishop Museum Special Publication 61. Honolulu: Bishop Museum Press.

————. 1996. *Ke Kumu Aupuni: Ka moʻolelo Hawaiʻi nō Kamehameha Ka Naʻi Aupuni a me Kāna aupuni i hoʻokumu ai.* Honolulu: ʻAhahui ʻŌlelo Hawaiʻi.

————. N.d. *Quotations from His Dictionary.* BM.

Ka manao o na alii [Thoughts of the chiefs]. 1825. Oahu: Mission Press.

Kameʻeleihiwa, Lilikalā. 1992. *Native Land and Foreign Desires: Pehea Lā E Pono Ai? How Shall We Live in Harmony?* Honolulu: Bishop Museum Press.

Kamehameha III and Kekauluohi. 1843. *To People.* Broadside, Feb. 25, 1843. BM.

Kanawai. 1846. *Kanawai i kauia e ka Moi, e Kamehameha III., ke Alii o ko Hawaii pae aina: ua hookoloia e na ʻLii ahaolelo a me ka poeikohoia, i ka makahiki iwakaluakumamakahi o kona noho aupuni ana, a i ke kolu a me ka ha o kona noho kuokoa ana, A.D. 1845 a me 1846. Ua huipuia mai na olelo ae i ke kuokoa ana, a me na kuikahi me ko na aina e.* Honolulu: printed by the mission.

Kāne, Herb Kawainui. 1997. *Ancient Hawaiʻi.* Honolulu: Hawaiian Paradise Trading Company (also available on-line).

Keesing, Roger M. 1989. "Creating the Past: Custom and Identity in the Contemporary Pacific." *The Contemporary Pacific* 1:19–42.

Keesing, Roger M. and Robert Tonkinson, eds. 1982. "Reinventing Traditional Culture: The Politics of Kastom in Island Melanesia." *Mankind* (special issue) 13(4).

Ke kanawai o Iehova [The Ten Commandments]. 1925. Oahu: Mission Press.

Kekāuluohi, Miriama (attributed). 1848. *E ola ke alii ʻke Akua.* BM.

Kepelino (Keauokalani). 1932. *Kepelino's Traditions of Hawaii.* Martha W. Beckwith, ed. and trans. Bernice P. Bishop Museum Bulletin 95. Honolulu: The Bishop Museum.

————. 1977. "Kepelino's 'Hawaiian Collection': His 'Iloʻiliili Hawaii' Pepa I, 1858." Bacil F. Kirtley and Esther T. Mookini, trans. and annotation. *The Hawaiian Journal of History* 11:39–68.

Koskinen, Aarne A. 1953. *Missionary Influence as a Political Factor in the Pacific Islands.* Annales Academia Scientiarum Fennica B78:1. Helsinki: Academia Scientiarum Fennica.

Kuykendall, Ralph S. [1938] 1989. *The Hawaiian Kingdom. Volume I: 1778–1854, Foundation and Transformation.* Honolulu: University of Hawaiʻi Press.

Lahainaluna. *Faculty Records 1835–1877.* Photocopy on shelf 373.9 L 14, HMCS.

Laslett, Peter. 1988. "Introduction." In John Locke, *Two Treatises of Government.* Peter Laslett, ed. Cambridge: Cambridge University Press.

Linnekin, Jocelyn. 1983. "Defining Tradition: Variations on the Hawaiian Identity." *American Ethnologist* 10(2):241–252.

————. 1990a. "The Politics of Culture in the Pacific." In Jocelyn Linnekin and Lin Poyer, eds., *Cultural Identity and Ethnicity in the Pacific.* Honolulu: University of Hawaiʻi Press.

————. 1990b. *Sacred Queens and Women of Consequence: Rank, Gender, and Colonialism in the Hawaiian Islands.* Ann Arbor: University of Michigan Press.

————. 1991a. "Text Bites and the R-Word: The Politics of Representing Scholarship." *The Contemporary Pacific* 3(1):172–177.

————. 1991b. "Cultural-Invention and the Dilemma of Authenticity." *American Anthropologist* 93(2):446–449.

Linnekin, Jocelyn, and Lin Poyer. 1990. "Introduction." In Jocelyn Linnekin and Lin Poyer, eds., *Cultural Identity and Ethnicity in the Pacific*. Honolulu: University of Hawai'i Press.

Loomis, Elisha. *Copy of the Journal of E. Loomis*. May 17, 1824–January 27, 1826. Original owned by Dr. Wm. D. Westervelt and placed in Hamilton Library, University of Hawai'i.

Loomis, Maria T. S. "Journal, 1819–1824." Typescript, J/HMCS.

Luomala, Katharine. 1990. "Foreword." In Martha Warren Beckwith, ed. and trans., *The Kumulipo: A Hawaiian Creation Chant*. Honolulu: University of Hawai'i Press.

Lyman, Chester Smith. *The Hawaiian Journals of Chester Smith Lyman, 1846–1847*. BM.

Lyons, Betsey C. "Journal of Betsey Curtis Lyons." Typescript, J/HMCS.

Macintosh, Stephen D. N.d. *Vocabulary of the Hawaiian Language*. BM.

McLoughlin, William G. 1978. *Revivals, Awakenings, and Reform: An Essay on Religion and Social Change in America, 1607–1977*. Chicago: University of Chicago Press.

Macrae, James. 1972. *With Lord Byron at the Sandwich Islands in 1825, Being Extracts from the MS Diary of James Macrae, Scottish Botanist*. Hilo, Hawai'i: Petroglyph Press.

Malo, David. 1837. "No ka hiki ana mai o ko ke Akua aupuni." *Ke Kumu Hawaii*, Nov. 22, 1837.

————. 1839. "On the Decrease of Population on the Hawaiian Islands." *The Hawaiian Spectator* 2:121–130.

————. 1987. *Ka Mo'olelo Hawaii (Hawaiian Antiquities)*. Malcolm Naea Chun, ed. Honolulu: The Folk Press and Kapiolani Community College.

————. [1951] 1991. *Hawaiian Antiquities (Moolelo Hawaii)*. 2d ed. (first ed. 1903). Nathaniel B. Emerson, trans. Bernice P. Bishop Museum Special Publication 2. Honolulu: Bishop Museum Press.

Manby, Thomas. 1929. "Journal of Vancouver's Voyage to the Pacific Ocean." *Honolulu Mercury* 1(1):11–25, 1(2):33–45, 1(3):39–55.

Masse, W. Bruce, Laura A. Carter, and Gary F. Somers. 1991. "Waha'ula Heiau. The Regional and Symbolic Context of Hawai'i Island's 'Red Mouth' Temple." *Asian Perspectives* 30(1):19–56.

Miller, Perry. 1967. *The New England Mind: From Colony to Province*. Boston: Beacon Press.

Miller, William. 1831. "Memorandum." Typescript, FOE, Sept. 25, 1831.

Minson, William H. 1952. *The Hawaiian Journal of Manuel Quimper*. MA thesis, University of Hawai'i, HL.

Missionary Album, The. 1969. *Portraits and Biographical Sketches of the American Protestant Missionaries to the Hawaiian Islands*. Honolulu: Hawaiian Mission Children's Society.

Mosblech, Boniface. 1843. *Vocabulaire océanien-français et français-océanien des dialectes parlés aux Iles Marquises, Sandwich, Gambier, etc.* Paris: Jules Renouard et Compagnie.

Newburgh, Rufus. 1835. *A Narrative of Voyage &c by Rufus Newburgh*. FOE, Apr. 28, 1835.

Niebuhr, H. Richard. 1954. "The Idea of Covenant and American Democracy." *Church History* 23:129–135.

Norton, Robert. 1993. "Culture and Identity in the South Pacific: A Comparative Analysis." *Man* (N.S.) 28(4):741–759.

Notes on Teaching. N.d. BM.

Nuckolls, Charles W. 1998. *Culture: A Problem That Cannot be Solved*. Madison: University of Wisconsin Press.

Obeyesekere, Gananath. 1992. *The Apotheosis of Captain Cook: European Mythmaking in the Pacific*. Princeton, N.J.: Princeton University Press, and Honolulu: Bishop Museum Press.

O ke kauoha maikai a ke Alii o Beritania, a Wiliama IV. ka Haleahaolelo, June 28, 1830. 1830. Oahu: Mission Press.

Pagden, Anthony. 1982. *The Fall of Natural Man: The American Indian and the Origins of Comparative Ethnology*. Cambridge: Cambridge University Press.

Philibert, Jean-Marc. 1986. "The Politics of Tradition: Towards a Generic Culture in Vanuatu." *Mankind* 16(1):1–12.

Piianaia, Abraham K. 1987. "Biographical Sketch of Davida Malo." In David Malo, *Ka Mo'olelo Hawaii (Hawaiian Antiquities)*. Malcolm Naea Chun, ed. Honolulu: The Folk Press and Kapiolani Community College.

Pocock, J.G.A. 1985. *Virtue, Commerce, and History: Essays on Political Thought and History, Chiefly in the Eighteenth Century*. Cambridge: Cambridge University Press.

———. 1999. "Nature and History, Self and Other: European Perceptions of World History in the Age of Encounter." In Alex Calder, Jonathan Lamb, and Bridget Orr, eds., *Voyages and Beaches: Pacific Encounters, 1769–1840*. Honolulu: University of Hawai'i Press.

Pogue, John F. 1858. *Ka Mooolelo Hawaii, i Kakauia e Rev. J. F. Pokuea, mamuli o ka Mooolelo Hawaii i Paiia ma Lahainaluna i ka M. H. 1838, Oia ke Kumu o keia, a ua Hoohuiia no nae*. Honolulu: Government Press.

Polanyi, Karl. [1944] 1957. *The Great Transformation: The Political and Economic Origins of Our Time*. Boston: Beacon Press.

Pukui, Mary Kawena. 1983. *'Ōlelo No'eau: Hawaiian Proverbs and Poetical Sayings*. Bernice P. Bishop Museum Special Publication 71. Honolulu: Bishop Museum Press.

Pukui, Mary Kawena, and Samuel H. Elbert. 1957. *Hawaiian-English Dictionary*. Honolulu: University of Hawai'i Press.

————. 1964. *English-Hawaiian Dictionary*. Honolulu: University of Hawai'i Press.

————. 1986. *Hawaiian Dictionary: Hawaiian-English, English-Hawaiian*. Revised and enlarged ed. Honolulu: University of Hawai'i Press.

Pukui, Mary Kawena, Samuel H. Elbert, and Esther T. Mookini. 1976. *Place Names of Hawaii*. Revised and expanded ed. Honolulu: University of Hawai'i Press.

Pukui, Mary Kawena, and Alfons L. Korn, trans. and ed. [1973] 1988. *The Echo of Our Song: Chants & Poems of the Hawaiians*. Honolulu: University of Hawai'i Press.

Rabinow, Paul. 1986. "Representations Are Solid Facts: Modernity and Post-Modernity in Anthropology." In James Clifford and George E. Marcus, eds., *Writing Culture: The Poetics and Politics of Ethnography*. Berkeley: University of California Press.

Ralston, Caroline. 1984. "Hawaii 1778–1854: Some Aspects of *Maka'ainana* Response to Rapid Cultural Change." *The Journal of Pacific History* 19(1):21–40.

————. 1993. "Chronology: Beach Communities and Port Towns." Appendix 2 in Max Quanchi and Ron Adams, eds., *Culture Contact in the Pacific*. Cambridge: Cambridge University Press.

Ranger, Terence. 1983. "The Invention of Tradition in Colonial Africa." In Eric Hobsbawn and Terence Ranger, eds., *The Invention of Tradition*. Cambridge: Cambridge University Press.

Remy, Jules. 1852–1855. *Vocabulaire français-havaiien. Recueillé dans l'archipel de Havaii pendant les années 1852–1855*. Microfilm of the original ms., HL.

Reynolds, Stephen. 1938. *The Voyage of the New Hazard to the Northwest Coast, Hawaii and China, 1810–1813*. F. W. Howay, ed. Salem, Mass.: Peabody Museum.

————. 1989. *Journal of Stephen Reynolds. Vol. 1: 1823–1829*. Pauline N. King, ed. Honolulu: Ku Pa'a Incorporated, and Salem, Mass.: Peabody Museum.

Richards, William. *Journal of Travels in the U.S.A., 1837*. AH.

————. 1839. *No ke Kalaiaina* (Adaptation of Francis Wayland's *Elements of Political Economy*). Lahainaluna: Press of the High School.

————. 1943. "William Richards' Report to the Sandwich Islands Mission on His First Year In Government Service, 1838–1839." *The Fifty-first Annual Report of the Hawaiian Historical Society for the Year 1942*. Bernice Judd, ed. Honolulu: Hawaiian Historical Society.

————. 1973. "William Richards on Hawaiian Culture and Political Conditions of the Islands in 1841." Marshall Sahlins and Dorothy Barrère, eds. *The Hawaiian Journal of History* 7:18–40.

Ricord, John. 1844. *Complaints and Opinions*. AG/AH.

Roberts, Julian M. 1992. "Pidgin Hawaiian: The Dominant Contact Language in Nineteenth-century Hawaii?" Typescript, HL.

Robson, David W. 1985. *Educating Republicans: The College in the Era of the American Revolution, 1750–1800*. Contributions to the Study of Education 15. Westport, Conn., and London: Greenwood Press.

Rohrer, James R. 1995. *Keepers of the Covenant: Frontier Missions and the Decline of Congregationalism 1774–1818*. New York: Oxford University Press.

Ross, Alexander. 1849. *Adventures of the First Settlers on the Oregon and Columbia River*. London: Smith, Elder.

Rudolph, Frederick. 1962. *The American College and University: A History*. New York: Alfred A. Knopf.

Ruggles, Samuel, and Nancy W. Ruggles. "Journal on Board the Brig *Thaddeus*, 1819–1820." Typescript and ms., J/HMCS.

Ryan, Alan. 1989. "Property." In Terence Ball, James Farr, and Russell L. Hanson, eds., *Political Innovation and Conceptual Change*. Cambridge: Cambridge University Press.

Sahlins, Marshall. 1981. *Historical Metaphors and Mythical Realities: Structure in the Early History of the Sandwich Islands Kingdom*. Association for Social Anthropology in Oceania Special Publication 1. Ann Arbor: University of Michigan Press.

———. 1985. *Islands of History*. Chicago: University of Chicago Press.

———. 1991. "The Political Economy of Grandeur in Hawaii from 1810 to 1830." In Emiko Ohnaki-Tiernay, ed., *Culture Through Time: Anthropological Approaches*. Stanford: Stanford University Press.

———. 1992. *Anahulu: The Anthropology of History in the Kingdom of Hawaii*. Chicago: University of Chicago Press.

———. 1996. "The Sadness of Sweetness: The Native Anthropology of Western Cosmology." *Current Anthropology* 37(3):395–428.

———. 1999. "Two or Three Things that I Know about Culture." *Journal of Royal Anthropological Institute* (N.S.) 5:399–421.

———. 2000. *Culture in Practice: Selected Essays*. New York: Zone Books.

Sandwich Islands Mission. 1819. *Instructions to the Missionaries*. ABCFM-HEA.

———. 1826a. *Proceedings at a General Meeting of the Sandwich Island Mission*. HP/HMCS.

———. 1826b. *To the Friends of Civilization and Christianity*. Broadside. Honolulu: The Mission Press. HP/HMCS.

———. 1830. "Resolutions Respecting Principles of Intercourse with the Chiefs, with Reference to Commercial, Political, and Civil Affairs, Sept. 1826." Appended in *The Minutes of a General Meeting of the Sandwich Island Mission Held at Honolulu, Jan. 1830*. Honolulu: Mission Press.

———. 1836a. *Memorials of the Sandwich Islands Mission on the Importance of the Arts in Christianizing the Heathen*. HP/HMCS. (Also printed in Bingham 1849, 490–496.)

———. 1836b. *Copy of Instructions to the Rev. William Richards*. Signed by Hiram Bingham. MSL, Richards to Depository, 1835–1839.

Schmidt, George P. 1957. *The Liberal Arts College: A Chapter in American History*. New Brunswick, N.J.: Rutgers University Press.

Schmitt, Robert C. 1968. *Demographic Statistics of Hawaii: 1778–1965*. Honolulu: University of Hawai'i Press.

———. 1977. *Historical Statistics of Hawaii*. Honolulu: The University Press of Hawai'i.

Shain, Barry A. 1994. *The Myth of American Individualism: The Protestant Origins of American Political Thought*. Princeton: Princeton University Press.

Shapiro, Michael J. 1993. *Reading "Adam Smith": Desire, History and Value*. Modernity and Political Thought 4. Newbury Park: Sage.

Smith, Lowell. *Lowell Smith's Journal*. BM.

Smith, Timothy L. 1976. *Revivalism and Social Reform: American Protestantism on the Eve of the Civil War*. Gloucester, Mass.: Peter Smith.

Statute Laws. 1846. *Statute Laws of His Majesty Kamehameha III. King of the Hawaiian Islands; Passed by the Houses of Nobles and Representatives, during the Twenty-first Year of His Reign; and the Third and Fourth Years of the Public Recognition, A.D. 1845 and 1846: To which Are Appended the Acts of Public Recognition, and the Treaties with Other Nations*, vol. 1. Honolulu: Government Press.

Stewart, Charles S. [1830] 1970. *Journal of a Residence in the Sandwich Islands, during the Years 1823, 1824, and 1825: Including Remarks on the Manners and Customs of the Inhabitants; an Account of Lord Byron's Visit in H.M.S. Blonde; and a Description of the Ceremonies Observed at the Interment of the late King and Queen in the Island of Oahu*. Honolulu: University of Hawai'i Press for the Friends of the Library of Hawaii.

Stewens, Sylvester K. [1945] 1968. *American Expansion in Hawaii, 1842–1898*. New York: Russell & Russell.

Stokes, John F. G. 1932. "The Hawaiian King (Mo-i, Alii-aimoku, alii-kapu)." *Papers of the Hawaiian Historical Society* 19. Honolulu: Hawaiian Historical Society.

Strauss, W. Patrick. 1963. *Americans in Polynesia 1783–1842*. East Lansing: Michigan State University Press.

Swidler, Ann. 1986. "Culture in Action: Symbols and Strategies." *American Sociological Review* 51(2):273–286.

Tate, Merze. 1960. "The Early Political Influence of the Sandwich Islands Missionaries." *The Journal of Religious Thought* 17:117–132.

———. 1964. "Sandwich Islands Missionaries and Annexation." *The Journal of Religious Thought* 20:137–145.

Thaddeus Journal. *Journal of the Sandwich Islands Mission, 1819–1821*. JC/HMCS.

Thomas, Nicholas. 1992. "The Inversion of Tradition." *American Ethnologist* 19(2):213–232.

———. 1994. *Colonialism's Culture: Anthropology, Travel and Government*. Cambridge: Polity Press.

———. 1999. "Liberty and License: The Forsters' Accounts of New Zealand Sociality." In Alex Calder, Jonathan Lamb, and Bridget Orr, eds., *Voyages and Beaches: Pacific Encounters, 1769–1840*. Honolulu: University of Hawai'i Press.

Thrum, Thomas G. 1904. "The Sandalwood Trade of Early Hawaii as Told by the Pioneer Traders, Voyagers and Others." *Hawaiian Almanac and Annual for 1905*, 43–74.

———. 1918. "Brief Sketch of the Life and Labors of S. M. Kamakau, Hawaiian Historian." *Twenty-Sixth Annual Report of the Hawaiian Historical Society for the Year 1917*. Honolulu: Paradise of the Pacific Press.

Thurston, Lucy G. 1934. *Life and Times of Mrs. Lucy G. Thurston, Wife of Rev. Asa Thurston, Pioneer Missionary to the Sandwich Islands*. Honolulu: The Friend.

Tinker, Reuben. *Journal, 1834–1838.* J/HMCS.

Tocqueville, Alexis de. 1948. *Democracy in America*. 2 vols. Henry Reeve, trans.; Francis Bowen, revisions; Phillips Bradley, corrections and ed. New York: Alfred A. Knopf.

Turnbull, John. 1805. *A Voyage Round the World in the Years 1800, 1801, 1802, 1803, and 1804*. 3 vols. London: Richards Phillips.

Twain, Mark. 1990. *Mark Twain in Hawaii: Roughing it in the Sandwich Islands*. Honolulu: Mutual.

Tyerman, Daniel, and George Bennet. 1831. *Journal of Voyages and Travels by the Rev. Daniel Tyerman and George Bennet, Esq. Deputed from the London Missionary Society, to Visit Their Various Stations in the South Sea Islands, China, India, &c., between the Years 1821 and 1829*. James Montgomery, ed. 2 vols. London: Frederick Westley and A. H. Davis.

Valeri, Valerio. 1985a. "The Conqueror Becomes King: A Political Analysis of the Hawaiian Legend of 'Umi." In Anthony Hooper and Judith Huntsman, eds., *Transformations of Polynesian Culture*. Auckland: The Polynesian Society.

———. 1985b. *Kingship and Sacrifice: Ritual and Society in Ancient Hawaii*. Paula Wissing, trans. Chicago: University of Chicago Press.

Vancouver, George. [1798] 1984. *The Voyage of Discovery to the North Pacific Ocean and Round the World 1791–1795*. 4 vols. W. Kaye Lamb, ed. The Hakluyt Society Second Series 163–166. London: The Hakluyt Society.

Wagner, Roy. 1975. *The Invention of Culture*. Englewood Cliffs, N.J.: Prentice Hall.

Wayland, Francis. 1837. *The Elements of Political Economy*. New York: Leavitt, Lord & Co.

———. [1841] 1963. *The Elements of Moral Science*. Joseph L. Blau, ed. Cambridge, Mass.: The Belknap Press of Harvard University Press.

Werbner, Pnina. 2001. "The Limits of Cultural Hybridity: On Ritual Monsters, Poetic Licence and Contested Postcolonial Purifications." *Journal of Royal Anthropological Institute* (N.S.) 7:133–152.

Werbner, Pnina, and Tariq Modood, eds. 1997. *Debating Cultural Hybridity: Multicultural Identities and the Politics of Anti-racism*. London: Zed Books.

Whitman, John B. 1979. *An Account of the Sandwich Islands: The Hawaiian Journal of John B. Whitman, 1813–1815*. Honolulu: Topgallant, and Salem, Mass.: Peabody Museum.

Whitney, Mercy P. "Journal on Board the Brig *Thaddeus* under Sail, 1819–1820." Typescript, J/HMCS.

———. *Journal, 1821–1860*. Ms., J/HMCS.

Wise, Henry A. 1849. *Los Gringos: Or an Inside View of Mexico and California, with Wanderings in Peru, Chili, and Polynesia*. London: Richard Bentley.

Wright, Louis B., and Mary I. Fry. 1936. *Puritans in the South Seas*. New York: H. Holt and Co.

Wyllie, Robert C. 1848. *Answers to Questions Proposed by His Excellency, R. C. Wyllie, His Hawaiian Majesty's Minister of Foreign Relations, and Addressed to all the Missionaries in the Hawaiian Islands, May, 1846*. Honolulu: Government Press.

Youngs, J. William. 1998. *The Congregationalists*. Westport, Conn.: Praeger.

Yzendoorn, Reginald. 1927. *History of the Catholic Mission in the Hawaiian Islands*. Honolulu: Honolulu Star-Bulletin.

Index

About the Author

Juri Mykkänen, who is currently a lecturer of political science at University of Helsinki, received his doctorate from the University of Hawai'i at Mānoa. This is his first book.